THE MATERIALITY OF RELIGION IN EARLY MODERN ENGLISH DRAMA

The Materiality of Religion in Early Modern English Drama is the first book to present a detailed examination of early modern theatrical properties informed by the complexity of post-Reformation religious practice. Although English Protestant reformers set out to destroy all vestiges of Catholic idolatry, public theater companies frequently used stage properties to draw attention to the remnants of traditional religion as well as the persistent materiality of post-Reformation worship. *The Materiality of Religion in Early Modern English Drama* explores the relationship between popular culture and theatrical performance by considering the social history and dramatic function of these properties, addressing their role as objects of devotion, idolatry, and remembrance on the professional stage. Rather than being aligned with identifiably Catholic or Protestant values, the author reveals how religious stage properties functioned as fulcrums around which more subtle debates about the status of Christian worship played out

Given the relative lack of existing documentation on stage properties, *The Materiality of Religion in Early Modern English Drama* employs a wide range of source materials—including inventories published in the Records of Early English Drama (REED) volumes—to account for the material presence of these objects on the public stage. By combining historical research on popular religion with detailed readings of the scripts themselves, the book fills a gap in our knowledge about the physical qualities of the stage properties used in early modern productions.

Tracing the theater's appropriation of highly charged religious properties, *The Materiality of Religion in Early Modern English Drama* provides a new framework for understanding the canonization of early modern plays, especially those of Shakespeare.

Elizabeth Williamson is Assistant Professor of English at The Evergreen State College, USA.

D1709830

Studies in Performance and Early Modern Drama

General Editor's Preface

Helen Ostovich, McMaster University

Performance assumes a string of creative, analytical, and collaborative acts that, in defiance of theatrical ephemerality, live on through records, manuscripts, and printed books. The monographs and essay collections in this series offer original research which addresses theatre histories and performance histories in the context of the sixteenth and seventeenth century life. Of especial interest are studies in which women's activities are a central feature of discussion as financial or technical supporters (patrons, musicians, dancers, seamstresses, wigmakers, or 'gatherers'), if not authors or performers per se. Welcome too are critiques of early modern drama that not only take into account the production values of the plays, but also speculate on how intellectual advances or popular culture affect the theatre.

The series logo, selected by my colleague Mary V. Silcox, derives from Thomas Combe's duodecimo volume, *The Theater of Fine Devices* (London, 1592), Emblem VI, sig. B. The emblem of four masks has a verse which makes claims for the increasing complexity of early modern experience, a complexity that makes interpretation difficult. Hence the corresponding perhaps uneasy rise in sophistication:

> Masks will be more hereafter in request,
> And grow more deare than they did heretofore.

No longer simply signs of performance 'in play and jest', the mask has become the 'double face' worn 'in earnest' even by 'the best' of people, in order to manipulate or profit from the world around them. The books stamped with this design attempt to understand the complications of performance produced on stage and interpreted by the audience, whose experiences outside the theatre may reflect the emblem's argument:

> Most men do use some colour'd shift
> For to conceal their craftie drift.

Centuries after their first presentations, the possible performance choices and meanings they engender still stir the imaginations of actors, audiences, and readers of early plays. The products of scholarly creativity in this series, I hope, will also stir imaginations to new ways of thinking about performance.

The Materiality of Religion in Early Modern English Drama

ELIZABETH WILLIAMSON
The Evergreen State College, USA

ASHGATE

Published by
Ashgate Publishing Limited
Wey Court East
Union Road
Farnham
Surrey, GU9 7PT
England

Ashgate Publishing Company
Suite 420
101 Cherry Street
Burlington
VT 05401-4405
USA

www.ashgate.com

British Library Cataloguing in Publication Data
Williamson, Elizabeth.
The materiality of religion in early modern English drama. – (Studies in performance and early modern drama)
1. Religion and drama. 2. Theater and society – England – History–16th century. 3. Stage props – England – History – 16th century. 4. English drama, 1500–1600 – Early modern and Elizabethan, 1500–1600 – History and criticism.
I. Title II. Series
792'.025'0942'09031-dc22

Library of Congress Cataloging-in-Publication Data
Williamson, Elizabeth, 1976–
The materiality of religion in early modern English drama / Elizabeth Williamson.
p. cm. – (Studies in performance and early modern drama)
Includes bibliographical references and index.
ISBN 978-0-7546-6827-5 (hardcover : alk. paper) – ISBN 978-0-7546-9476-2 (ebook)
1. Theater–England–History–16th century. 2. Theater–England–History–17th century. 3. Theater–Religious aspects. 4. Religious articles in the theater. 5. Idolatry in the theater. 6. Theaters–Stage-setting and scenery–England–History–16th century. 7. Theaters–Stage-setting and scenery–England–History–17th century. 8. English drama–Early modern and Elizabethan, 1500-1600–History and criticism. 9. English drama–17th century–History and criticism. 10. Religion in literature. I. Title.

PN2590.R35W56 2009
792.0942'09031–dc22

2009006718

ISBN 9780754668275 (hbk)
ISBN 9780754694762 (ebk)

Mixed Sources
Product group from well-managed forests and other controlled sources
www.fsc.org Cert no. SA-COC-1565
© 1996 Forest Stewardship Council

Printed and bound in Great Britain by
MPG Books Group, UK

Contents

List of Figures

Acknowledgements

This project began with the help of many wonderful mentors and friends at the University of Pennsylvania and could not have been completed without the support of my colleagues at The Evergreen State College. Peter Stallybrass's generative thinking shaped the direction of my research; he also went far beyond the call of duty to find fellowship support for me in the final year of my Ph.D. work. Margreta de Grazia, Phyllis Rackin, Sean Keilen, and Cary Mazer all provided invaluable feedback at various stages of the writing process, and Erika Lin, Marissa Greenberg, Miriam Jacobson, and Jennifer Higginbotham slogged through fifty-page chapters out of what I can only suppose is sheer loyalty. Jean Howard and Jane Degenhardt gave me the confidence to resurrect the thesis as a book project; they continue to be models of collegiality and intellectual integrity for me in everything I do, and I cannot imagine what my professional life would look like without them. Several portions of this project were delivered at annual conferences; I am particularly grateful to the organizers of the annual Shakespeare Association of America meetings, whose hard work provides seminar members from graduate students to full professors with an exceptional environment for scholarly feedback.

Countless staff members at libraries and archives, most especially John Pollack and Daniel Traister at the University of Pennsylvania Rare Books Library and Georgianne Ziegler at the Folger Library, have been extraordinarily helpful in assisting me with my hunt for theatrical relics. Anthony Dawson, whose keynote address delivered at the 2005 Elizabethan Theatre Conference influenced the final phase of my thinking about this book in fundamental ways, was kind enough to allow me to cite his unpublished work. Jerry Singerman gave me vital guidance as I was reworking the project and honing the book proposal. And the humanities faculty at Evergreen graciously entrusted me with the coordination of our curriculum planning in 2007-2008 so that I could earn time off from teaching to complete the manuscript. I also owe a debt of thanks to my editor Erika Gaffney for her patience with me as a first time author and her enthusiastic support of the project. All the images in the book are reprinted with the generous permission of the Folger Library and the Huntington Library.

To David, who sees the writer in me, and to my parents, without whom this book would never have had a material existence, my debts are uncountable.

Introduction
Mere Properties:
The Materiality of Religious Objects

During the recent excavation of the Rose Theatre site in 1988-89, London archaeologists uncovered a small treasure trove of early modern objects, including two sixteenth-century finger rings, a button, several dress pins, a serving fork, a man's shoe, a stove tile, a sword scabbard, a dress hook, a spur fragment, a baluster, several money-box tops, a half-groat, and a manicure pin. One of the most suggestive artifacts was the fragment of a rosary made of bone with copper alloy links. This object, currently housed in a display case at the Museum of London, is described as being possible evidence of "the continued existence of Roman Catholicism after the Reformation," since the beads have been dated 1550-1600. "Or," the curator goes on to hint, "they are possibly a stage prop." For the student of early modern drama, this is a hypothesis too tempting to ignore. Although the use of rosaries was banned in the 1540s, they could be found in private homes and chapels throughout the sixteenth and early seventeenth centuries, and in many ways they were ideal objects of covert devotion: small, portable, and easily concealed. In Middleton's *A Game at Chess* (1624), the Black Knight gleefully describes how he has taught his followers to smuggle "hallowed oil, beads, medals, pardons, / Pictures, Veronica's heads in private presses," and indeed the fear that Catholic goods, especially small ones, were being secretly fabricated or brought into the country from overseas continued to haunt church officials well after Protestantism had been reestablished as the state religion under Elizabeth I.[1] References to characters "at their beads" appear in several contemporary plays, including Middleton's *Your Five Gallants* (1607), in which two young lovers exchange rosary beads as a token of their chaste devotion to one another.[2]

---

[1] Thomas Middleton, *A Game at Chess*, ed. T. H. Howard-Hill (Manchester: Manchester University Press, 1993), 4.2.48-9.

[2] References to beads appear in Shakespeare's *2 Henry VI* (1591), *Look About You* (1599), Dekker's *If It Be Not a Good Play the Devil Is In It* (1612) and Mountfort's *The Launching of the Mary* (1632). Other plays that call for a character to carry beads on stage include Chettle and Munday's *Death of Robert Earl of Huntington* (1598) and Dekker and Ford's *The Noble Spanish Soldier* (1622). Lisa McClain argues that in the aftermath of the Reformation "material objects such as the rosary played a key role in English Catholics' quest for salvation given the frequent absence of traditional avenues to grace." Many were smuggled into England from Catholic countries "with a merchant's regular shipment of goods or with a tradesman's supply of raw materials" (*Lest We Be Damned: Practical*

All this is to say that Philip Henslowe might very well have acquired a set of rosary beads and stored them in the tiring house at the Rose along with the other, larger items documented in his 1598 inventory. Such speculation is impossible to confirm, but we can read this artifact as symbolic of the surprising proximity of traditional religious objects to the theater and to the lives of London playgoers. Texts such as *A Game at Chess* present objects associated with Catholic worship as part of anti-papist jibes, but other plays deal in more subtle ways with the fluctuating value of items such as rosaries, crosses, and prayer books. In many cases these objects were recognizably Catholic; in others, their presence revealed an overlap between pre- and post-Reformation religious practice. Inspired by these play scripts, and by the survival of objects such as the Rose Theatre rosary, this book is an attempt to come to terms with some of the ways the companies used religious implements—or things that looked like them—in their theatrical fictions. Literary scholars have long acknowledged a kind of analogy between the survival of biblical dramas and the continuing practice of Catholicism in post-Reformation England. This book draws a somewhat more obvious, but less obviously ideological, comparison between the material artifacts of traditional religion and their counterparts on the public stage, arguing that the strategies employed by theater practitioners in turn reflected the remarkable shifts in value that occurred as religious objects left English churches and were destroyed, repaired, and reincorporated into new contexts. This rosary, along with the textual traces that survive in stage directions and in lines of dialogue, serves as a reminder that theater companies frequently addressed the shifting status of religious objects as part of their engagement with the culture that surrounded them. Playgoers' responses to such objects would necessarily have been inflected by their own personal experiences as well as by political events; both the persistence of material forms of devotion and the variety of ways in which that materiality manifested itself in the decades following the Reformation provide suggestive clues about the kind of emotional charge the players were attempting to access when they brought religious objects into the theater.

The End of Popery

In examining the plays that deploy religious objects during the early seventeenth century, this book deals with two related phenomena: the imaginative function of stage properties, inspired in part by the objects they referred to, and their actual presence on stage. Unfortunately, the stage properties used in the public theaters of Shakespeare's London are, for the most part, poorly documented. We know very little of their construction or their value, which is why Henslowe's inventory of the stage properties owned by the Admiral's Men—including a hell mouth,

Innovation and Lived Experience Among Catholics in Protestant England, 1559-1642 [Routledge: New York, 2004], 81, 158).

two tombs, a crosier staff, an altar, one pope's mitre, one "owld Mahemetes head," and two steeples[3]—has received so much critical attention. It seems unlikely that this list included all the objects in the tiring house at the Rose; rather, these are all items that were valuable enough to record and required a significant financial investment to replace or repair. But fabrication is itself a deceptively simple word. The 1581 patent of commission for Edmund Tilney, Master of the Revels, enjoins him to retain a wide spectrum of artisans, including "painters, imbroderes, taylors, cappers, haberdashers, joyners, carders, glasiers, armorers, basketmakers, skinners, sadlers, waggen makers, plaisteres, fethermakers, as all other propertie makers and conninge artificers and laborers."[4] From this and other documents associated with the Office of the Revels, we can draw some conclusions about how public theater properties might have been made, although they would necessarily have been produced on a less grandiose scale.

An entry from 1582-83, for instance, lists some of the physical materials required to create stage properties for court entertainments, including "paste bord, paper, and paste" as well as "[t]ynfoyle," while one entry from 1576-77 adds such items as brown paper, flour to make the paste, glue, linen rags, clay, and wainscot. In the first year of Edward's reign, the Office of the Revels was commissioned to purchase "a greate past burde gyldyd with ffyne golde for the making of Crownes & Crosses for the poope" for three shillings four pence.[5] Based on the more expensive model recorded in the Revels documents, we can approximate how the Admiral's Men might have commissioned an object such as a crosier or cross staff to be built. We might also compare such records to a 1557-58 entry in the churchwardens' accounts for St. Matthew Friday Street in London: "P'd for a crose & a staffe & payntyng yt for lante iiijs."[6] The point is that the theater companies had access to the same technologies the churchwardens did, and that they could reproduce religious objects as well as inheriting them from the spoiling of parish churches.

We can also look backward to the material compiled by the editors of the Records of Early English Drama (REED), primarily those entries dealing with the biblical plays performed in towns such as Wakefield and Chester, in order to learn about how local guilds produced, maintained, and repaired the properties that

---

[3] Andrew Gurr, *The Shakespearean Stage 1574-1642* (Cambridge University Press: Cambridge, 1970), 123-4.

[4] E. K. Chambers, ed., *The Elizabethan Stage*, vol. 4 (Oxford: The Clarendon Press, 1974), 485.

[5] Albert Feuillerat, ed., *Documents Relating to the Office of the Revels in the Time of Queen Elizabeth* (Vaduz: Kraus Reprint, 1963), 359, 261; *Documents Relating to the Revels at Court in the Time of King Edward VI and Queen Mary* (Louvain: A. Uystpruyst, 1914), 6.

[6] W. Sparrow Simpson, "Churchwardens Accounts for the parish of St. Matthew, Friday Street, in the City of London, from 1547-1603," *Journal of the British Archaeological Association* 25 (1869): 356-81, 368.

were central to their dramatic productions. These records, like the ones from the Office of the Revels, mention cheap materials such as "pawper mache," and small but remarkable items such as "a newe sudere [handkerchief] for god," purchased for seven pence.[7] But these documents also describe more expensive processes associated with producing parish drama, such as an entry from Coventry that records the payment of two shillings sixpence to "Hewyt" for "paynting & gylldying the fawchyne, the pillar, the crose & Godes cote" or the four shillings eight pence paid for "v dosyn of goldefoyle" and the transportation of it in 1560-61 at New Romney in Kent. As the REED editors have repeatedly shown, the cycle plays continued in places such as Coventry long after the first wave of attacks against religious drama. The reference to painting and gilding the cross and god's coat is from 1565, and two years later a parish inventory records both "godes crose" and "the spyrytes crose."[8] These records also document the purchase, storage, repair, and sale of church ornaments such as altars, candlesticks, and crosses. They provide information about the business of making properties for a dramatic enterprise that was nearly contemporaneous with the public theater, while simultaneously revealing the proximity of church goods to players' goods, objects that were linked through material technologies that did not entirely disappear with the advent of the Protestant Reformation.

Admittedly, religious objects make up a relatively small number of the stage properties referenced in early modern play scripts; consequently, only a few scholars have paid any attention to them.[9] Nor is it difficult to understand why such items rarely appear in records of early modern performance: reformers had outlawed Catholic church furnishings and devotional aids because they were thought to provoke idolatrous behavior. Yet the fact that religious objects appear at all in the drama points to a striking paradox at the heart of post-Reformation culture. Although Protestant statutes specified that churches and homes were to be entirely cleansed of potentially distracting material objects, in practice English worshipers continued to rely heavily on the physical accoutrements that anchored their faith. For their part, Protestant theologians had to wrestle with the problem of maintaining a healthy respect for the sacramental nature

---

[7] J. J. Anderson, ed., *Newcastle Upon Tyne* (Toronto: University of Toronto Press, 1982), 55; R. W. Ingram, ed., *Coventry* (Toronto: University of Toronto Press, 1981), 96.

[8] Ingram, 239-40; James M. Gibson, ed., *Kent: Diocese of Canterbury* (Toronto: The British Library and University of Toronto Press, 2002), 78.

[9] Exceptions include Gary Taylor's "Divine [ ]sences," *Shakespeare Survey* 54 (2001): 13-30 and Peter Mullany's *Religion and the Artifice of Jacobean and Caroline Drama* (Salzburg: Institut fur Englische Sprache und Literatur, Universitat Salzburg, 1977). Taylor's work is a highly suggestive but very brief survey of some often overlooked plays. Mullany's monograph deals with many of the works I address here, but he ultimately dismisses the theater's treatment of religion as pandering to its audience's taste for spectacle and exoticism—a classically secularizing account published years before the better known examples by Greenblatt and Montrose.

of Christian belief while preventing the communion and other forms of devotion from becoming idolatrous. In bringing religious materials on stage, therefore, the playing companies were doing more than simply expressing scorn or nostalgia for the recognizable elements of Catholicism. They were taking advantage of audience members' residual interest in the materiality of religion, revealing ongoing contradictions between post-Reformation theory and practice while taking full advantage of the highly visual, object-centered nature of their own medium.

The standard language of Protestant propaganda describes religious objects such as crucifixes, altars, and rosary beads as dangerous remnants of papist superstition that should be eliminated at all costs. According to this logic, articulated most clearly in the Elizabethan book of homilies, religious objects provoke idolatry whenever they are brought out in public, and should thus be considered dangerous even when presented as part of secular performances. The surviving statutes tacitly acknowledge this problem, but they also indicate that it would be just as problematic to dramatize the elements of reformed English worship as it would be to resurrect Catholicism on stage.[10] The first of these laws, issued in 1559, forbids any unauthorized play "wherin either matters of religion or of the governaunce of the estate of the common weale shal be handled or treated, beyng no meete matters to be wrytten or treated upon."[11] Although the prohibition on religious subjects was not absolute, the language of mainstream Protestantism was one of decent conformity, and like her father before her Elizabeth sought to stamp out any potentially seditious ideas that might be contained in a play about contemporary religious practice.

At the heart of the reformers' desire to critique and control the stage was their distaste for what they saw as its deceptive superficiality. Like the Roman Catholic church, the theater was accused of relying on outward shows—what Bishop John Jewel called the "scenic apparatus" of the church[12]—to seduce spectators away from more substantive forms of contemplation. Peter Lake and Michael Questier clearly lay out the binaries operating in Protestant polemic between the carnal and the transcendent, the image and the word:

> If true religion was determinedly logocentric, acting on true believers principally through the word of God, both read and preached, popery and theater seduced their victims into sin and damnation through inherently fleshy appeals to the other senses, appeals directed as much, if not more,

---

[10]   The plays by John Bale and other early reformers discussed in Paul Whitfield White's *Theatre and Reformation* (Cambridge: Cambridge University Press, 1993) do address contemporary Protestantism, but they deal primarily with theology and not with ritual practice.

[11]   Chambers, 263.

[12]   Joseph Leo Koerner, *The Reformation of the Image* (London: Reaktion, 2004), 175.

to the eye as to the ear and appealing even to the ear through the inherently corrupting forms of musical, rhetorical and linguistic play and display.[13]

Catholicism had been rejected because it relied too heavily on material objects and gestures, and by the same token the theater was seen as an enterprise that attracted customers through gorgeous visual displays. Both antitheatricalist and anti-Catholic polemics contended that the ordinary English playgoer (or churchgoer) put too much stock in false shows, mistaking the fiction for reality. The danger of using visual representations to depict religious concepts was that they could be mistaken for the real thing, directing one's worship toward the image rather than its referent. In Jonathan Gil Harris and Natasha Korda's apt formulation: "Protestant iconoclasm and antipathy to the theatre operated in tandem with a pronounced hostility to *objects*: the props of religious and dramatic ritual alike served—as did the paltry Eucharist biscuit—to distract attention from more godly, hidden truths, by virtue of their very visibility."[14] Although Luther had taken a rather moderate stance on religious images, maintaining that they could be contemplated without being abused, English Calvinists held that men and women would inevitably succumb to superstitious thoughts when confronted with material representations of religious subjects. Consequently, these reformers underscored their reliance on the word of God rather than on false images of his divinity, seeking to draw the believer's attention away from the crucifix—the image that had dominated pre-Reformation spirituality—by replacing it with the decalogue, focusing in particular on the second commandment, which bars the worship of graven images.

It is not entirely accurate to claim, however, that Protestantism eschewed all material objects and practices or that traditional practices and objects were successfully removed from the lives of all English citizens. As Anthony Dawson writes, Protestantism was "not entirely anti-visual nor anti-performance," and old habits of thought were hard to overcome.[15] Those who had grown up in the Catholic church were accustomed to conceiving of their deity in representational terms, using material objects to assist them in their devotions. Moreover, only a small percentage of English citizens were literate, meaning that they were unable to have unmediated access to the word of God. The community of readers that the reformers had envisioned when they commissioned the first vernacular translations of the Bible and the prayer book thus constituted only a small fraction of the nation's believers. Nor did the Protestant establishment manage to eliminate

---

[13]   *The Anti-Christ's Lewd Hat: Protestants, Papists and Players in Post-Reformation England* (New Haven: Yale University Press, 2002), 453.

[14]   Jonathan Gil Harris and Natasha Korda, eds, *Staged Properties in Early Modern Drama* (Cambridge University Press: Cambridge, 2002), 5.

[15]   Anthony B. Dawson and Paul Edward Yachnin, *The Culture of Playgoing in Shakespeare's England: A Collaborative Debate* (Cambridge: Cambridge University Press, 2001), 135.

all material objects from the visible church, for many of them were simply modified: the altar became the communion table, the mass book became the Book of Common Prayer, and the architecture of the churches themselves remained largely unchanged. As I discuss in Chapter 3, many Catholic objects survived the Reformation altogether and were lovingly preserved in private homes and chapels throughout the sixteenth and early seventeenth centuries. For some members of the aristocracy, it was even possible to hear a traditional Latin mass and to receive communion at the hands of a Catholic priest.

Any study of the late sixteenth and early seventeenth centuries must also attempt to acknowledge the considerable local fluctuations in the enforcement of Protestant reforms. During the period in which the public theater companies were beginning to flourish as commercial entities, Londoners experienced an especially violent wave of iconoclasm, and later, during the first third of the seventeenth century, they witnessed the resurgence of more traditional forms of worship, along with the resulting backlash against such changes on the part of strict Protestants. With each new monarch came a new set of laws about religious practice, but despite or perhaps because of these changes in official policy many of the material objects associated with traditional religion survived and were adapted to new purposes. By using religious stage properties, then, the theater was responding to the ongoing danger posed by what polemicists called the "ornaments of superstition." But play scripts did not operate simply as mirrors for popular culture or governmental policy; the drama had its own investment in materiality, and in some cases the translation of these religious objects into the theater actually enhanced the emotional power of its secular fictions. Ultimately, the drama's use of religious stage properties was limited by their controversial status, but throughout its development as a commercial medium the theater continued to be inspired by the persistence and adaptability of post-Reformation religion.

The reformers' attempts to distance themselves from the material trappings of Catholicism are neatly captured in an elaborate foldout from Michael Sparke's *Crumms of comfort* (1628) (Figure 0.1) depicting the "before" and "after" of English religion.

Figure 0.1   "The night of popish superstition," *Crumms of comfort*, 1628 (P4^v-
             P5^r). By permission of the Folger Shakespeare Library

The upper half of the illustration represents the "night of Popish superstition,"
in which crowds of monks bear the host in procession while Protestant martyrs
burn under a blackened sky. In the foreground, two tonsured priests minister to
a dying woman, perhaps Queen Mary herself. As part of a ceremony known as
the *commendatio animae*, one of them holds a crucifix in front of her face as
a symbol of salvation. Behind them on an altar the various implements of the
priests' craft are clearly displayed: a large candlestick, an altar cross with the
body of Christ affixed to it, a large processional cross, and a set of rosary beads.
Below this image is a scene lit by a large sun in the left-hand corner and labeled

"The returne of the Gospells light." Here a minister preaches to an attentive group of parishioners, while in the distance a pair of Protestant divines crown the new queen. In the foreground, five godly Protestant men can be seen handing Elizabeth a copy of the English Bible. The contrast between these two images, like those in the title page of Foxe's *Acts and Monuments* (1563), could not be plainer: the superstitious worship of the host and the abuse of the image of the crucified Christ have been replaced by a godly sermon and the vernacular Bible, thus ensuring the salvation of the English people. It was politically necessary for Protestant writers and polemicists to claim a radical break from traditional religious practice, but as I explain in Chapter 4, the Bible itself is a also physical object, one that Elizabeth made a show of kissing during her first appearance as queen in a gesture that echoed the priests' kissing of the missal during the mass. Protestantism, like the theater, often relied on the power of images, and neither the reformers nor the players could afford to ignore the impact of material objects and practices on the lives of ordinary believers.

The purging of traditional religion occurred not all at once but gradually, in fits and starts. As the articles of visitation demonstrate, church officials in some dioceses were still seeking out the remnants of popery well into the early seventeenth century, and in the decades leading up to the Civil War the reformers began to lose ground as Archbishop Laud and his supporters initiated their project of restoring beauty and sacrality to English churches. In 1637 the churchwardens of the London parish of St. Mary Axe conducted an elaborate hallowing ceremony for their new pieces of church plate; Henry Mason, the rector, took the opportunity to warn the assembled congregation against abusing any of these items: "let the curse of this sacred altar, and the curse of my Lord and Master Jesus Xt, bee upon that man, or that woman, that shall purloyne them away, alienate them, or either of them, from their sacred use." Strict Protestants reacted against this trend toward more elaborate church furnishings by beginning a new wave of iconoclastic attacks and encouraging parishioners to reject these "innovations." At St. Benedict Gracechurch the churchwardens sold off "ye popish altar cloth" for one pound eight shillings in 1642, and paid a group of workmen another one shilling sixpence "for defacing superstitious things in the church."[16] As John Sommerville notes, church furnishings were often sold off by the parishioners themselves "so that the proceeds would actually be used for religious purposes" rather than augmenting the royal war chest.[17]

---

[16] Charles Bevois Boulter, *History of St. Andrew Undershaft, St. Mary Axe, in the City of London, with Description of the Monuments and the Coloured Glass Therein* ([London, privately printed], 1935), 62; James Peller Malcolm, *Londinium Redivivum, or, An Antient History and Modern Description of London*, vol. 1 (London: Printed by J. Nichols, 1802), 317.

[17] *The Secularization of Early Modern England: From Religious Culture to Religious Faith* (New York: Oxford University Press, 1992), 63.

By reading accounts of Reformation-era iconoclasm, we learn that not only were religious objects removed from the churches, they were also put to new uses—one altar stone in East Newlyn was even turned into a cheese press. Some items were sold off for the value of their materials while others were purchased or stolen by the faithful to prevent further desecration. According to Susan Brigden, who has documented the impact of the Reformation on the lives of ordinary Londoners in the sixteenth century, "only Catholic sentiment or a traditional piety could explain why little broken, wooden images were bought for a few pence."[18] Many parishioners preserved these objects in hopes of repairing and restoring them, as they had done under Mary. Other sacred implements, including pieces of church plate, were unceremoniously melted down. Items that had cost the churchwardens tens of pounds to purchase and repair were turned back into their constituent materials, which could then circulate more easily in the marketplace.[19] The act of reducing these sacred objects to a collection of commodifiable materials seemed to confirm the reformers' notion that they were no more than "dead" things.

My interest in the objects associated with traditional religion in England is thus driven by the stories they tell about the intricacies of post-Reformation worship. I am also drawn to religious objects because they are so well documented, comparatively speaking. Their physical characteristics and the uses to which they were put in the decades following the Reformation provide a set of clues about the materiality of the stage objects that are absent from theatrical inventories. From churchwardens' accounts, legal records, personal letters, and images such as Sparke's, we learn that there were several kinds of crosses, some more controversial than others. We also learn the crucial difference between small objects, like beads, that could be circulated in secret, and large objects, like stone altars, that were problematic precisely because they were immovable. The records of private and public forms of devotion, both of which varied widely even within the vicinity of London itself, help document the kinds of objects that continued to circulate despite the best efforts of government officials. By reading the historical materials on post-Reformation religion alongside the information gleaned from stage directions and recorded dialogue, we can piece together a picture of what it might be like, in the context of early modern culture, to see these objects brought on stage.

Although the 1620s, 30s and 40s mark the most widespread use of traditional religious objects since the Reformation, this movement followed a period of several decades in which James I adopted a relatively tolerant attitude toward traditional religion, allowing groups of worshipers to retain possession of the devotional

---

[18]   Robert Whiting, *The Blind Devotion of the People: Popular Religion and the English Reformation* (Cambridge: Cambridge University Press, 1989), 74; *London and the Reformation* (Oxford: Clarendon Press, 1991), 432.

[19]   As John Phillips writes: "the considerable opportunities now open for the small man to buy church property must have provided a welcome material gloss to the theological arguments for Protestantism" (*The Reformation of Images: Destruction of Art in England, 1535-1660* [Berkeley: University of California Press, 1973], 74).

objects they had been introduced to as children. In "The Parochial Roots of Laudianism Revisited," Alexandra Walsham lays out the existing evidence relating to the question of whether the residual Catholic practices that survived Elizabethan reforms bled into or gave rise to the return of some forms of more traditional worship under Archbishop Laud. Although Walsham tentatively concludes that there may indeed be a connection, her main focus is on the incredible diversity of religious practices in the early seventeenth century and the importance of considering the history of individual communities. As monarchs, James and his son Charles urged the importance of uniformity, but they were ultimately more interested in levying fines and taxes on Catholic recusants than in burning them at the stake.[20] Nor were they entirely at fault for the persistence of traditional religious implements in seventeenth-century England; all of these narratives, those of survival and those of return, testify to the difficulty of erasing the material elements of Catholicism from the imaginations of English men and women. Laud would never have described himself as a recusant, a term that referred to an adherent of the traditional religion who refused to give up her Catholic roots. Rather, he and other anti-Calvinists expressed a persistent interest in the ritual aspects of Catholicism while remaining safely within the general rubric of conformity.

My focus on the survival, as well as the gradual return, of objects traditionally associated with Catholicism, allows me to draw on the work of historians such as Alexandra Walsham, Eamon Duffy, Patrick Collinson, and Nicholas Tyacke, who emphasize the slow and often unsteady progress of Protestant reform. In some instances, the drama seems to support Duffy's argument that Catholic practices persisted because they were inextricable from family histories and local customs, but few early modern plays express a straightforward sense of nostalgia for bygone times. More frequently, the scripts subtly remind us that English Protestants never entirely gave up all the physical aspects of worship, and that there was an ongoing slippage between "proper" reformed behaviors and "improper" Catholic ones. And though the objects vary, the reference points for these dramatic representations are often surprisingly contemporary. My aim in this book is to use what we know of the objects that survived in churches and in private homes to make up for the paucity of information about the religious stage properties owned by public theater companies, supplementing my readings of the plays with the extensive research conducted by scholars of early modern religious practice. I rely, for instance, on Collinson's description of the various stages of Protestant iconoclasm, as well as on Tyacke's account of the ellision between various forms of "reformed" worship during the early 1600s and Walsham's sophisticated analysis of anti-Calvinism.[21]

---

[20] "The parochial roots of Laudianism revisited: Catholics, anti-Calvinists and 'parish Anglicans' in early Stuart England," *Journal of Ecclesiastical History* 49, no. 4 (1998): 620-51, 648.

[21] See Collinson, *The Birthpangs of Protestant England* (New York: St. Martin's Press, 1988); Duffy, *The Stripping of the Altars* (New Haven: Yale University Press, 1992); Tyacke, "Archbishop Laud," in Kenneth Fincham, ed., *The Early Stuart Church 1603-1642*

In subsequent chapters, I posit specific explanations for the appearance of certain kinds of stage properties and practices during particular historical moments, but in general my research suggests that the early decades of the seventeenth century are significant for three reasons. First, the public theater was better established in these later decades, and production values, especially for long-standing companies such as the King's Men, would be more elaborate. Second, the early 1600s represent a short reprieve from the fervid iconoclasm that characterized both the 1590s and the 1640s. A third, related reason is that the early 1600s saw a gradual return of more traditional religious practices, a phenomenon that may have encouraged theatrical companies to stage plays in which religious objects play crucial roles.

Just as there is no clear line between Protestant and Catholic practice during this period, the theater is anything but monolithic in its treatment of religious subjects. Responding to Martha Tuck Rozett's contention that the theater provided spectators with the sense of ceremony now missing from the reformed church, and to similar claims put forward by Louis Montrose and Stephen Greenblatt, Huston Diehl and Michael O'Connell have laid out two very different but equally influential models of the relationship between theatrical production and post-Reformation religion. Diehl has argued that the reformed communion and the ideology behind it often impacted the content of public theater productions, and she identifies moments in the surviving scripts that evoke Protestant models of religious behavior. Responding to Diehl's statement that both Protestantism and theater are receptive to the power of words to "move, persuade, and transform," O'Connell argues that plays by authors such as Shakespeare and Jonson are responding directly to the antitheatricalists' attacks on the drama's superficiality.[22] "How did this continuing attack on theater as 'idolatrous,'" he asks, "affect the self-understanding of an art that is visual as well as verbal?" His work proposes a tension between word and image that arises when what he calls "technologies of representation" are in flux. In other words, the theater provoked anxiety among Protestants because it presented a new kind of visuality, one that relied upon "actual human bodies standing for other bodies."[23] O'Connell's attention to the "technology" of theater is particularly useful to my own work on stage properties, and throughout the book I use the related concepts of "material" and "affective" technologies, which I outline in Chapter 1, to parse the relationships between religious and theatrical practice.

(Stanford: Stanford University Press, 1992), 51-70 and Walsham, "Parochial roots of Laudianism."

[22]   "Vital Cultural Practices: Shakespeare and the Mysteries," *Journal of Medieval and Early Modern Studies* 29, no. 1 (Winter 1999): 149-68, 151. See Diehl, "Observing the Lord's Supper and the Lord Chamberlain's Men: The Visual Rhetoric of Ritual and Play in Early Modern England," *Renaissance Drama* 22 (1991): 147-74, and *Staging Reform, Reforming the Stage* (Ithaca: Cornell University Press, 1997).

[23]   O'Connell, *The Idolatrous Eye: Iconoclasm and Theater in Early-Modern England* (New York: Oxford University Press, 2000), 11, 5, 9.

One of my objectives in focusing on stage properties is to find a new, more specific model for the theater's appropriation of religious themes and materials that complicates Stephen Greenblatt's theory of the stage as a mechanism for "emptying out" religious meaning from Catholic objects and rituals.[24] Although Greenblatt himself has moved past this approach, it is useful to remember why this narrative of secularization is so seductive. As Arthur Marotti and Kenneth Jackson argue, critics with Marxist sympathies have long attempted to reduce religion to politics in order to focus on the power structures operating on early modern subjects.[25] More recent work, however, has returned to the basic sympathy between religion and the theater: both were institutions that operated somewhere between the realm of entertainment and didacticism, and the theater was not above appropriating religious materials and resonances into its fictional narratives in order to elicit an emotional response—a process that Anthony Dawson, following Mikhail Bakhtin, calls "disassociation." Referring primarily to the work of the novel, Bakhtin describes disassociation as "a destruction of any absolute bonding of ideological meaning to language."[26] For Dawson, this separation entails finding a new language to describe religious experience, a language that "allow[s] the theatre to extend the range of its reference and hence assert its validity as an independent social practice." Like Peter Lake's study of puritan tropes across literary and nonliterary genres, Dawson's argument focuses on the multiplicity of "languages and voices" operating in the theater, suggesting that the rearrangement of these discourses "helped to separate religious language from its ideological centre" and emphasized the medium's "separateness from religious culture."[27]

My own work focuses on objects rather than on discourse *per se*—the value of the stage property is determined by language, but because it has its own material life it also bears a more complex relationship to meaning than the "authoritative discourses" Dawson discusses. Nonetheless, his emphasis on how the theater reframed religious experience without entirely superceding it is vital to my approach. This book also seeks to extend Dawson's argument by suggesting that acts of Protestant iconoclasm actually paved the way for the theater's own processes of disassociation by removing the implements of traditional religion from their original contexts, thus making them available, imaginatively if not physically, to the playing companies. When objects are translated into the public theater, either directly or indirectly, they necessarily take on new meanings, but

---

[24] See "Resonance and Wonder," in *Learning to Curse* (New York: Routledge, 1990), 161-83.

[25] "The Turn to Religion in Early Modern English Studies," *Criticism* 46, no. 1 (Winter 2004): 167-90.

[26] *The Dialogic Imagination: Four Essays* (Austin: University of Texas Press, 1981), 369.

[27] "The Secular Theatre," in *Shakespeare and the Cultures of Performance*, ed. Paul Yachnin and Patricia Badir (Aldershot, England; Burlington, VT: Ashgate, 2008), 83-100, 86.

their old ones are not always expunged. Rather, each play text performs its own set of negotiations, through dialogue and stage settings, that determines the extent to which a given object can be related to its original context. For this reason, I take theatrical history to be as important to our understanding of the period as the study of material culture *per se*.

This diachronic view of stage properties will be immediately recognizable to readers of Greenblatt's work. In addition to citing the well-documented examples of priests' vestments being sold to acting companies, he also meditates on more specific instances, such as a stage property that might once have been Cardinal Wolsey's hat.[28] In an essay entitled "Resonance and Wonder," Greenblatt explores the aura that adheres to this hat, an aura that originated in the highly theatrical ceremonies of the Catholic hierarchy. The object, he claims, was lost to history after the Reformation, but was eventually given to Christ Church, Oxford by an eighteenth-century theater company. For Greenblatt, the company's appropriation of the cardinal's costume, or part of it, represents one of its more important theatrical innovations. By imagining the actors' efforts to translate the object to the stage without bringing religion itself into the theater, Greenblatt provides a compelling narrative about the way drama works. But as Anne Barton and John Lee have shown, Greenblatt's method relies on eliding the surviving facts about the realities of cultural production when they threaten to complicate his theories.[29]

The object in question here—the "round red priest's" hat Greenblatt came across in Oxford—did have a theatrical history of its own, but not the one he describes. According to the card attached to it, the hat belonged at one time to Horace Walpole and was purchased in 1842 by the actor Charles Kean, who used it repeatedly in productions of *Henry VIII* (1613). The hat thus tells us something about theater generally, but not about Shakespeare's theater. Nor does the display at Christ Church claim that the hat was ever Wolsey's.[30] So although Greenblatt's re-reading of the hat sheds light on the material relationships between the theater and other forms of early modern cultural production, the life cycle of the hat-as-prop, insofar as historians and archivists can reconstruct it, reminds us that we must keep an eye on the material history

---

[28]   Greenblatt, *Learning to Curse*, 161.

[29]   Anne Barton, "Perils of Historicism—Learning to Curse: Essays in Early Modern Culture by Stephen J. Greenblatt," *The New York Review of Books* 38, no. 6 (March 28, 1991): 53; John Lee, "The Man Who Mistook His Hat: Stephen Greenblatt and the Anecdote," *Essays in Criticism: A Quarterly Journal of Literary Criticism* 45, no. 4 (October 1995): 285-300.

[30]   The sale catalogue produced at the time of Kean's death confirms that he bought the item from Walpole but describes the object as follows: "this hat was found in the great wardrobe by Bishop Burnet when he was clerk of the closet. It was left by his son Judge Burnet, to his housekeeper, who gave it to her ladyship, and she gave it to Horace Walpole" (A. N. L. Munby, *Sale Catalogues of Libraries of Eminent Persons* [London: Mansell with Sotheby Parke-Bernet Publications, 1971], 531).

of the theater as well, and the material history of theater is precisely what is at stake in my readings of early modern play scripts.[31] By beginning with the example of the Rose Theatre rosary I acknowledge my debt to Greenblatt, but ultimately I hope to use this and other evidence to emphasize a continuity, rather than a disconnect, between public theater performance and popular devotional forms. Through its use of certain highly charged stage properties, the drama was actively pursuing the question of whether material objects still had a place in the religious culture of early modern England.

Many parishioners managed to profit from the reformers' redistribution of church resources, but others struggled desperately to keep up with the fluctuations in the value and meaning of religious objects. Having destroyed or reshaped their Catholic ornaments at the request of Edward's ministers, they were promptly instructed to restore them under Mary, and then to eliminate them again when Elizabeth came to the throne. A group of citizens in Long Melford complained that their church goods had been "scattered abroad and delivered to sacrilegious persons, which paid little or nothing for them" during the first wave of iconoclastic attacks, and that many of them had been "spoiled and mangled."[32] Among those "sacrilegious persons," we may count theatrical entrepreneurs such as Henslowe, for when priests' vestments made their way into theatrical productions in the late sixteenth century, these objects that had helped shape and define the ceremonies of the Catholic church were put to new use by players imitating priests.[33] Similarly, it is possible that the theater companies were capable of acquiring alienated church furnishings. Such transactions, if they took place at all, do not survive in the documentary record, but not all transactions are physical ones and not all objects are straightforwardly commodifiable. As anthropologists Igor Kopytoff and Arjun Appadurai argue in their examination of the social life of objects, any given thing can be "singularized" or made sacred, but it can also be commodified, made indistinguishable from an object with a similar market value, as it passes

---

[31]   Andrew Sofer makes a similar case for the importance of stage properties as part of an ongoing theatrical tradition in *The Stage Life of Props* (Ann Arbor: University of Michigan 2003), but he is primarily interested in the theatrical experience of the objects rather than their historical specificity. Similarly, my work departs from the phenomenological approach taken by Frances Teague in *Shakespeare's Speaking Properties* (Lewisburg: Bucknell University Press; London; Cranbury, NJ: Associated University Presses, 1991), but I am indebted to her discussion of the way the function of properties is often distinct from the function of the objects they reference. See, for instance, her discussion of knives, 18ff.

[32]   Christopher Haigh, *English Reformations: Religion, Politics, and Society Under the Tudors* (Oxford: Clarendon Press, 1993), 210.

[33]   Glynne Wickham adduces two instances from 1574 where liturgical vestments were sold outright (*Early English Stages 1300-1660* [London: Routledge and Paul, 1959], 2). Churchwardens in Maldon and Braintree rented out vestments as costumes before they sold off wardrobes in 1564 and 1579, and at New Romney, Kent, the pageant organizers bought "copes and vestures" to make players' costumes in 1560 (O'Connell, "Vital Cultural Practices," 118).

into larger spheres of social exchange.[34] Nor were there easy answers to questions about what a religious object was worth or what meanings could be attached to it, especially after the Reformation dislodged these objects from their original context. Accordingly, this book seeks to map out a broad spectrum of possibilities associated with the circulation of stage properties and the corresponding circulation of sacred objects.

In 1553 a local man named Helier stole a cross from his church in Silverton and proceeded to plant it in a hedgerow, where he hung "pictures of Our Lady and St. John" from its arms.[35] This early example of performance art was intended to mock the structure of rood crosses, which frequently included the figures of the two saints in addition to the body of Christ. Helier's actions thus present a clear example of the process whereby "Protestant imagery not only draws upon, but pointedly redefines traditional Catholic images that remained fixed in people's minds."[36] On the other hand, there was no guarantee that every passerby would read this display as the triumph of Protestantism over superstition. The very act of removing objects such as crosses from parish churches prompted processes of revaluation that did not always end with their being dismissed as false idols. Similarly, although religious objects might be used in a stage play to indicate a Catholic character's hypocrisy, there was no way of ensuring that other meanings might not be layered on top of more familiar, stereotypical ones. In a surprising number of cases, the playing companies actually took advantage of the complex range of emotions associated with traditional worship, complicating the anti-Catholic stereotypes linking material objects to idolatry. Acknowledging its own investment in ephemeral objects, the theater frequently pointed out gaps in the project of Protestant reform, gaps that revealed a structural similarity between the materiality of performance and the materiality of religious practice.

The Quality of Playing

My work on early modern drama is inspired by the advances in historical scholarship made during the last ten to fifteen years, but several generations of literary scholars have noted that much of what we know about theatrical performances during this period comes either from the Protestant statutes that attempted to control them or

---

[34]   Igor Kopytoff, "The cultural biography of things: commoditization as process," in *The social life of things: commodities in cultural perspective*, ed. Arjun Appadurai (Cambridge; New York: Cambridge University Press, 1986), 64-91. A key term for Kopytoff is what he calls cultural biography of a thing: "the story of the various singularizations of it, classifications and reclassifications in an uncertain world of categories whose importance shifts with every minor change in context" (90).

[35]   Whiting, 79.

[36]   John N. King, *Tudor Royal Iconography: Literature and Art in an Age of Religious Crisis* (Princeton: Princeton University Press, 1989), 122-3.

the antitheatricalist complaints designed to undermine them. Accordingly, E. K. Chambers devotes a substantial portion of his multi-volume study, *The Elizabethan Theatre*, to "Documents of criticism and control." More recently, O'Connell has described pre-Reformation drama as "merely one element in the complex of worship and religious practice" marked for elimination by Protestant reformers.[37] Although the cycle plays were eventually stamped out, a new form of popular theater was emerging, one that could not always be prevented from engaging with religious subjects. Despite regulations such as the one Elizabeth's parliament passed in 1559, the Privy Council was still complaining thirty years later that "the players take upon themselves to handle in their plaies certain matters of Divinyties and of State unfitt to be suffred, for redress whereof their Lordships have thought good to appointe some persones of judgement and understanding to viewe and examine their playes before they be permitted to present them publickly."[38]

Both the original statute and the complaint lodged by the Privy Council seem to suggest that the objectionable plays were treating matters of doctrine; yet they fail to mention the presence of "papist" objects. The assumption on the part of lawgivers may have been that religious objects were so controversial that even the playing companies would choose not to use them. But as with the slippage between Protestant practice and Catholic practice, there was a variety of more or less obvious ways the players could represent religious subjects. A 1603 sermon by Henry Crosse bewailing the representation of biblical figures in the theater introduced another potential threat: "Must the holy Prophets and Patriarkes be set upon a Stage, to be derided, hist, and laught at? Or is it fit that the infirmities of holy men should be acted on a Stage, whereby others may be inharted to rush carelessly forward into unbrideled libertie?"[39] While focusing primarily on the profane treatment of religious men, perhaps his own contemporaries, Crosse's language introduces a familiar element of many antitheatrical discourses, the idea that sinful actions depicted on a stage will cause audience members to "rush carelessly forward" into similar activities. Implicit in his critique is the fear that, in addition to adopting a libertine attitude toward their own lives, spectators will be encouraged by the players to scorn religious authority.

In response to the ongoing practice of introducing religious subjects and figures into the theater, the crown issued another "Acte to Restraine Abuses of Players" in 1606. This statute specified that "any person or persons doe or shall in any Stage play, Interlude, Shewe, Maygame, or Pageant jestingly or prophanely speake or use the holy Name of God or of Christ Jesus, or of the Holy Ghoste or of the Trinitie, which are not to be spoken but which feare and reverence [such person or persons] shall forfeite for everie such Offence by hym or them committed Tenne Pounds." This document does not address the representation of religious subjects, but rather the very appearance of God's name in the public theater.

---

[37]   O'Connell, "Vital Cultural Practices," 23.

[38]   Chambers, 306.

[39]   Ibid., 247.

The law, it seems, could not be any clearer about the necessity of preventing common players from recklessly invoking sacred names, persons, or doctrines. Yet in 1608, William Crashaw was still describing actors as "children of Babylon that will not be healed." "[N]ow," he announces, as if this had not been a problem all along, "they bring religion and holy things upon the stage: no marvel though the worthiest and mightiest men escape not, when God himselfe is so abused."[40]

Despite the valuable information they provide about contemporary responses to the theater, however, it is important not to take the antitheatricalist diatribes too much at face value. Crashaw, like Crosse, seems primarily to be remarking on plays with direct or indirect references to contemporary political figures; in 1609 he again complained that the actors "play with Princes and Potentates, Magistrates and ministers, nay with God and Religion, and all holy things."[41] What is important about these "Documents of criticism and control" is that they reveal precisely how difficult it was to confine the playing companies to uncontroversial subjects. But if it was impossible for the authorities to prevent religious matters and personages from appearing on the public stage, the plays that flew in the face of royal edicts did more than just challenge the authority of the Protestant state. Because they were performed publicly and to large crowds, their reception was entirely unpredictable. Nominal religious conformity was a crucial element of Elizabethan and Jacobean policy, and the theater challenged this conformity by allowing spectators to react, on their own terms, to the objects being presented on stage.

Some Protestant writers, most notably William Prynne, sought to place these profane activities within a providential framework in which the players' blasphemy would, of necessity, bring down divine retribution on their heads. Another one of Prynne's strategies was to draw connections between pagan actors and contemporary ones, as this remarkable anecdote from *Histrio-mastix* (1633) makes clear:

> It is recorded of one Porphory a Pagan Stage-Player, that he grew to such an height of impiety, as he adventured to baptize himselfe in jest upon the Stage, of purpose to make the people laugh at Christian Baptisme, and so to bring both it and Christianity into contempt; and for this purpose he plunged himselfe into a vessell of water which he had placed on the Stage, calling aloud upon the Trinity: at which the Spectators fell into a great laughter. But loe the goodnesse of God to this prophane miscreant; it pleased God to shew such a demonstration of his power and grace upon him, that this sporting baptisme of his, became a serious laver of regeneration to him: in so much that of a gracelesse Player, he became a gracious Christian, and not long after, a constant Martyr.[42]

---

[40]   Ibid., 338-9, 249.

[41]   Ibid., 254.

[42]   *Histrio-Mastix: The Players Scourge, or, Actors Tragaedie* (London: Printed by E[dward] A[llde, Augustine Mathewes, Thomas Cotes] and W[illiam] I[ones], 1633), 119-20.

With this example, Prynne endeavors to turn the spontaneity and flexibility of the theater, and of audience response, against the player himself. Although the pagan actor intends his gestures to be blasphemous, and although they produce the desired effect among members of his audience, they paradoxically result in his very genuine conversion. This is the type of positive moral influence Heywood's *Apology for Actors* (1612) claimed for the theater. Plays, Heywood writes, are socially useful because they are capable of showing "action, passion, motion, or any other gesture, to moove the spirits of the beholder to admiration."[43] Prynne, too, is aware of the affective power of theatrical performance. He even reproduces an early defense of Catholic drama, Lindanus's assertion that "Stage-playes have a certaine shape of Images; and oft times move the pious affections of Christians, more than prayer it selfe." For this very reason, Prynne argued fervently that the souls of men and women were automatically imperiled when they stepped into the Globe or the Phoenix, where their senses were bombarded with images and sounds that moved them not to piety but to sin. "In Play-houses," Prynne contends, "there is a contagion of manners, where people use to learne filthy things, to heare dishonest things, to see pernicious things… [t]here the quier and singing of the Stage player allureth the hearing, but conquereth the wholesome affection."[44] Focusing in particular on religious stage properties, this book explores the variety of "affections," they may have excited among audience members, and how these emotional responses further problematize the categories "Catholic" and "Protestant."

In *Plays confuted in five actions* (1582), one of the most powerful denunciations of the role material objects played in the popular theater, Stephen Gosson attacks the trifles that occupy a central place in dramatic fictions:

> Sometime you shall see nothing but the adventures of an amorous knight, passing from countrie to countrie for the love of his lady, encountering many a terible monster made of broune paper, & at his returne, is so wonderfully changed, that he cannot be knowne but by some posie in his tablet, or by a broken ring, or a handkircher or a piece of a cockle shell, what learn you by that? When the soul of your playes is eyther meere trifles or Italian baudry, or wooing of gentlewomen, what are we taught?[45]

Here Gosson prefigures the question posed by Prynne: what does the audience take with them when they leave the theater? Objects such as the finger in *The Changeling*, the skull in *Hamlet*, and the asp in *Antony and Cleopatra* were at the center of playgoers' impressions of early modern theater. Thus, Gosson's attack captures a genuine insight: these things are not trifles, but rather provide important access points to the play text. Gosson's rhetoric deserves further attention,

---

[43] *An apology for actors* (London: Okes, 1612), B3ʳ.

[44] Ibid., 764-5, 347.

[45] Stephen Gosson, *Playes confuted in five actions* (London: n.p., 1582), C6ʳ.

however—in part because he is employing the language of trifles and trinkets that, as I discuss in the final section of the book, was deeply tied to anti-Catholic polemics. Gosson specifically derides plays in which characters become unrecognizable when separated from their properties. These fictions, drawn primarily from Italian romances, suggest that things such as handkerchiefs can function as the anchors for fantasies of uniqueness, despite the fact that a given handkerchief may have been used as a nose-wipe in another play and even though the actor playing the hero might have appeared as a Turk in the previous scene. In other words, Gosson seeks to expose the hypocrisy at the heart of the play's fantasy of uniqueness by directing his readers' attention to the banality of the objects used to construct this ideal of singularity. "When the soul of your plays is eyther meere trifles or Italian baudry," Gosson asks, "what are we taught?" The word "trifles" is associated here with frivolous foreigners and foolish women, but it also registers a certain nervousness about the effect such plays might have on their audiences. If the audience were to focus on such apparently trivial objects, including their origins and life histories, what might they learn?

Around the same time that Prynne was revitalizing Gosson's initial critique, Richard Brome produced a play that combined the antitheatricalists' anxieties about pagan idols, seductive players, and dangerous fantasies in one metatheatrical plot. *The Antipodes* (1638), named for the mythical region in which social behaviors are precisely the opposite of those in England, argues for the curative power of theater, but it also flirts with the realization of Prynne's greatest fear: that those who enter the playhouse will, in fact, lose the ability to distinguish spectacle from reality. Brome's play also references the contention of writers such as Gosson that stage properties are mere trifles by making its own properties part of a powerful, and ultimately positive, theatrical fantasy. Both the main and secondary plots of *The Antipodes* emphasize the importance of sexual pleasure in marriage, but eroticism is not the only form of sensuality the text celebrates. Its central figure, Sir LeToy, is a man who loves "the quality of playing" above all else, spending his money not on his own costume but on apparel for his actors.[46] As the events of the play unfold, LeToy's company provides an innovative cure for two psychologically unbalanced characters: a young man who is obsessed with travel and an old man who is overly jealous of his wife. The play thus concretizes Heywood's claim that the drama can provoke positive emotions in its audience.

In an effort to cure Peregrine, the youth with an unhealthy appetite for travel narratives, and to restore his sexual interest in his wife, his family members conspire with LeToy and a famous doctor to convince him that he has, in fact, traveled to the Antipodes. There he meets his wife in the guise of a foreign princess and, with renewed vigor, marries and beds her. But Peregrine is not merely a passive participant in the scenario that has been constructed for his benefit. He expresses distinct preferences about how his world is to be furnished—he chooses a sword

---

[46] *The Antipodes*, ed. Ann Haaker (Lincoln: University of Nebraska Press, 1966), 1.5.72.

property, an attractive scabbard with no sword in it, over a real one—and soon after reaching the Antipodes, he sets about to conquer it by attacking the material trappings of the fiction itself. According to the lead actor in LeToy's company:

> He has got into our tiring house amongst us,
> And ta'en a strict survey of all our properties;
> Our statues and our images of gods, our Planets and our constellations,
> Our giants, monsters, furies, beasts, and bugbears,
> Our helmets, shields, and vizors, hairs, and beards,
> Our pasteboard marchpanes, and our wooden pies.
> …Whether he thought 'twas some enchanted castle,
> Or temple, hung and pil'd with monuments
> Of uncouth and of various aspects,
> I dive not to his thoughts. Wonder he did
> A while it seem'd, but yet undaunted stood;
> When on the sudden, with thrice knightly force,
> And thrice, thrice puissant at me he snatcheth down
> The sword and shield that I played Bevis with,
> Rusheth amongst the foresaid properties,
> Kills monster after monster, takes the puppets
> Prisoners, knocks down the Cyclops, tumbles all
> Our jigambobs and trinkets to the wall.
> Spying at last the crown and royal robes
> I' th' upper wardrobe, next to which by chance
> The devil's vizors hung, and their flame-painted
> Skin coats; those he remov'd with greater fury,
> And (having cut the infernal ugly faces,
> All into mammocks) with a reverend hand,
> He takes the imperial diadem and crowns
> Himself King of the Antipodes, and believes
> He has justly gain'd the kingdom by his conquest.
> (3.6.2-31)

I cite this speech in full because it provides a detailed account of how early modern stage properties were made from materials such as "past board" and wood, but also because the actor, Byplay, self-consciously adopts the language of antitheatricalism, calling some of the properties "jigambobs and trinkets." His narrative also evokes the romance plots, such as those inspired by the famous Bevis of Hampton, which were wildly popular on the stage and in ballad literature. Finally, it recalls the 1617 Shrove Tuesday attack on the Cockpit playhouse in which several apprentices destroyed a large number of costumes and props; their exploits were celebrated in a ballad that echoes Peregrine's triumphant righteousness.[47]

---

[47] Ibid., 69.

What is most extraordinary about this account, however, is its revelation about Peregrine's fantasy of exploration, which relies explicitly on material objects. In fact, the young man is so fully convinced of the power of certain stage properties that when he tears down the "temple" in the tiring house he believes he has conquered the entire country. Having made himself the *de facto* ruler of the Antipodeans, as represented by LeToy's actors, Peregrine sets out to normalize their social customs. His re-imposition of English mores and his abolishment of the carnivalesque behaviors of the Antipodeans also facilitate his own return to psychological health by curing him of his fascination with foreign cultures. Here, as in the schooling of Loveless the jealous husband, the play points up the positive influence of dramatic fictions in contemporary culture. It is not insignificant that this process of instituting "Englishness" in the fictional Antipodes begins with the destruction of "[o]ur statues and our images of gods." Even though iconoclasm is construed as a normative English virtue, Peregrine's belief in the efficacy of destroying idols highlights the irony of iconoclastic attacks, which often reinforce the aggressor's belief in the power of the objects themselves. Layered on top of this commentary on iconoclasm is the fact that Peregrine mistakes what Byplay himself calls "jigambobs" for the furnishings of a real pagan temple, thus fulfilling the antitheatricalists' predictions. Only those with weak wits, the play argues, will mistake stage properties for the things they are intended to represent, and Peregrine's response to the fabricated objects presented to him is modeled after that of an unusually receptive spectator. His "affections" are thus subject to superficial displays, fulfilling Prynne's predictions about the seductive power of the theater, even as his destruction of the idols and his reformation of the Antipodeans' social behaviors conform to a strict Protestant model of godly action.

Brome's play is first and foremost a celebration of the theater, particularly if we take LeToy as its protagonist, but this celebration is dependent on a demystification of critiques like Prynne's, for in Peregrine's case the experience of being carried away by his fantasy ironically brings him back to a more normative way of living. A further level of irony is suggested by the doctor's assertion that in the Antipodes "all their poets are puritans... And players, too," and that these men are the "sob'rest/ Precisest people pick'd out of a nation" (1.6.197, 198-9). Although it deals most directly with theatrical representations of pagan culture, *The Antipodes* serves as a useful introduction to my discussion of Christian objects in the public theater plays that preceded it, for it provides an account of the contents of a tiring house, including detailed clues about how stage properties were constructed. Moreover, it articulates a complex response to Prynne's complaint about the theater's negative impact by making these pagan properties central to Peregrine's eventual cure. And it reminds us that even when the religious objects presented on stage are "pagan" they may still have a great deal to do with the experience of English worshipers in post-Reformation England, especially because Peregrine's attack on the "temple" is reminiscent of Protestant iconoclasm. Although I do not want to dismiss the significance of the disassociative strategies whereby pagan implements were substituted for more controversial Christian objects, I would argue that many plays, including those that stage rituals involving pagan altars, need to be read within the context of the religious culture in which they were produced—a culture in which the status of both Catholic objects and the material practices that went with them were hotly contested.

Properties in Action

The dramatic texts that figure most prominently in this book, by playwrights such as Fletcher, Ford, Massinger, and Webster, are infrequently performed on the modern stage, but we can also learn something about the religious resonances embedded in a variety of early modern scripts by studying recent productions of Shakespearean drama.[48] In particular, the traditional sets and costumes used at the new Shakespeare's Globe in London provide us with one method of assessing the performance possibilities recorded in the surviving play scripts. Many of the Globe Theatre Company's productions feature Elizabethan garments that were made using early modern tools and materials, and for these productions the theater professionals at the Globe have devised stage settings that reflect, to the best of their knowledge, those of the versatile repertory companies of Shakespeare's day. Though centered around an unusual casting principle—all the actors were female—the 2003 production of *Richard III* performed by the Women's Company serves as a particularly good example of the Globe's ability to create "authentic" performance values. In fact, the program notes specifically assert that the setting, costumes, and music were all within the reach of the Admiral's Men in 1593. Apart from small items such as pens, paper, hats, and jewelry, the properties were primarily made of paint, cloth, and/or wood and included a bed, several tables, Hastings's head, a throne, two books, two crosses, and a crucifix. The latter objects, in particular, played noteworthy roles in the company's depiction of Catholicism and were used to draw attention to false piety as a crucial aspect of Richard's hypocritical behavior. Although this was a modern interpretation, it provides a suggestive example of the way in which a script with unexceptional stage directions can be said to invite the use of religious stage properties. In other words, productions such as the *Richard III* performed by the Globe Women's Company remind us that dramatic depictions of religious practice are often implied rather than specifically called for.

One type of property, a set of wooden crosses, was brought on during the scene in which Richard positions himself as a model of pious devotion for the benefit of the citizens of London. The scene is both a typical example of Gloucester's hypocrisy and a jab at traditional Catholicism, as the 2003 production made clear.

---

[48] Here and elsewhere in the book I consciously avoid engaging with recent critical debates about the status of Shakespeare's own religious belief. Though Stephen Greenblatt, in particular, has thrown important new light on the subject in recent years, questions of biography have little bearing on the performance-centered approach I am using here.

Both within the fiction and on a literal level, these simple wooden crosier staffs served as props for the bishops, described by Buckingham as "two deep divines."[49] For her part, the actor playing Richard was dressed in a white robe and cowl that made her look like an El Greco saint. She held rosary beads in one hand and an upside-down prayer book in the other. The crosses, which served as extensions of the bishops themselves, also framed the actor's body as she raised her arms in imitation of Christ. Whether consciously or not, this blocking pattern invoked the triangular structure of wooden crucifixes, like the one Helier placed in the bush. The image of the episcopal figure holding a cross staff would itself have been a highly familiar one: at least four public theater plays from the period, including *Doctor Faustus*, call for characters to enter with crosiers.[50] The image of the bishop with his crosier might also have been recognizable to playgoers because of anti-papal broadsheets, or, conversely, the stained glass windows in parish churches. Among the many images William Dowsing destroyed during his 1643 campaign to stamp out idolatry in East Anglia and Cambridgeshire was one of "the three kings coming to Christ with presents, and three bishops with their mitres and crosier staffs."[51] The Globe Theatre Company's production clearly referenced this iconic symbol of the Catholic church hierarchy, but it also demonstrated Richard's hypocrisy in appropriating it. The bishops were hooded, never showing their faces, and they turned away as if in silent disgust at the end of the scene. The production thus suggested that these characters were paid actors who, like the men employed to murder the princes, took Richard's money but played their roles somewhat unwillingly.

The second stage property used to enliven the play's portrait of Catholic devotion was a small, standing crucifix. Although, as I explain in Chapter 3, there was some slippage during the early modern period between the terms "cross" and "crucifix," the properties used in this production effectively illuminated their material differences. The crosses used in Act 3 resembled the processional crosses depicted in *Crumms of comfort*; they did not contain the figure of Christ, and neither the bishops nor Richard himself made reverence to them. Conversely, the small crucifix, which figured prominently in the reconciliation scene prior to Edward's death in Act 2, clearly included the body of Christ and was used as a devotional tool to which various characters performed obeisance. It looked, in fact, like a portable altar cross, one of the first objects banned by the reformers in the sixteenth century. This property was apparently made of wood that had been painted gold. It had a square base, was approximately a foot high and—as those of

---

[49]   *The Riverside Shakespeare*, ed. G. Blakemore Evans and J. J. M. Tobin, 2nd ed. (Boston: Houghton Mifflin, 1997), 3.7.75. All citations to Shakespeare's plays refer to this edition.

[50]   These include Marlowe's *Doctor Faustus* (1592), Haughton's *Grim the Collier of Croyden* (1600), Dekker's *The Whore of Babylon* (1606), and *The Two Noble Ladies* (1622). Such properties also appear frequently in the REED volumes.

[51]   Margaret Aston, *England's Iconoclasts* (Oxford: Clarendon Press, 1988), 78.

us standing in the pit could see clearly—the figure of Christ was affixed to it. The crucifix was carried on stage by the ailing King Edward, who made a display of kissing it passionately as he spoke of his impending death. Members of the 2003 audience might or might not have been aware that Edward's devotions referenced the practice depicted in the Sharpe foldout, for as part of a "good death" Catholics were instructed to hold the image of their redeemer before them, to kiss it, and to use it as a weapon for warding off the devil. Here again, the property operated on two levels: first, as a reference to traditional religion, and second, as proof that the material trappings of Catholicism were often used to disguise hypocrisy as genuine piety.

After announcing his intention to reconcile his kinsmen before his death, Edward placed the crucifix on the ground, near the front of the stage. Here it sat, ignored by all the other characters—except Gloucester, who ostentatiously removed his sword, knelt in front of it, and crossed himself before addressing the assembled nobles. During this extrapolated stage business, the crucifix remained at eye level to audience members in the yard, who could not help but see it as a prominent aspect of the stage setting before Richard entered and well after he finished his supposed devotions. For these spectators, in particular, the crucifix foregrounded the rest of the scene, and on a stage otherwise uncluttered by objects the crucifix took on an even greater significance. When the actor playing Richard knelt down in front of it, she had the opportunity to exchange knowing looks with the audience, who were encouraged to savor her self-conscious wickedness. But although this production, like the play itself, celebrated the versatility of Richard's performance, it also reinforced Protestant stereotypes linking Catholicism with duplicity. The connection between Richard's appearance with the bishops and his ostentatious gestures toward Edward's crucifix both supported antitheatrical, anti-Catholic tropes that linked the performance of piety in the Catholic church with the superficial shows put on by public theater actors—perhaps in part because this is still the most familiar stereotype of Catholic practice available to English-speaking Protestants.

Throughout the production, religious stage properties were used to concretize the practices and principles Richard so blithely violates. They formed the anchor for the play's exploration of traditional faith systems, but they also demonstrated the ways in which Richard was able to use the performative aspects of religion in order to cover up his unholy thoughts. In fact, the impact of these religious properties relied in part on modern audience members' ability to place the bishops' wooden crosses and the king's gilded crucifix within the context of traditional religion. Edward's behavior in kissing the crucifix, for instance, could only be fully appreciated if spectators had some knowledge of Catholic practices. But as with all successful theater, neither scene rested entirely on the meaning of its stage objects, and the audience could derive as much about Richard's character from his sly looks as from his behavior toward the crucifix.

The stage directions available in the surviving text of *Richard III* are minimal at best: the one in Act 3 simply specifies that Richard should appear "*aloft*" with two "*bishops*" and does not mention any stage objects, while the stage direction in Act 2, scene 1 indicates only that the king is sick (3.7.94 sd.). Therefore, in addition to providing us with a twenty-first-century attempt to recreate the religious resonances of a play first performed at the height of Elizabethan iconoclasm, this production reminds us that the Admiral's Men were themselves extrapolating from the script. Shakespeare's published plays have notoriously thin stage directions, but in performance the actors were not even given the quarto to work from, at least not initially. Instead, they were handed a series of roles or parts for each actor to memorize. What I find useful about the Globe Theatre Company's production, therefore, is not that it proves conclusively that the Admiral's Men could have carved a wooden crucifix and painted it gold, or that they could have paid a carpenter to make them a crosier staff. Rather, it provides one example of how an individual group of actors could interpret Richard's hypocrisy as a misappropriation of sacred objects, choosing the necessary stage properties to support their interpretation rather than relying on the playwright to specify them.

This project began with an interest in unusual stage directions, the ones that mention religious objects explicitly, but it has also led me to consider the variety of more subtle ways the public theater responded to the reformers' attacks on the material trappings of Catholicism. Thus, while Shakespeare is typically cagey about bringing religious subjects on stage, he has contributed in important ways to my thinking about the staging of religious objects. And although I am fascinated by playwrights such as Philip Massinger who push the boundaries of the theatrical medium by addressing religious questions head on, I acknowledge, as early modern performers did, the limits of their creative enterprise. Those limitations were physical as much as political, and the constraints placed on the repertory companies often prompted the ingenious reuse of key properties. Objects such as crosiers, which were the exclusive property of bishops, might have been familiar cues that allowed playgoers to identify the characters as Catholic prelates, and their very familiarity may in turn have led to their subsequent absence from quarto and folio stage directions.

When I first began to compile lists of stage properties with religious associations I posed a series of questions about what was happening within the space of the theater: "What were these objects *doing* on the secular stage? Were they always controversial, or could they be presented in ways that rendered them acceptable within a particular fictional framework?" There are, of course, multiple answers to these questions. Individual playwrights and playing companies had different investments in religious objects and varying solutions to the problem of their controversial status. But, as I argue throughout the book, they all reveal the theater's reliance on material objects, an investment it shared with adherents of mainstream Protestantism as well as with members of the recusant community. What is surprising about these plays is not that they somehow attempt to resurrect Catholicism. Rather, their subversive potential, where it exists, springs from their ability to draw an analogy between their own material technologies and those that characterized post-Reformation religion. No simple model of appropriation maps onto actual stage practices of the London theater companies, but the particular materiality of each type of stage property corresponds to a strategy by which the theater companies addressed their audiences' persistent engagement with the physical aspects of Christian worship.

The Materials of Performance

My examination of the surviving play scripts has revealed a variety of references to religious stage properties as well as a wide range of attitudes toward those objects within the fictions. In order to reflect the specificity of the processes by which religious objects were appropriated by the playing companies, each chapter addresses a particular property: tombs, altars, crosses, and books. The first two chapters deal with relatively large stage objects and with what I call "material technologies"—physical structures and gestures inherited from Catholic ritual and dramatic forms. In terms of the frequency with which they appear in the surviving plays from the period, tomb and altar properties are relatively rare, but they do participate in clear generic and historical patterns. In other words, they are used in materially similar ways from one production to another and tend to refer more directly to ritual practice.

The next two chapters deal with smaller, more intimate properties, whose function is almost entirely determined by the dramatic context into which they are introduced and which appear far more frequently in the theater as well as outside it. Crosses and religious books were both more important to daily religious practice than large ritual objects and more adaptable to post-Reformation contexts. Accordingly, these items are presented in a number of different ways in the surviving play scripts and operate more as "affective technologies," a phrase I use to describe the emotional resonance that the public theater companies managed to translate from a religious medium to their own secular plots. These chapters reference private religious practices rather than ritual *per se* and thus speak more directly to the circulation of sacred objects in post-Reformation England. A discussion of their shifting status leads into the coda, where I explore what happens to stage properties once they leave the theater.

Chapter 1 examines the theatrical appropriation of sepulchers or tombs, which were also used as properties in the guild-sponsored plays depicting the resurrection of Christ. Strictly speaking, they derived from the Easter ceremonies of the Catholic church and other dramatizations of Christ emerging from his tomb, but such practices had long since been outlawed, and the stage properties I examine here did not directly reference their religious antecedents. Large enough to contain an actor's body, or to conceal a trapdoor through which he could emerge, they were likely made of wood painted to look like stone or marble. Some tomb properties had hinged or moveable lids, while others might have included life-sized effigies to make them look more like contemporary grave sculptures. Henslowe lists not one but two tombs in his inventory, and I argue that such properties supplied the necessary conditions for a character's sudden return to life, a convention that became a stock feature of Jacobean tragicomedies. I also suggest, however, that this convention was firmly rooted in the pre-Reformation drama, whose stage directions provide a rich account of the theatrical possibilities of such a stage object.

Drawing on Michael O'Connell and Lawrence Clopper's insights about the continuing influence of the cycle plays on post-Reformation culture, I examine a series of public theater plays in which a character emerges from his or her tomb. Shakespeare's career is representative of the commercial theater's interest in staging resurrections, and his experimentation with this well-established trope culminates in *The Winter's Tale* (1610) at the moment when Hermione's statue suddenly "comes to life." These moments of resurrection provided a connection between the medieval and early modern dramatic forms, just as the persistence of certain physical objects provided a bridge between pre- and post-Reformation modes of worship. More specifically, I make the claim that in order to understand the theater's use of these properties as anything other than simply parodic we need to consider their role in a continuing theatrical tradition. Consequently, I read Webster's *The Duchess of Malfi* (1614) and *The Winter's Tale* as plays that inherited a powerful material technology from their medieval predecessors which they endowed with a new type of emotional charge.

Like tomb properties, altars were also large enough to serve as the focus of a particular scene and to be associated with dominant generic traditions. But unlike tombs, which consisted of a box with or without a lid, the onstage altars I address in Chapter 2 were created by placing smaller objects—candlesticks, cloths, crucifixes, and even statues—upon a table-like structure. Thus the basic unit used to construct the altar also appeared in banquet scenes and could even double as a writing desk. The *OED* defines a property, in the theatrical sense, as "any portable article, as an article of costume or furniture, used in acting a play," but stage altars were more than portable; they were also adaptable.[52] The surviving stage directions tend to describe altars as large visual set pieces that are either "set out," "laid out," or suddenly "discovered," having been assembled ahead of time, suggesting that they had to be constructed by adding the appropriate ornamentation. Notably, one of the main goals of the Protestant reformers was to strip the altar of its popish trappings and eventually replace it with a simple wooden table that reflected the communion's function as a commemorative meal rather than a sacrifice. Thus the material technology used in the theater, by which an altar was transformed into an ordinary table and back again, actually mirrored some aspects of Protestant iconoclasm. Because of these and other underlying analogies between stage altars and church altars, the plays I discuss in this chapter can be readily analyzed within the framework of contemporary debates over proper Christian worship.

---

[52] *Oxford English Dictionary* (Oxford and New York: Oxford University Press, 1989-), online edition, copyright 2008, "property," 3. Subsequent references to the *OED* will be listed parenthetically in the text.

In this second chapter, then, I move from dramatic forms to ceremonial forms in order to suggest that the early modern theater, with its reliance on a small number of highly adaptable properties, used those objects to reference ongoing debates over the status of "idolatrous" Catholic altars and "godly" Protestant communion tables. For although altars could not be carried around the stage or passed from one character to another, they had immense mobility within the repertory system precisely because they could be so easily reconfigured. This flexibility in turn allowed them to highlight the different uses of ritual objects. Jonson's *Sejanus* (1603) and Middleton's *A Game at Chess* (1624), for instance, reveal the connections between theater and religious ritual, while Fletcher, Field, and Massinger's *The Knight of Malta* (1618) and Ford's *The Broken Heart* (1630) stress the slippage between the communion table and the altar, presenting a more positive view of the role such objects played in individual communities. Ultimately, these scripts reveal a dynamic, overarching analogy between religious practice and dramatic practice. By building altars on stage the actors were able to address the constructed nature of the implements of the mass, drawing attention to structural similarities between the technologies of the theater and those of the church.

Crosses, by far the most controversial religious objects to be incorporated into early modern scripts, appeared in a variety of material forms. If the altar was constituted by what was put on it, the degree of controversy elicited by the cross depended on its physical qualities, its size and dimensionality. The public theater companies avoided bringing wooden roods on stage, and when they did use crosses they were typically small ones. With this third chapter, then, the book shifts away from large, ritual objects to objects associated with personal acts of devotion. But even with domestic crosses it was difficult to dissociate the materialization of the object from the worship of the anthropomorphized image of Christ. Consequently, crosses were often used to decorate actors' shields and breastplates. This particular appropriation made the cross less problematic through its association with Christian soldiers, especially those fighting abroad against a Muslim enemy. Crosses also appeared as processional items or as hand-held properties that might have been made of wood or paste board. Occasionally, a play script calls for a cross or crucifix to decorate an altar; these objects might have resembled the painted wooden object made for the Women's Company at the Globe. And in several cases, crosses appear as small, jeweled objects worn about the neck.

In this third chapter I argue that in order to deploy such a controversial symbol on the public stage, the theater companies presented a number of cross properties that were somehow adapted from their original religious context. Some, for instance, displaced these properties into foreign contexts and associated them with the actors' bodies, making them markers of personal virtue rather than idols to be worshiped. This strategy is especially evident in plays with nationalistic overtones. European characters fighting in the Holy Land wore crosses on their tunics, and in such settings the cross became a less problematic symbol of generic Christianity. The crucifix stood on the opposite end of the spectrum from these painted military emblems, and it was deeply offensive to Protestant reformers because it contained a three-dimensional image of the body of Christ. The final section of this chapter reveals, however, that small crucifixes survived in private homes and on the stage throughout the early 1600s. Although these household crucifixes did not directly reference religious ritual, they were nonetheless endowed by dramatic fictions with a powerful affective value.

Unlike the properties which seem to have been fabricated specially for the playing companies, the objects I discuss in Chapter 4 were most likely "real" books. There are at least two reasons the early modern playing companies might have chosen to employ actual books in scenes that call for a character to read a prayer manual or Bible. First, small quartos were relatively easy to buy or borrow, and thus in plays such as *Richard III* any book would do. Second, in plays such as Heywood's *If You Know Not Me, You Know Nobody* (1604) that actually depicted a character handling an English Bible, it would have been potentially sacrilegious to use anything other than a copy of the scriptures. Although later generations of theater professionals would commission authentic-looking prayer books to be made for them, it seems clear that in the theater of Shakespeare's day the actors were handling actual codexes—though whether they were in fact the books called for in the script is another question altogether. This basic uncertainty at the heart of scenes that use book properties in turn reflects an instability in the use of books as emblems of reformed devotion, and in Chapter 4 I explore the self-conscious use of books as stage properties, arguing that they are often deployed in pointed references to the performative nature of piety.

The immaterial word of God was at the heart of the Protestant belief system, but as plays such as *Richard III*, *Arden of Faversham* (1591), and *Hamlet* (1600) make clear, the undeniable materiality of books revealed the irony of using physical images and objects to convey the abstract ideals Protestants attached to the act of reading. Theatrical practice thus mirrored the doctrinal crux at the heart of Protestant devotion by exposing the contradiction involved in designating books and the bodily practice of reading as indicators of an immaterial quality called faith. This chapter also deals extensively with the gendered nature of reading, or, more properly, with gendered representations of reading. The reformers prided themselves on the fact that members of the middling classes and women now had access to the word of God, thanks to the Book of Common Prayer and the widespread publication of English bibles; moreover, the model of the godly Protestant household relied upon having an obedient, literate woman as its anchor. By stressing the performative nature of these roles, plays such as *Arden of Faversham* explore the paradox at the heart of Protestant reading practices, which depended upon the physical materiality of the book as much as Catholic worship did, and which were often difficult to distinguish from the false or idolatrous behaviors associated with popery.

The book concludes with an examination of the afterlife of stage properties. Early modern properties often had little economic value, but in plays such as *Othello* they take on important roles within the fiction. The infamous handkerchief gains and loses value as it passes from hand to hand: it appears as a love token in one scene and a magical charm in the next. I read this play alongside William Pietz's work on the history of the fetish and Igor Kopytoff's ideas about the cultural biography of objects in order to interpret the effects of these exchanges. Ultimately, the handkerchief reveals the difficulty of attaching any value, economic or religious, to an object circulating between multiple social spheres. I also suggest that the fluctuating value of this stage property reflects the material processes through which the status of all stage properties shifts as they move from the tiring house to the stage and back again. This section also considers *Othello* as a text that helps us understand the stage properties that were enshrined as relics through their association with famous Shakespearean actors. The collectors who attempted to fix the value of these eighteenth- and nineteenth-century properties were resisting the ephemeral nature of the theater and reversing the logic by which properties were labeled "mere" things to be used and discarded. In this final section, then, I return to Harris and Korda's concern about the scholarly tendency to dismiss stage properties, but I also argue that the material history of the theater does not always speak to the centrality of these objects. They are given value through specific processes, both within the fiction and within the broader framework of the theatrical enterprise, but those processes can also be reversed. The fluctuating value of stage properties thus tells us more about the theater's particular investment in material objects than it does about the function of properties as stable repositories of meaning.

The study of material culture teaches us that objects often have their own life histories, and the properties I address here lead double lives. On one level they provide material clues about early modern staging practices, while within the fictional world created by the drama they serve as highly charged reference points to the culture in which the plays were first produced. Ultimately, they provide compelling evidence for the claim that the binaries such as Catholic/Protestant and even sacred/secular were far less meaningful during this period than critics have previously supposed. The resonance that adhered to these properties was neither entirely holy nor entirely unholy, and the theater's innovative use of these objects testifies to their complex, and highly adaptable, engagement with the most pressing religious issues of the day.

* * *

Because this book pays special attention to patterns within the repertory system, dates of all early modern play scripts are given in parentheses. These dates are approximate, and are cued to Alan Dessen and Leslie Thomson's *Dictionary of Stage Directions in Early Modern Drama*. First references to the plays are given in footnotes, and subsequent line numbers are included parenthetically. When modern editions with line numbers are not available, early modern quartos have been used. The spellings in quotations from early modern texts have been modernized throughout.

Chapter 1
"Things Newly Performed":
Tomb Properties and the Survival of the
Dramatic Tradition[1]

I want to begin by outlining a set of theatrical traditions. Throughout the book I argue that post-Reformation religious practice contained many material traces of traditional religion and that these traces can also be found in the plays performed in the commercial theater. Here, in the opening chapter, I address the theatrical technologies that the playing companies used to present scenes of resurrection on the public stage, technologies they inherited from the guild sponsored biblical dramas outlawed by Protestant reformers. Importantly, this continuity in theatrical practice speaks more to the tomb property's status as a familiar stage device than it does to any explicit engagement with questions of religious practice. It also presents the clearest example of my attempt to move away from studying the referential quality of dramatic dialogue and toward an examination of the plays' structure, in particular their use of certain highly charged stage properties. Like other scholars writing about religious elements in early modern drama, I cannot ignore the extraordinary spectacle at the end of Shakespeare's *The Winter's Tale* (1610)—in which Hermione, thought to be dead for sixteen years, is brought back to life through Paulina's "art"—but I want to contexualize this scene within a broader set of tragicomic patterns, focusing on what is missing from the play's final scene (the tomb) rather than what it represents (a living statue).

This chapter's primary claim is that the public theater's use of the tomb property was an inheritance from the so-called cycle plays, but that this inheritance did not affect its status as a secular institution. In resisting the idea of a clean break between pre- and post-Reformation theater, I am drawing on John Sommerville's definition of secularization as the compartmentalization rather than the elimination of faith. In his words, the Reformation makes religion "a thing to think about rather than a way of thinking" by moving Christian practice out of the dominant cultural position and into various subcultures, leading to an increasing "differentiation of religious symbols and institutions."[2] Sommerville's take on the project of secularization is important on several levels. First and foremost, it provides an alternative to the

---

[1]   Parts of this chapter are reprinted from Kenneth J. E. Graham and Philip D. Collington, eds *Shakespeare and Religious Change.* Basingstoke: Palgrave Macmillan, forthcoming, 2009. Reproduced with permission of Palgrave Macmillan.

[2]   Sommerville, 70, 11.

narratives that posit a definitive rift between pre- and post-Reformation culture, while acknowledging that Protestant iconoclasm did contribute to the gradual dissipation of collective religious practice in England. It also provides a broader framework for understanding the approach taken by historians, such as Alexandra Walsham, who have argued that we cannot discuss the impact of the Reformation unless we examine its effects on a local level. Finally, it helps us realize that most parishioners experienced the Reformation as an epistemological upheaval rather than a theological one: whatever one's attitude toward traditional religious practice, it was no longer possible to take religious values and practices for granted. Tessa Watt has suggested that we cannot view religion in sixteenth- and seventeenth-century England as "a category isolated from other aspects of experience."[3] Her point is that religious ways of thinking continued to be part of popular culture, especially popular visual culture. But it is also true that English worshipers were forced to be much more self-conscious about the way they practiced their faith, and it was this self-consciousness, together with the fragmentation of religion into subcultures, that characterizes the move toward secularization. Following Sommerville's lead as well as Watt's, my readings of early modern play scripts simultaneously attend to the continuity of religious experience and to the corresponding shifts in the way individual believers framed that experience.

Scholars of the drama tend to be interested in the transition from a unified religious culture to a nation of religious subcultures because it opened up a space for what Steven Mullaney calls "a more aesthetically complex and ideologically resonant theater" to develop.[4] Critical accounts such as Mullaney's pay close attention to the commercial theater's political subtlety but leave undisturbed the assumptions that characterize the evolutionary approach to English drama, which Lawrence Clopper has criticized as "an intellectual scam to maintain a distinction between us, we moderns, and them, those medieval people."[5] To say that the early modern theater was ideologically complex is to imply that medieval dramatic forms were merely didactic, when in fact the interpenetration of sacred and secular concerns, as well as an acknowledgement of the tensions between them, were prominent features of the guild-sponsored plays. This chapter thus presents an account of the particular historical moment in which plays such as *The Winter's Tale* were produced while acknowledging the fact that both the theatrical and the religious aspects of that historical moment were part of a continuing tradition. The Reformation, I argue, had a profound impact on English theater, but it was not altogether successful in creating a clear break with established practices and conventions. Keeping this claim—one of the book's central premises— in mind, I turn to the question of just how the commercial companies that emerged

---

[3]   *Cheap Print and Popular Piety: 1550-1640* (Cambridge: Cambridge University Press, 1991), 328.

[4]   *The Place of the Stage* (Chicago: University of Chicago Press, 1988), 52.

[5]   *Drama, Play, and Game* (Chicago: University of Chicago Press, 2001), 269.

in sixteenth-century London might have struck a balance between the Catholic theatrical tradition and the secularizing tendencies of their own subculture.

Responding to Stephen Greenblatt's now famous thesis about the theater's ability to "empty out" the religious content from the subjects it appropriates, Anthony Dawson has suggested that certain "habits of thought"—inspired, for instance, by debates about the status of the eucharist—continued to revolve around religious questions, and that these habits of thought in turn informed the plays written for the public theater.[6] This view of the early modern theater as one whose vocabulary was still conditioned by questions of religion is an attractive one, validated by the persistence of biblical dramas in places such as Coventry as well as by the slippage between "Catholic" and "Protestant" practice that characterized nearly every aspect of post-Reformation worship. The theater had been physically separated from the institution of the church, but this does not mean that religious "resonance," as Greenblatt calls it, was entirely absent from the early modern stage. Dawson, whose recent work draws attention to Sommerville's revisionist history of secularization, has pointed out that the theater's recontextualization of the affective power of religious ritual actually helped facilitate its development as a distinct cultural institution.[7] This understanding of the drama has much in common with Greenblatt's; both scholars argue that the commercial theater was somehow more secular than the parish dramas yet it was nonetheless interested in questions of religion. Dawson, however, focuses on the theater's eagerness to appropriate the authority associated with religious discourse, its desire "to extend the range of its reference and hence assert its validity as an independent social practice," whereas Greenblatt, at least in his early work, perceives the theater as having somehow already subsumed that authority.[8] Greenblatt participates in what Ken Jackson and Arthur Marotti have described as the new historicist attempt to demystify religion and focus instead on the discourses, both economic and political, that governed the lives of early modern subjects. This approach, as Debora Shuger and others have reminded us, glosses over the ways in which economics and politics are tied up with religion, both in the medieval period and in the decades following the Protestant Reformation. Even Shuger's critique, however, necessarily privileges early modern literature for the perceived complexity of its ideological engagement.

Seeking to avoid the teleological implications of such approaches, I focus here on the continuities between the pre- and post-Reformation theater, specifically their shared theatrical technologies. In subsequent references to the drama in this chapter, therefore, I have removed the terms "medieval" and "early modern" altogether, instead using language that refers to the particular conditions of performance under which the script in question was produced, either in London's commercial theaters or in the guild-sponsored parish drama. By narrowing my interest to stage

---

[6]   Dawson and Yachnin, 26.

[7]   Dawson, "The Secular Theatre," 86.

[8]   Ibid., 87.

properties, I am also seeking a more detailed vocabulary for describing theatrical appropriation. Greenblatt's discussion of appropriation as a mode of exchange in which objects with a particular charge move "from one culturally demarcated zone to another" is somewhat vague, but other terms, including his definition of "symbolic acquisition," are far more suggestive. "Here," says Greenblatt, "a social practice or other mode of social energy is transferred to the stage by means of representation." Importantly, this process of symbolic acquisition begins, but does not end, with the transfer of a material object—"something is implicitly or explicitly given in return for it."[9] Thinking specifically of the theater's appropriation of the practice of exorcism, Greenblatt notes that the actors cannot simply import this set of gestures and discourses without transforming them into a farce.

Other examples might reveal a more complex set of negotiations between the imported object's existing meaning and its function in the drama, but, as I argue throughout the book, the point is that the act of appropriation both shapes and is shaped by the preexisting qualities of the thing itself. An object with a recognizable ritual function, for instance, cannot easily be separated from that context when it appears in the drama, whereas an item associated with personal religious practice might easily take on multiple meanings when brought onto the stage. In the case of the tomb, its preexisting qualities are determined not just by its role in religious practice but by its previous history as a stage property. Its use in both pre- and post-Reformation theatrical genres, I argue, is governed by a set of "material technologies." In what follows I explain what I mean by the phrases "material technology" and "affective technology." Here and throughout the book I use these terms to call attention to stage objects as traces of a continuous set of cultural and theatrical practices and to describe the relationship between stage properties and particular categories of religious objects.

Tomb properties were a regular feature of the so-called mystery plays, which depicted Jesus's birth, death, and resurrection. Practically speaking, these properties had to be large and stable enough to house an adult male; they may also have included a moveable lid. Stage directions in the English cycle plays of the fifteenth and sixteenth centuries are notoriously thin, but one continental script provides evidence about how such a property might have been used. This script instructs the actor to "*cunningly and suddenly rise up from the tomb through a wooden trapdoor which will close itself again as soon as he has risen, and our Lord shall sit down on the tomb without touching or knocking it in any way*," suggesting the presence of a trap door as well as a fixed, but not entirely stable, box representing the tomb itself.[10] Similarly, public theater characters are often described as being "in" a coffin or tomb, as in *The Knight of the Burning Pestle* (1607), *How a Man May Choose a Good Wife From a Bad* (1602), and *Law-tricks* (1604).

---

[9]   *Shakespearean Negotiations* (Berkeley: University of California Press, 1988), 7, 9-10.

[10]   Peter Meredith and John E. Tailby, eds, *The Staging of Religious Drama in Europe in the Later Middle Ages* (Kalamazoo: Medieval Institute Publications, 1983), 97.

Fedele and Fortunio (1580) actually specifies that the actor should "lift" his head or torso up out of the tomb, while *The Knight of Malta* (1618), *The Turk* (1607), *Love's Sacrifice* (1632), and *The Valiant Welshman* (1612) call for characters to "rise" from the tomb. Similar devices were also used in civic pageants and in masques such as *Prince Henries Barriers* (1610) and *Chrysanaleia* (1616) to create moments in which a character springs back to life. In public theater plays, including *Antonio and Mellida* (1599) and *A Chaste Maid in Cheapside* (1613), the character's resurrection is specified not in the stage directions but in the dialogue.[11] The "material technology" of the tomb, then, is defined by the presence of the stage property and the conventional relationship between the object and the actor's body, which varies slightly from one performance to another. The lighting effects and gestures that accompany the moment of resurrection can also be described as material technologies. These techniques are not coded as either religious or secular; they are simply the tools used by actors to create a visual image. Together, the body and the tomb supply the conditions under which theater practitioners work to access the emotional charge of the religious event.

The term "affective technology" represents the emotional quality that the theater managed to translate from a religious medium to its own secular plots. Because it has to do with audience members' individual responses rather than religious policy *per se*, the concept of affect is particularly helpful for teasing out the continuity between various theatrical practices rather than focusing on the distance between the historical contexts in which they were produced. Admittedly, the sources and nature of theatrical affect are very difficult to pin down. It is easier to argue that a scene has a certain emotional quality than to identify the constituent elements that create that quality. Raymond Williams's thoughts about affect may, however, be usefully applied here. Williams remarks that in the moment of its production, before it becomes ossified as ideology, the "true social content" of any artwork "cannot without loss be reduced to belief-systems, institutions, or explicit general relationships, though it may include all these as lived and experienced." Instead, he advises us to consider cultural productions that fall outside the dominant ideology as either residual or emergent, arguing that we can distinguish emergent art forms because they manifest a particular "structure of feeling," a shift in the experience of culture related to "affective elements of consciousness and relationships." In other words, the "structure of feeling can be specifically related to the evidence of forms and conventions" that suggest a new art form is taking shape.[12] Taking a cue from Williams, I argue that the "affective technology," although it cannot be aligned with a specific religious sensibility, is a marker of the theater's recent innovations in its relationship with the Catholic tradition, including the cycle plays. Under the right conditions, the use of tomb properties opens up a new "structure of feeling," based, as I explain below, on the interplay between absence and presence, but also

---

[11] Alan C. Dessen and Leslie Thomson, eds, *A Dictionary of Stage Directions in English Drama, 1580-1642* (Cambridge: Cambridge University Press, 1999), 232-3.

[12] *Marxism and Literature* (Oxford: Oxford University Press, 1977), 132-3.

on the productive tension between the Catholic past and the secularized present. Not all of the resurrection scenes in public theater plays include an affective component, but those that do indicate that performers still knew how to access the visceral power of biblical imagery.

With the rise of cultural materialism and the establishment of the REED project, scholars have begun to reexamine the work of Shakespeare and his contemporaries in light of older dramatic models, specifically those associated with pre-Reformation Christianity. The source materials contained in the REED volumes have enabled a new generation of early modernists to revisit the arguments put forward thirty years ago by scholars such as Glynne Wickham and David Bevington, who first outlined the developmental model criticized by Clopper. My analysis of resurrections on the London stage is similarly informed by an examination of fourteenth- and fifteenth-century theatrical forms, and suggests that commercial playwrights were able to draw upon the affective power of a theatrical tradition that was still familiar to them and to their audiences by replicating certain conventions inherited from the resurrection plays. It differs, however, from the approach taken by Wickham, Bevington, and others in that I consider the public theater as part of a continuing tradition of theatrical practice rather than a cultural zenith. To use Joseph Roach's formulation, performance operates in these play scripts as both "quotation and invention" and serves to "hold open a place in memory into which many different people may step according to circumstances and occasions."[13] Roach is referring here to the way in which performance helps us communicate with the dead through a set of repeating rituals, but his work also supplies a useful model for thinking about Londoners' collective memory of the Catholic dramatic tradition.

This chapter presents a kind of matrix of resurrection scenes, allowing me to sketch out the parameters of the theatrical conventions Shakespeare drew from in writing the final scene of *The Winter's Tale*. In attempting to align the play with broader trends in early modern drama, most scholarly readers have turned to other plays that include statues, specifically, statues that move.[14] The play was also influenced, however, by the material technology associated with the tomb property; its resurrection is the result of generic conventions that, like Hermione's statue, were "many years" in the making, and by focusing on its link to the Catholic dramatic tradition, we can begin to see *The Winter's Tale* not as the last in a long line of statue plays but as a text that falls squarely in the middle of a significant group of resurrection plays, all of which reference and refigure existing theatrical conventions (5.2.96). As Darryll Grantley has argued, many of the "problems" associated with reading plays such as *The Winter's Tale* "arise from critical approaches that do not take sufficient account of the tradition of religious drama

---

[13]   *Cities of the Dead* (New York: Columbia University Press, 1996), 33, 36.

[14]   Bruce Smith, for instance, labels *The Winter's Tale* "the culmination of statue allusions and actual statue scenes throughout Shakespeare's earlier plays" ("Sermons in Stones: Shakespeare and Renaissance Sculpture," *Shakespeare Studies* 17 [1985]: 1-23, 18).

and art."[15] Moving away from the notion of Shakespeare's play as the singular innovation of a theatrical genius, we can see that it encapsulates and evokes a series of older dramatic forms, all of which were designed to negotiate the tricky problem of representing the miraculous.

Performing Absence

The emotional dynamic that links Catholic resurrection plays to the scripts performed in the London public theaters is the interplay between absence and presence, a narrative element that can be traced back to biblical accounts. The scriptural story of the resurrection clearly indicates that the emotional power associated with Christ's resurrection derives not only from his miraculous transfiguration, but also from the disciples' inability to entirely understand it. Christ's return evokes a sense of pathos as well as joy, especially in the twenty-fourth chapter of Luke, which is characterized by the starkly human responses of the apostles. This chapter is also marked by an increasing sense of confusion and deprivation. After visiting the sepulcher and handling the empty grave clothes, Peter is left bewildered, "wondering in himself at that which was come to pass."[16] When Christ first appears to the apostles, their confusion deepens, for on the road to Emmaus he presents himself in the guise of a fellow traveler and they fail to recognize him as their Lord. Only when they invite him to supper and he blesses the bread are they at last able to identify him, but this moment of recognition is immediately followed by one of profound loss: "And their eyes were opened, and they knew him; and he vanished out of their sight" (24:31). Although Christ's appearance to the apostles confirms the reality of the resurrection, their various encounters with him serve to mystify rather than explain his enduring presence. In fact when they find him standing among them later the same day, they are "terrified and affrighted," thinking that they have seen "a spirit" (21:37).

The events described in Luke are noteworthy because they foreground the conflicted emotions of the disciples, but also because the resurrection itself is pointedly missing from the narrative. If we read Luke as a narrative fiction, we can see that it employs absence strategically as a way of heightening the reader's experience of the event. This narrative technique provokes our emotions because Christ is suddenly present when we expect him to be absent and absent when we expect him to be present, both in the tomb and later when he suddenly disappears

---

[15] *"The Winter's Tale* and Early Religious Drama" *Comparative Drama* 20:1 (Spring 1986): 17-37, 18. Grantley anticipates my argument, and Michael O'Connell's arguments about the residual impact of the mystery cycles, by suggesting that Shakespeare "invests his spiritual play with something of the theological and mythic power of the earlier scriptural drama without having particularly to depart from the historical specificity of his own characters and narrative" (29).

[16] 24:12. All bible passages are taken from the King James translation.

in front of his disciples' very eyes.[17] The drama's source material thus also openly acknowledges the difficulty of describing the miraculous process by which Jesus becomes *Christus resurrectus*. In England, the performance of the resurrection was also associated with the liturgical drama, which expressed the trope established in Luke by celebrating the miraculous absence of Christ's *corpus* from the tomb on Easter Sunday. The charge associated with the tomb in this dramatic form derives both from the joy surrounding the miracle and from the sense of loss expressed by the three Maries who come to visit the tomb looking for their lord. This powerful emotional moment was carried over into the cycle plays, in which the moment of Christ's resurrection was often accompanied by a general sense of pathos and confusion, even in the post-resurrection scenes where Christ appears to his apostles to comfort them.

In one sense the cycle plays represent a departure from the biblical narrative, because they depict the moment in which Christ bursts from his tomb, leaving his grave clothes behind. In the liturgy, the absence of the body is crucial to the symbolic representation of the miracle—the fact that Christ is missing proves his divinity. The premise remained the same in the cycle plays, but because these dramas were more realistic than symbolic the actors were faced with the challenge of representing the resurrection in believable terms while using a human actor to portray Christ. In response to this challenge, the performers in the guild-sponsored plays heightened the confusion and sorrow of the other characters, suggesting that, at least on one level, Christ is still "missing." This dramatic tension between Christ's absence and the disciples' longing for his presence created good theater and took some of the pressure off the representational problem of making a human actor look like Christ. Thus, the emphasis on absence was simultaneously an element of the underlying theology, a material solution to a practical problem, and a means of manipulating audience response.

The reenactment of Christ's resurrection, which appears in various dramatic forms, has long been associated with the origins of modern drama in England. The important shift in recent scholarship, as Clopper suggests, has been to question the distinction between "medieval" and "early modern" theatrical practices. In Michael O'Connell's words, the tradition of staging the resurrection was still a "vital cultural practice" in the early seventeenth century, a material convention that was not yet dead and thus continued to inform and enhance the dramas being staged in the London public theaters.[18] If we agree with O'Connell that there exists

---

[17]   For another account of the interplay between absence and presence, specifically in the York cycle, see Sarah Beckwith, *Signifying God* (Chicago: University of Chicago Press, 2001), 86-7. As Anthony Dawson has shown, the particular "presence" of the actor in the public theater, no less than the medieval theater, can be understood through the language of transubstantiation (Dawson and Yachnin, 26).

[18]   In "Vital Cultural Practices: Shakespeare and the Mysteries," O'Connell makes a very specific argument, gestured at elsewhere by Clifford Davidson, that Shakespeare had a memory of the Coventry plays from his childhood or adolescence. On the basis of this assumption,

some continuity between the dramatic and narrative elements of the religious theater and those of the London playing companies, it is possible to see that not all the plays of the period are concerned with "removing the experience of death from a sacred to a neutral zone," as Michael Neill has suggested.[19] On the contrary, the audience's familiarity with the trope of the resurrection established by the guild-sponsored drama allowed commercial playwrights to draw upon the affective power of the events depicted in the Bible. The physical presence of the property provided an access point to this continuous tradition and to the emotional charge associated with it. The fact that the New Testament served as the source for public theater resurrections indicates the power of the story, as well as the limitations of reading play scripts as either "sacred" or "secular."

The dichotomies of sacred/secular and Catholic/Protestant likewise fall short when considering the status of medieval parish dramas. Following Bing D. Bills, Lawrence Clopper argues that they "were not characterized as 'popish' until the latter years of their existence or after their demise." In their own performance context, within the parish community, they were seen as expressions of civic pride and communalism as well as religious belief. It was only after "the Puritan antagonism toward theater" took hold that the plays were dismissed by representatives of the crown as dangerous remnants of Catholicism.[20] Thus, to read every reference to the cycle drama as potentially "Catholic" is to accept a post-Reformation terminology that did not necessarily apply in places such as Chester and Coventry. It is likewise an oversimplification to assume that every reference to the use of tombs in the religious drama was straightforwardly "sacred," or to interpret public theater productions as more sophisticated forms of commercial entertainment that supplanted a simpler, didactic drama intended only to convey the meaning of biblical stories. On the contrary, many of the dramas produced in London's commercial theaters can be construed as having an interest in the sacred because they work to access the power of the religious narrative through the use of specific material technologies.

Admittedly, any comparison of the guild-sponsored theater and the commercial theater reveals key structural differences as well as a continuity in their use of material technologies. Post-Reformation playgoers, unlike their fifteenth-century counterparts, paid directly for their entertainment in the form of ticket sales. The material conditions of the London theater were also fundamentally different from those of an earlier drama that was primarily occasional. The public theater companies used permanent, purpose-built playing spaces, and their performances

---

he points out the thematic commonalities between, for example, the harrowing of hell plays and *Macbeth*. But he also raises larger methodological issues about the extent to which concerns about accuracy and a general lack of interest in religious issues have prevented new historicists from crossing the artificial boundary between historical periods.

[19] "'Feasts put down funerals,'" in *True Rites and Maimed Rites*, eds Linda Woodbridge and Edward Berry (Urbana: University of Illinois Press, 1992), 47-74, 51.

[20] Clopper, *Drama, Play, and Game*, 274.

were funded by ticket sales rather than by civic and guild monies. But the primary reason scholars have tended to separate "medieval" plays from "early modern" ones is that, chronologically speaking, they fall on either side of the English Reformation. Confined by the reformers' suspicious attitude toward the dramatization of religious themes, the theater that developed in England in the 1570s and 80s was necessarily limited in its use of tombs and resurrections. However, by glancing briefly at the stage history of the cycle plays we can gather some clues about what was possible on the London stage. In addition to supplying the generic conventions appropriated and transformed by the commercial playing companies, accounts of fifteenth- and early sixteenth-century performances shed light on the physical conditions under which something like the moment of Christ's resurrection could be recreated. The dramatic record suggests that Catholic performers were aware of the representational pitfalls involved in depicting the resurrection, and that as a result they developed various strategies for producing suspense and wonder that accentuated the actor's own movements.

As records of performance conditions, early English play scripts are tantalizingly short of detail. Accounts of the French theater, by contrast, provide very suggestive hints about possible solutions to the problem of staging the resurrection. The Paris play, for instance, calls for Jesus to appear "*clad in white or quite naked, accompanied by the angels*," and for him to "*cunningly and suddenly rise up from the tomb through a wooden trapdoor.*"[21] Informed by such evidence, David Bevington suggests that in the Chester play, the action surrounding the supper at Emmaus might have been similarly arranged on two levels, and that Christ's sudden exits and entrances may have been effected using a curtain and a trap door.[22] This direction pointedly emphasizes the fallibility of the actor playing Christ, who is warned against knocking over the temporary structure set up to represent the sepulcher. In a play text associated with Mons, the actor playing Jesus is directed to rise "*and put his right leg out of the tomb first.*" This seemingly irrelevant detail about the order in which Christ's legs should appear reminds us that the author of the stage direction was thinking about the best possible way of presenting the actor's body. He may even have been aware of the dominant trend in the visual arts, which nearly always depicted Christ stepping from the tomb right foot first. Unlike carvers and illuminators, however, the Mons author was able to call for a particular set of effects, specifying that "*there should issue with him a great brightness and smoke of incense and light.*"[23] Resurrections on the London stage may have employed similar effects, and in fact one contemporary commentator pokes fun at the "[d]rummers" who make "[t]hunder in the Tyring-house" and the "twelvepenny Hirelings" who make "artificial Lightning in their

---

[21]   Meredith and Tailby, 97.

[22]   *Medieval Drama* (Boston: Houghton Mifflin, 1975), 628.

[23]   Meredith and Tailby, 114.

Heavens," but *The Second Maiden's Tragedy* (1611) is the only play that explicitly calls for a special kind of lighting.[24]

The visual tradition in England gives us some of the information that is missing from the theatrical record about the imaginative possibilities of representing the resurrection. Sculptures and carvings of Christ were among the first objects abandoned by the Protestant reformers, but as Tessa Watt has shown, the image of the resurrection continued to figure prominently in broadside ballads as well as in secretly printed Catholic prayer manuals. Thus the visual record demonstrates the persistence of images of the resurrection, which continued to appear in printed books long after they were removed from churches and cathedrals. Illustrations of the resurrection in Catholic primers tend to emphasize the supernatural quality of Christ's body by depicting the surprised reactions of the soldiers at his feet. Similarly, in the resurrection image from an instructional manual printed in 1597, Christ stands on the lid of the tomb while the soldiers shield their faces and draw back in wonder (Figure 1.1). Elsewhere, Watt has reproduced a resurrection image from a 1629 broadsheet entitled *Two pleasant ditties, one of the birth, the other of the passion of Christ / To the tune of Dulcina Of Nativity*, which typifies the remarkable flexibility with which English printers incorporated images of the resurrection into a variety of new materials. These images demonstrate the persistence of resurrection themes in popular visual culture, but they also testify to the challenge of making an ordinary actor appear supernatural. The theater had one distinct advantage—because it was live it could take advantage of sudden appearances to intensify the power of the moment—but it continued to wrestle with the basic problem of how to present the actor's body as "resurrected."

---

[24] Andrew Gurr, *Playgoing in Shakespeare's London* (Cambridge: Cambridge University Press, 1996), 243. Many of the plays discussed in this chapter were produced in the more intimate hall playhouses—including the first and second Blackfriars, Whitefriars, and the Cockpit—where the actors might have more control over special effects such as lighting and sound, but R. B. Graves reminds us not to overstate this point: "one might suppose that indoor lighting produced quite a different effect, yet it must be realized that the mixture of window light and candle light in the permanent hall playhouses was nearly as difficult to control as the light outdoors" (*Lighting the Shakespearean Stage 1567-1642* [Carbondale: Southern Illinois University Press, 1999], 112).

OF THE RESVRREC- 72
TION.

Figure 1.1   Loarte, Gaspar de, "Of the resurrection," *Instructions and advertisements*, 1597 (72ʳ). This item is reproduced by permission of The Huntington Library, San Marino, California

Although dramatic and artistic representations must ultimately be considered separately, each of them grew out of the Catholic liturgy, and the liturgical elements, like the biblical narrative, self-consciously acknowledge the limits of representation. As part of the Easter service, recorded in texts such as the *Rites of Durham*, the host is buried, sometimes within a hollow built into the image of Christ, and then secretly removed so that the priest can demonstrate the absence of the *corpus* on the following day. Other dramatic forms employ actors rather than the wooden figure of Christ, but they are similarly concerned with the absence of Christ's body and the bewilderment of the disciples who do not recognize him when he appears to them after the resurrection has taken place. One of the earliest examples of these dramatic liturgical forms is the *visitatio sepulchri*, a piece of staged dialogue accompanied by the singing of hymns in which the three Maries come to see the body of their Lord, only to be told by an angel that *"non est hic"*—he is not here.

In an English version of this ceremony, taken from the tenth-century *Regularis Concordia* of St. Ethelwold, the stage directions repeatedly highlight the distance between the actors representing the resurrection and the actual biblical event. The brother portraying the angel is to enter *"as if on other business"* before approaching the sepulcher, while the three "Maries" are to enter *"in the manner of seeking for something."* Finally, after a short piece of dialogue, the Maries, who are referred to using the masculine pronoun to indicate the monks' status as actors, reach into the tomb and take out the shroud, *"as if demonstrating that the Lord has risen and is not now wrapped in it."*[25] Some parishes apparently discovered a middle ground between the actor and the wooden crucifix, for there is evidence that one aspect of popular theatrical performance in pre-Reformation England was the resurrection puppet show. As part of a sermon against idolatry delivered in November of 1547, Bishop Barlowe of Saint David's is said to have "shewed a picture of the resurrection of our Lord made with vices, which put out his legges of the sepulchre and blessed with his hand and turned his heade"; he subsequently allowed several boys from the audience to destroy it.[26] Equally suggestive is William Lambarde's 1581 account, which claims that the inhabitants of Witney attracted visitors to their fair by staging "the hole Action of the Resurrection" with "certein small Puppets, representing the Parson of the Christe, the Watchmen, Marie, and others." Although he characterizes the show at Witney as a "pleasant spectacle," Lambarde notes that in it Christ is "rather played with then preached."[27]

---

[25] Bevington, 27-8. The wording here is from Karl Young's translation of the original Latin.

[26] Charles Wriothesley, *A Chronicle of England During the Reigns of the Tudors, from A.D. 1485 to 1559*, vol. 2. (Westminster: Printed for the Camden Society, 1875), 1.

[27] William Lambarde, *Dictionarium Angliae Topographicum et Historicum* (London, 1730), 459-60. Pamela Sheingorn notes that other parishes, including St. Mary Redcliffe, Bristol, might have had a similar device for presenting "the tableau of the resurrection" in the liturgical drama that preceded the mystery plays. This parish, for instance, had

Among contemporary representations of the resurrection, these puppet shows were the most overtly anti-realistic, but even in a more reverent context neither the resurrection nor Christ's appearance to the disciples would have been easy to stage convincingly, which is presumably why the Mons direction calls for extra lighting effects. Meg Twycross, who supervised a modern production of the York plays, reports that the resurrection "is an outrageous thing to have to present on stage, especially an open-air stage with no possibility of dimming the lights." She also suggests that if the resurrection is presented slowly, with the sound of thunder and chanting, the effect could be quite impressive. More speculatively, she argues that for a contemporary audience member, "the actual emergence of a Christ-figure from the tomb must at first have seemed like the ritual come to life."[28] There may be an element of nostalgia coloring this description, for in the cycle plays the act of resurrection itself is described with tantalizingly brief stage directions like "*Christus resurget*" and "*Tunc Jhesu resurgente*," along with references to the singing of a relevant hymn, a participatory exercise as much as an auditory effect. The soldiers hired to guard the tomb are on stage during the act of resurrection, but because they sleep through the miracle they are often forced to report the theft of the body without understanding what has occurred. As in the narrative from Luke, the soldiers' confusion mirrors the difficulty of depicting the resurrection, and consequently their remarks focus on the miraculous absence of Christ's corpse rather than attempting to describe the presence of his resurrected body. The cycle plays give us hints about how actors solved the problems associated with staging the resurrection, but more importantly they reveal that these problems were not unique to the commercial theater.

Like Luke 24, most of the resurrection dramas highlight the considerable emotional potential in Christ's meetings with the apostles, but the characters' pained responses to his sudden disappearance are especially poignant in the Chester play. The surviving records and scripts relating to the Chester play also provide one of the most compelling examples of the continuity between the cycle plays and the London commercial theater, for the cycle was still being performed in the mid-1570s.[29] Additionally, the particular emotional quality of its dialogue provides the best evidence for the claim I have been making about the drama's use of absence as well as presence, loss as well as joy. It is only after Jesus vanishes

---

"[a]n ymage of god almyghty Risyng oute of the same Sepulchre with all the Ordynance that longeth therto. That is to say A lath made of Tymbre And the yren worke there to & cetera" (*The Easter Sepulchre in England* [Kalamazoo: Medieval Institute Publications, 1987], 58-60).

   [28]   "Playing The Resurrection," in *Medieval Studies for J. A. W. Bennett*, ed. P. L. Heyworth (Oxford: Oxford University Press, 1981), 271-96, 289-90.

   [29]   Lawrence Clopper, ed., *Chester* (Toronto: University of Toronto Press, 1979), 298. References to the Chester play itself are taken from R. M. Lumiansky and David Mills, eds, *The Chester Mystery Cycle* (London: published for the Early English Text Society by Oxford University Press, 1974).

that Luke and Cleophas understand who the "traveler" they have been speaking with really is: "Alas, alas, alas, alas! / This was Jesus in this place." The focus in the Chester plays is on "*non est hic*" and on the apostles' inability to see their Lord, particularly when Christ literally "disappears from their eyes" (ll. 129-30).

Nor does this initial encounter prepare the apostles for their next meeting, in which they mistakenly believe they are in the presence of a ghost rather than Christ himself. Cycle plays, especially the one from Chester, tend to take advantage of the fact that the biblical narrative does not require the disciples to witness the act of resurrection. The Chester script makes the most of the sense of sorrow and confusion that mark their post-resurrection meetings with Jesus, and even the soldiers, who are often characterized in other plays by fright or outrage, convey some of this sense of loss. The Chester dialogue also provides crucial hints about the staging of the resurrection. "Owt, alas!" the first soldier exclaims when he awakens, "[w]here am I?/ So bright abowt ys herebye/ that my harte wholey/ owt of slough ys shaken." The third soldier is even more descriptive, crying "[a]las, what ys thys great light/ shyuning here in my sight?/ Maned I am, both mayne and might" (ll. 186-9, 210-12). Christ has already disappeared by the time they become aware of his absence, but they realize immediately that "Jesu ys rysen" by the after-effects of the miracle, which include the "great light" mentioned by the third soldier; thus, their "alas" seems to register some understanding of what they have missed (l. 212). The script should not convince us, however, that the audience saw the "great light" which the soldiers failed to see. The dialogue's insistence on the sudden brightness accompanying the resurrection may indicate that these English performers were not able to recreate the spectacular effects of the French theater, and thus had to describe it verbally. In other words, the performers who produced the English mystery plays may have relied more on their audience's familiarity with the biblical narrative, and on their own imaginative powers, than on spectacular special effects.

Clifford Davidson has concluded that the Chester cycle, which he specifically calls "popish," was "doomed" the same way all sacred images were doomed in sixteenth-century England, but I am more convinced by arguments that view these and other plays as part of a continuing tradition of dramatic performance that survived the Reformation because they were adapted to suit the times.[30] According to the existing records, the Chester plays were performed in 1560-61, 1565-66, 1566-67, 1567-68, 1571-72, and finally in May of 1575. One of the witnesses to the last performance of the cycle in 1575 speculated that some parts of the play were excised "because of the superstition in them," but Clopper points out that it is difficult to find anything particularly superstitious in the text, or anything that can be related to tensions between Catholicism and Protestantism. It is more likely, he argues, that the plays were initially criticized for the way they presented the

---

[30] "'The Devil's Guts,'" in Clifford Davidson and Ann Eljenholm Nichols, eds, *Iconoclasm vs. Art and Drama* (Kalamazoo, 1989), 92-144, 111.

godhead, or for their association with specific Catholics.[31] The fact that the Chester cycle was produced at all in the 1560s and 70s makes it a noteworthy example of the kind of adaptation that was available to performers after the Reformation, and a precursor to the more drastic recontextualization of biblical subject material that went on in the public theaters a few decades later. In Clopper's apt phrase, we need to be aware of the commercial drama's "indebtedness to and sharing with the persistent 'medieval' traditions."[32] These traditions do not necessarily give us all the material clues we need to reconstruct early modern stage performances, but they do remind us that the commercial playing companies were confronting the same set of representational issues their counterparts faced in producing the cycle plays.

Any use of a tomb property, which would still have been associated with the religious subject material of the cycle plays, would have been necessarily controversial in post-Reformation England. As a result, the companies were forced to negotiate absence on a structural as well as a thematic level. Some plays point directly to the Catholic tradition by drawing an obvious parallel between their secular resurrection and the depiction of Christ's resurrection, thus producing a satirical effect. Other plays alter or eliminate certain physical aspects of the staging tradition in order to hold onto the emotional charge associated with it. The popularity of this theatrical tradition—that is, the presentation of acts of resurrection within secular fictions—is indicated by the variety of forms in which it appeared, but also by the fact that playwrights such as Shakespeare consciously departed from the conventional use of a tomb property. As the London companies began to develop more and more sophisticated ways of exploiting their own medium, it was natural that they should turn to one of the cycle plays' most evocative tropes.

Staging Affect

In his edition of *The Duchess of Malfi* (1614), John Russell Brown playfully speculates that Webster might have found a tomb property lying disused in the tiring house, recognized its dramatic potential, and decided to write a play around it.[33] The surviving scripts, however, belie his supposition. Tomb properties were employed in a wide variety of public theater plays, and these stage resurrections ranged from the satirical to the tragic. Moreover, the tombs that appear in public theater plays are associated with certain generic conventions—the jealous lover, the virtuous wife who is not truly dead, the missing person who reappears in

---

[31]   Clopper, *Drama, Play, and Game*, 298. For an apt summary of the current state of scholarly research on the topic of the guild plays and their survival, see Beatrice Groves, *Texts and Traditions: Religion in Shakespeare 1592-1604* (Oxford: Clarendon Press, 2007), 33-9. "The guilds," she remarks, "were certainly tenacious in retaining their costumes and props" (39).

[32]   *Drama, Play, and Game*, 269.

[33]   *The Duchess of Malfi* (Manchester: Manchester University Press, 1997), 25.

another guise—that shed light on *The Winter's Tale* as well as *The Duchess of Malfi* and several other play texts discussed below. Throughout the sixteenth and early seventeenth centuries, companies such as Shakespeare's developed increasingly sophisticated theatrical practices that played off a longstanding theatrical tradition while actively responding to each other's dramatic innovations. Yet to stress the connection between public theater scripts is not to argue that the plays are all doing the same kind of cultural or dramatic work. Actors were not imitating each other any more than they were imitating the guild members who participated in parish resurrection plays. The commercial players used their tomb properties in a variety of ways, each of which reflected the script's particular attitude toward religious practice. All the plays discussed in this chapter, however, express a common understanding of the theatrical possibilities latent in the property, possibilities that were demonstrated by contemporary use as well as by the role they played in the guild-sponsored drama.

In the London theater, the group of generic conventions surrounding the use of tomb properties was mainly associated with tragicomedies, and included a particular set of stage actions and practices; thus, the plot features that would later form the basic framework for *The Winter's Tale* appear as early as 1598 in *Much Ado About Nothing*. This play dramatizes the tragic effects of male jealousy, presenting the woman wrongly accused of sexual infidelity who seems to die and is later mourned by her penitent lover. Like the later play, this one flirts with the possibility of the young man's remarriage before resurrecting his beloved and returning her to him. These two Shakespearean scripts also resemble each other in that they do not call for their wronged heroines to emerge from tomb properties. Other more typical tomb scenes include those in Heywood's *How a Man May Choose a Good Wife from a Bad* (1602) and Day's *Law Tricks* (1604). In each of these tragicomedies, a husband attempts to poison his virtuous wife, but the poison has been replaced with a sleeping potion, and the wife emerges from her tomb to wonder at her situation before finally forgiving him and appearing at his trial to save him from execution. Heywood's play introduces an additional trope, one that appears later in *The Second Maiden's Tragedy*, in which there is a conflation of resurrection and haunting, for when Mistress Arthur appears in the courtroom, everyone takes her for a ghost, as the apostles do when they first see the resurrected Christ. For its part, Day's play adds an echo scene reminiscent of the one in *The Duchess of Malfi*, except that in this case the audience knows the echo to be fake: it is merely the lady's servant playing a trick on her grieving husband. Chapman's *The Widow's Tears* (1604)—in which a jealous husband feigns death and then, dressed as a stranger, woos his own wife in his tomb—is one of the darkest examples of this particular convention.[34] Even a cursory glance at the plots

---

[34]   As Alice Dailey has shown, this play also parodies biblical resurrection narratives. "Easter Scenes from an Unholy Tomb: Christian Parody in *The Widow's Tears*," in *Marian Moments in Early Modern British Drama*, eds Regina Buccola and Lisa Hopkins (Aldershot, England: Ashgate, 2007), 127-39.

of the public theater plays that employ tomb properties reveals that not all of them are interested in accessing the power of the Christian tradition, but all of them do take advantage of existing conventions—both theatrical and religious—and the resonance surrounding them.

Another more familiar resurrection appears in Middleton's *A Chaste Maid in Cheapside* (1613), a play which inverts the trope of the jealous husband and the wronged wife by calling for two young lovers, believed dead, to be brought back to life simultaneously. In contrast to this festive comedy, John Mason's *The Turk* (1607) presents a darker view of sexual fidelity, in which the wronged wife goes on a murdering rampage of her own after she is "resurrected" by her lover. This play owes as much to revenge tragedies as it does to the developing tradition associated with the tomb property, but in diverging from the convention of the saintly woman who has been unjustly treated, Mason is also putting pressure on the gender norms enacted in other public theater resurrections. Among the most extreme examples of the gendered nature of such resurrections is Shirley's *The Martyred Soldier* (1618), in which a pagan tyrant attempts to rape a Christian martyr whose material body has been taken up to heaven, only to find that he is making love to a corpse. These texts tend to exert more pressure on male jealousy than they do on female chastity, and many of the plays from this period explore the tragic potential of a husband's obsession with his wife's fidelity rather than the problem of adultery *per se*. *Othello* (1604), too, falls within this tradition, and we can read Desdemona's final speech, in which she pronounces her husband's pardon several minutes after he has smothered her, as a kind of mock resurrection. The difference in Shakespeare's play, of course, is that the moment is characterized by pathos rather than humor. As I explain in more detail below, Webster's *The Duchess of Malfi* presents a similarly wrenching example of a "false" resurrection.

At the opposite end of the spectrum from *Othello* and *The Duchess of Malfi* is the staged resurrection in Fletcher, Field, and Massinger's *The Knight of Malta* (1618). This is in fact a "true" resurrection, in which the heroine is given a sleeping potion and awakes to find herself in her own tomb. Yet the play's treatment of the event is curiously parodic. When the hero and his companion Norandine hear the lady moaning, the latter automatically assumes that it is some "*devill in the wall*," some trick or conjuration; his nervous exclamations can be read as a comic version of the responses of the bewildered soldiers in the cycle plays.[35] But even when Miranda and Norandine discover the source of the noise, they are fooled several times into thinking that the lady is really dead as she repeatedly rises up and falls back down again in a swoon. This type of satirical distance between the theatrical event and its religious antecedent was one convenient strategy adopted by commercial playwrights, who, not limited to one mode or the other, alternated between poking fun at the Catholic tradition and attempting to appropriate its affective power to intensify their secular plots.

---

[35]   *The Dramatic Works in the Beaumont and Fletcher Canon*, ed. Fredson Thayer Bowers, vol. 8 (Cambridge: Cambridge University Press, 1966), 4.2.33.

Anthony Munday's sixteenth-century court drama *Fedele and Fortunio* (1584) presents its tomb scene as part of a series of humorous anti-Catholic tropes, making it one of the plays that point directly to the representational problems at the heart of Catholic religious drama in order to separate itself from that particular tradition. *Fedele and Fortunio* is, to my knowledge, the first example of a London company using a tomb in this fashion, and therefore it cannot, like the plays discussed elsewhere in this chapter, be seen as responding to an existing public theater convention. Furthermore, it was performed for an elite Elizabethan audience rather than for large crowds at an amphitheater. But we cannot accept the play's satirical elements entirely at face value as catering to members of the Protestant aristocracy. The very act of bringing the tomb on stage might have evoked conflicted memories of the guild-sponsored drama from many contemporary playgoers.

Although *Fedele and Fortunio* was among the first public theater plays to use a tomb property in this manner, its use of the tomb is relatively complex. Munday, who was also writing antitheatrical critiques at the time, complements his use of the resurrection trope by juxtaposing it with another example of false religiosity, the practice of black magic. The play's send-up of the act of resurrection begins when Victoria, who is in love with Fortunio, solicits the help of a witch named Medusa to win his affection. Dressed as nuns, the two women sneak into a church where they perform a pagan ritual with a wax image of Victoria's beloved. At the culmination of this ceremony, they throw their tapers into an open coffin, hoping to summon a group of supernatural helpers. Instead, they manage to set fire to Crackstone the clown, who emerges from the tomb in which he has been hiding with a candle in each hand and one in his mouth.[36] The women run screaming from the church, thinking they have seen the devil—an appropriate response, given that they have just been summoning dark spirits to do their bidding. All the elements of the scene, from the nuns' costumes to the man made of virgin wax, undermine any suggestion that this theatrical resurrection is to be taken seriously. It is only fitting that these would-be witches, who impersonate nuns and commit sacrilege against the dead, are eventually bested by a fake demon.

Munday's spoof on popular superstition offers further support for Stephen Greenblatt's examination of Protestant rhetoric in "Shakespeare and the Exorcists." In the passages Greenblatt reproduces from Samuel Harsnett's tract, the author suggests that the best way to demystify the tricks and superstitious rituals associated with Catholicism, including the falsification of demonic possession, is to reveal them as mere theater. "Acknowledging theatricality," as Greenblatt puts it, "kills the credibility of the supernatural."[37] In *Fedele and Fortunio*, Munday stages just such an act of demystification, debunking both the pagan love ritual and the audience's naïve desire to see the act of resurrection for themselves. Reginald Scot's *Discoverie of Witchcraft*, first published the same year as Munday's play,

[36] *A Critical Edition of Anthony Munday's Fedele and Fortunio*, ed. Richard Hosley (New York: Garland, 1981), 2.2.99 s.d.
[37] *Shakespearean Negotiations*, 109.

similarly exposes the tricks behind the magic acts performed by sixteenth-century witches. This text sets out to disabuse its readers of the notion that witches are anything other than cony-catchers who pretend to conjure spirits and perform miraculous deeds using elaborate properties. Thus Scot describes the trick of "beheading" a live person in such detail that the reader, given the right tools, could reproduce it herself. Such a person, Scot reassures his readers, would "greatlie advance the power and glorie of God, discovering [the jugglers'] pride and falshood that take upon them to worke miracles, and to be the mightie power of God."[38] Similarly, Munday's play encourages its audience to witness and reaffirm the charlatanism of papists and pagans, drawing upon the well-established rhetoric of anti-Catholic satire.

As Huston Diehl has argued, there was ample ideological space for Protestantism in the theater, but what is most intriguing about moments of resurrection on the public stage is that very few of them can be read in a straightforward sense as either anti- or pro-Catholic, due to the emotional resonance of the convention I have been describing. Most of the plays that use tomb properties do so in more subtle ways than Munday, who was writing at the height of Elizabethan iconoclasm, could ever have done. Yet despite the complicated aspects of the plays' treatment of religious themes, antitheatricalists often misconstrued the theater's power over its audience as a kind of papist trick. For many Protestants, the problem with the public theater was that it claimed to represent truth, rather than acknowledging itself as fiction. This type of criticism was analogous to the charge that the Catholic priest, a mere "game-player" in Thomas Becon's phrase, actually attempted to convince his audience that the host really was Christ's body in a literal sense.[39] Other kinds of evidence demonstrate the bias inherent in these attacks—Jeffrey Knapp suggests, for example, that the public theater was self-consciously providing an alternative to the current religious climate. Given the contentiousness of that climate, however, it is easy to see why incorporating religious themes and tropes into the public theater necessitated caution and subterfuge.

Like those governing religious practice, the laws against treating sacred subjects on the stage were not easy to enforce, but they did change the nature of the public theater. Post-Reformation playgoers paid out of pocket to see performances that had been officially sanctioned by the Office of the Revels, and were aware that any depiction of explicitly religious material could be deemed illegal as well as blasphemous. But preventing public criticism of royal policy was only one of the reasons for exerting tighter controls on theatrical production. Beginning in the 1560s, church authorities began to crack down on the cycle plays for their superstitious content, issuing orders such as the one in 1575 that instructed the citizens of Wakefield not to allow the persons of the trinity to be represented

---

[38]   *The Workes of the Most Famous and Reverend Divine Mr. Tomas Scot* (Holland, 1624), 248.

[39]   *The Catechism of Thomas Becon. With Other Pieces Written by Him in the Reign of King Edward the Sixth* (Cambridge: Cambridge University Press, 1844), 259.

during civic productions. Lawrence Clopper has demonstrated, however, that this type of injunction was specific enough to allow the plays themselves to continue in an amended form, as many of them did, well into the 1570s.[40] Like the public theater itself, the cycle plays survived because they continued to adapt themselves to the demands of the political climate in which they were produced. Continuing Protestant attacks ironically provide further evidence for the claim that post-Reformation audiences were still very much interested in religious subjects; but just as the enforcement of Elizabeth's articles of religious conformity was neither immediate nor comprehensive, the application of legal controls was typically uneven when it came to the playing companies.

Although I ultimately want to argue for Shakespeare's place within a longstanding dramatic tradition, it is also important to acknowledge the shifts in the enforcement of anti-Catholic statutes that affected the public theater's treatment of religious topics. The emphatic iconoclasm of the mid-Elizabethan period had more or less subsided by the time James took the throne in 1603, and in the early years of his reign theological debates took on a new tenor as he flirted with the idea of establishing a political alliance with Catholic Spain. As I suggest throughout the book, this period was characterized by the surprising prominence of religious themes and properties on the London stage. Reformers such as William Crashaw, who published his sermon against the stage in 1608, thus had some reason to complain that the companies now "bring religion and holy things upon the stage."[41] Even before Crashaw's critique, forms of unauthorized popular drama had prompted the 1606 *Acte to Restraine Abuses of Players*, which levied a fine of ten pounds against any actor who abused even the holy name of God.[42]

In the later years of his reign, the relative flexibility of James's religious policies and the resulting upturn in religiously-inflected play scripts prompted a renewed interest in reforming the excesses of the stage. This reactionary trend culminated in polemical writings such as William Prynne's *Histrio-mastix* (1633),

---

[40]   *Drama, Play, and Game*, 282, 292. There is abundant evidence for the persistence of the cycle plays throughout the first half of the sixteenth century and for the existence of transitional forms. There was, for example, an East Anglian revival of biblical drama in the "early years of Elizabeth's reign" (Alexandra Johnston, "Cycle Drama in the Sixteenth Century," in Albert H. Tricomi, ed., *Early Drama to 1600* [Binghamton: Center for Medieval and Early Renaissance Studies, State University of New York, 1987], 1-15, 5). In York, the common council was still urging the mayor to grant permission to perform the Corpus Christi plays in 1579-80, and the Corpus Christi play at Kendal apparently survived into the seventeenth century (Johnston, 7). Although we have comparatively few play scripts from the Coventry cycle, we do know that the parish continued to present its play through 1578. In 1599, the Mercers were still repairing their pageant house, though this may have been done in anticipation of its sale a few years later. Clopper points out that although religious plays were not performed in London, they were printed there; one example is *The Life and Repentaunce of Marie Magdalene* in 1566 (*Drama, Play, and Game*, 285).

[41]   Gurr, *Playgoing in Shakespeare's London*, 230.

[42]   Chambers, 338.

a voluminous compilation of the offenses committed by players, both pagan and papist, throughout western history. Prynne condemns, for instance, the "desperate madnesse" of Catholics who turn the history of Christ's life, including the resurrection and the ascension, into "a meere prophane ridiculous Stage-play." Fortunately for Prynne, the London playing companies were not in the business of staging the Passion, but he still maintains that the very act of performing in public was enough to produce a negative effect on any playgoer. "Alas, what goodnesse, what profit doe men reape from stage playes, that should any way engage their affections to them? Do [plays] not enrage their lusts, adde fire and fewell to their unchast affections; deprave their minds, corrupt their manners, cauterize their consciences," he demands.[43] It is worth noting, as Michael O'Connell does, that sixteenth-century critiques of the guild-sponsored drama followed this same logic, arguing that actors merely toy with and therefore profane religious narratives and themes. Despite the fact that religious content was the exception rather than the rule on the London stage, Prynne and other antitheatricalists were understandably anxious about the power that plays exerted over the emotions of their audiences. For Prynne, in other words, the continuity between the wicked Catholic past and the otherwise enlightened present was the theater itself, and its ability to provoke uncontrollable emotional responses that were anything but godly. Like many iconoclasts, Prynne was highly sensitive to the power of the visual and dramatic arts. More so than any of his puritan colleagues, he understood that the drama's ability to provoke affective responses among members of its audience was, if not recognizably papist, dangerously uncontrollable.

Although Webster's *The Duchess of Malfi* does include familiar elements of anti-Catholicism, it is also one of the most convincing examples of the kind of play that would have upset William Prynne. It may seem a strange text to include in this chapter, because its tomb property does not conform to the types of material technologies I have been describing, but for precisely that reason it illuminates the ways in which the theater was able to get around the problem of representing absence in order to access the emotional affect of the resurrection. In Act 5, scene 3, the Duchess's ghost appears to her husband in the form of an echo issuing from her tomb, seeking to warn him of her brothers' deadly plot against his life. But Antonio, who believes he is merely walking through a ruined monastery, does not know that she has been killed and remains uncertain about what he has actually witnessed. There is no stage direction calling for an actor playing a ghost to rise up out of a coffin; consequently, modern readers tend to associate the property with a typical seventeenth-century funerary tomb and with contemporary allegories of memorialization, rather than with the theatrical trope inherited from the religious drama. Reading *The Duchess of Malfi* alongside Webster's tribute to the young prince Henry, Michael Neill interprets the tomb scene as a meditation on memory, and the play as a secular monument to the Duchess herself. According to Neill, "the tomb was a survival from the mystery cycles," but it appears only as

---

    [43]   Prynne, 733, ii.

"a secular equivalent of the old resurrection motif." Whereas in the cycle plays "the tomb would have been a sign of spiritual triumph ... in the new popular theatre it quickly developed an extended range of secular meanings."[44] Following Greenblatt, Neill draws an absolute distinction between the affect of Catholic drama and the more rational, nonreligious commercial theater, ignoring the possibility that the otherwise secular playing companies might still be interested in accessing the power of religious images.

Historians of the Reformation have recently demonstrated that not all the Catholic rituals and beliefs surrounding death and resurrection had been effectively secularized by the seventeenth century. As Watt reminds us in her discussion of the traditional religious symbols that appear in printed books and broadsides, "the 'secularization' of imagery cannot be explained in terms of 'secularization' of society as a whole, or mere lack of interest in religious art."[45] Narrative images of the resurrection continued to be widely produced, and although these images were not created to be adored but to serve as visual tools for learning about the life of Christ, their use could never have been fully controlled. The term "secular" as modern scholars tend to use it thus fails to describe the complex ways in which the drama engaged with a newly-fragmented religious culture. What we can say, however, is that the power of the resurrection had been converted to a new set of purposes. In the case of Webster's play, what was retained was not the image of Christ himself, but the emotional charge surrounding his sudden reappearance. The sense of pathos associated with such resurrections is not unique to this period—rather, the public theater companies were merely rediscovering what many guild performers already knew. The King's Men understood that it was difficult to convincingly stage the resurrection, no matter what the context. They also knew, or hoped, that a focus on absence rather than presence would mask the representational problem and intensify the emotional quality of the scene. They therefore departed from the material technology they inherited from the cycle plays, while continuing to rely on their audience's familiarity with these conventions.

As we have seen, one of the most convincing examples of the persistence of the cycle plays in the sixteenth and early seventeenth centuries can be found in Chester, whose revised banns are recorded in David Rogers's 1609 *Breviary*. Rewritten sometime during Elizabeth's reign, the late banns go out of their way to assert that the Chester play will not succumb to the standard pitfalls associated with religious drama. "Noe man can proportion the godhead," the author of the new banns observes, reassuring the audience that "all those persones that as godes doe playe/ In Clowdes [shall] come downe with voyce and not be seene."[46] In other words, although the producers of the Chester Whitsun play probably continued to present the person of Christ, they were no longer attempting to bring the godhead

---

[44] *Issues of Death: Mortality and Identity in English Renaissance Tragedy* (Oxford: Oxford University Press, 1997), 309-10.

[45] Watt, 165.

[46] Clopper, *Chester*, 248.

on stage. Webster's play deals not with the trinity, but with a single spirit-like character—the Duchess herself—and it does not present a resurrection *per se*. Yet it employs a similar dramatic strategy. In an attempt to maintain the sacred aura of the scene in which an echo emerges from the Duchess's grave to comfort and advise her grieving husband, *The Duchess of Malfi* keeps its title character more or less off stage. It is her voice, not her body, that is most prominently displayed, and it is precisely because the Duchess is not present through much of the scene at the monastery that the play can sustain its strong religious overtones without lapsing into parody.

The sacred aura that adheres to the scene in the ruined abbey in Act 5 is carefully foreshadowed by the play's treatment of the Duchess's banishment and martyrdom. Although the Duchess is initially presented as an iconoclast—a woman who disparages the social rules governing marriage and tells her lover Antonio that she is not the painted statue on her husband's tomb—the suffering she endures at the hands of her brothers and Bosola eventually casts her in a more explicitly Catholic light. When, in Act 3, her elder brother Ferdinand first accuses her of betraying his trust by secretly taking a husband he is unaware that the man in question is her steward, Antonio, and that she has already borne three of his children. Nonetheless, he spends much of the third act envisioning various deaths for the two lovers: "If thou do wish thy lecher may grow old / In thy embracements, I would have thee build / Such a room for him, as our anchorites / To holier use inhabit. Let not the Sun / Shine on him, till he's dead."[47] Fleeing his wrath, Antonio and the Duchess travel to the Shrine of Our Lady of Loreto, under the guise of making a pilgrimage. As John Russell Brown has suggested, the setting for this scene represents a kind of anti-type to the ruined abbey. The shrine provided pilgrims with a chance to ask for Mary's intervention, and it was reputedly "dominated by a statue of the Virgin which was said to be a miraculously true likeness." This later scene, Brown notes, "is also in a holy place, and the echo's effect is almost miraculous, but it all takes place among ruins, not in a goodly shrine."[48] Thus the play represents two very different religious sites, one in active use and one decrepit, both of which are employed to promote sympathy for the Duchess. It is hard not to think here of the English Reformation, and of the violence done to family tombs by those who found Catholic monuments, even those not associated with saints, to be incitements to superstition. Whereas the shrine is presented as the well-loved destination of pilgrims, Antonio worries that the tombs of the dead, who "[l]oved the church so well, and gave so largely to 't," have become exposed to the elements after years of neglect (5.3.15).

---

[47]   *The Duchess of Malfi*, ed. John Russell Brown, 3.2.100-104.

[48]   Brown, *The Duchess of Malfi*, 15. Huston Diehl reminds us that Orazio Torsellino's account of the Loreto shrine, published in English in 1608, celebrates it as a living testament to the power of the Virgin, including the ability to revive the dead ("'Strike All that Look Upon With Marvel,'" in *Rematerializing Shakespeare*, eds Bryan Reynolds and William West [New York: Palgrave Macmillan, 2005], 19-34, 22).

In Act 3, scene 4 the shrine at Loreto is put to diabolical use by the Duchess's brother the Cardinal, who interrupts the family's pilgrimage by publicly banishing them and stripping the Duchess of her lands and title. The next scene shows the Duchess and Antonio mourning the tragic events to come and unable to comfort each other. "Your kiss," she tells him, "is colder / Than that I have seen an holy anchorite / Give to a dead man's skull" (3.5.88-90). Her words echo Ferdinand's threat but also prefigure the horrific scene in which he gives her a severed hand, telling her it is her husband's. During her subsequent imprisonment and separation from her family, the Duchess's suffering is described as exquisitely serene: "she seems / Rather to welcome the end of misery / Than shun it …. She will muse four hours together: and her silence, / Methinks expresseth more then if she spake" (4.1.3-5, 9-10). Despite being held against her will, the Duchess has effectively taken on the role of anchorite, and she remains unmoved by the screams of the madmen her brother places outside her window. As she herself professes, "[n]ecessity makes me suffer constantly, / And custom makes it easy," to which her maid Cariola replies that she already resembles "some reverend monument / Whose ruins are even pitied" (4.2.29-30, 33-4). In Act 1 the Duchess rejects the image of herself as a static figure on her husband's tomb, but by Act 4 her body has become a spectacular presence on stage precisely because of its immobility.

Bosola, who unwillingly takes on various roles as the Duchess's chief tormentor, tells his victim that he has been sent to bring her "[b]y degrees to mortification" (4.2.176). Heightening both Bosola's remorse and the sense of pathos surrounding her death, which her brother repents too late to save her, the play goes so far as to have the Duchess regain consciousness several lines after she has been strangled, to utter the words "Antonio" and "Mercy" before slipping away again (4.2.349, 353). In the context of Webster's depiction of the Duchess's martyrdom, this event feels miraculous, but the play is actually employing a device that was a stock element of public theater tragedies and tragicomedies. Desdemona's sudden revival, in which she gathers just enough strength to absolve her husband of her death, is only one of the most famous examples of the near or false resurrection on the public stage. Crucially, in *The Duchess of Malfi*, this event signals to the audience that the play could choose to resurrect the Duchess, but that it will not. Webster is whetting his audience's appetite, preparing them emotionally for a very different kind of resurrection scene that does not involve the Duchess's coffin but still manages to access the emotional power typically associated with the use of tomb properties in the Catholic drama. As we will see, this decision to leave out the tomb while maintaining a sense of solemnity and pathos surrounding the resurrection is one that also figures prominently in the final scene of *The Winter's Tale*.

Foregrounded by the play's depiction of the Duchess's suffering and by the anticipation surrounding her near-resurrection, the scene in which the echo attempts to warn and comfort her husband is immediately recognizable as one with supernatural overtones. These overtones are further emphasized by Delio's description of a folk tale associated with the ruined abbey. The clarity of the echo produced on this site, he tells Antonio, has prompted many believers to suppose it is "a spirit / That answers" (5.3.8-9). When they hear it for themselves, Antonio and Delio disagree about the source of the sound, whether it is in fact his "wife's voice" or merely "the dead stones" giving counsel, but the scene itself, which lists the echo as its own speaking part, is clearly interested in the possibility that it has its own liveliness (5.4.0, 26, 36). A few lines later, when Antonio begins to hear his own words returned back to him—"'Tis very like my wife's voice. *Echo. Ay, wife's voice*" (5.3.26)—he begins to believe that the Duchess is somehow present. While Delio remains suspicious, Antonio responds passionately to the Echo's pronouncement that he shall "[n]ever see her more." "I marked not one repetition of the echo / But that," he marvels, "and on the sudden, a clear light / Presented me a face folded in sorrow" (43-5). Delio dismisses his vision as "[y]our fancy, merely" and encourages him to leave his "ague" behind, but this line recalls Bosola's morbid fantasy that the Duchess, whom he was unable to call back from life, is still with him (46-7). "Still methinks the Duchess / Haunts me. There, there!" Bosola exclaims at the end of Act 5, scene 2, before admitting sadly that "'[t]is nothing but my melancholy" (5.2.344-6). In this brief moment, the Duchess seems to revive, and her killer glimpses the possibility of his own salvation: "her eye opes, / And heaven in it seems to ope, that late was shut" (4.2.346-7). But just as the scene in the abbey denies both Antonio and the audience the physical presence of a resurrected spirit, this earlier scene tantalizes its audience with the possibility of a tragicomic ending only to frustrate that expectation. Whether during the original production the boy actor playing the Duchess appeared in both scenes, each character's speech evokes the same feelings of sadness and awe, emotions that mirror those of the apostles. This play is not merely staging Antonio and Delio's disagreement over the nature of the echo in order to call attention to differences of opinion between faithful Catholics and dubious Protestants. Their inability to reach a single conclusion about the nature of what they have experienced actually helps recreate the sense of pathos associated with the depictions of Christ's resurrection in the Bible and the cycle plays within the context of a contemporary tragedy.

Just as the play denies its audience the satisfaction of a proper resurrection, it presents a tomb scene without an actual body. Antonio's reference to a "clear light" has convinced some scholars that the actor playing the Duchess should appear briefly on stage.[49] The evidence, however, does not support this hypothesis,

---

[49]   John Russell Brown observes that "[i]n itself an Echo was not particularly rare in plays of the time, but a stage direction at the head of the scene—'Echo from the Duchess' grave'—indicates that more is required here than a voice coming mysteriously from somewhere off-stage" (25). Robert Gibbons argues in his introduction to the New Mermaids edition that "[i]n contrast to the highly exclusive and very occasional Jacobean court masque, in which Italian expertise in scenic theatre and lighting was, at great cost, copied ... [the theatrical effects in the public theater were] largely emblematic" (*Duchess of Malfi* [London: A&C Black, 2001], xxxix). He also notes more cautiously than Brown that for the "face folded in sorrow" Webster "may have intended a special visual effect" (xxix).

which appears especially tenuous in light of the highly detailed stage direction from *The Second Maiden's Tragedy*, in which the ghost of the Lady appears to tell her lover Govianus about the theft of her body:

> *On a sudden, in a kind of noise like a wind, the doors clattering, the tombstone flies open, and a great light appears in the midst of the tomb; his* LADY, *as went out, standing just before him all in white, stuck with jewels, and a great crucifix on her breast.*[50]

This elaborate description is particularly evocative of the guild-sponsored resurrection plays. Following Luke but also John, these plays call for Christ to appear suddenly standing among the apostles when he appears to them for the second time after the resurrection. Similarly, the Lady's ghost in *The Second Maiden's Tragedy* is described as "*standing just before him.*" Rather than expecting the boy actor to leap or step out of the tomb, an operation that could have proved extremely awkward in practice, the play heightens the impact of his entrance through special effects and by his sudden proximity to Govianus.[51] In addition to the Mons stage direction, which refers to "*a great brightness and smoke of incense and light,*" there is evidence that other European resurrection dramas called for similar special effects. A Spanish play from the fourteenth century, for instance, calls for an earthquake to accompany Christ's emergence. But although it seems to resemble these earlier European scripts, *The Second Maiden's Tragedy* is extraordinary among public theater plays because of the spectacular, and spectacularly polemical, nature of its staged resurrection.

Webster's play is nearly unique in that it eschews the standard material technology associated with the tomb, pointing around the thing to the power associated with it. In terms of its setting, the reactions of the other characters, and the Duchess's remarkable absence from the scene, *The Duchess of Malfi* takes full advantage of the emotional affect associated with the tradition of staging the resurrection by avoiding any direct reference to the biblical narrative. It is able to do so, I argue, because of its audience's awareness of the existing generic conventions associated with stage resurrections. Bracketed on either side by Bosola's sense of being haunted and by Antonio's vision of a face "folded in sorrow," the echo's incorporeality allows the empty tomb to become the focus of the scene. Generally more cautious and more reverent about the business of staging a resurrected spirit,

---

[50]   *The Second Maiden's Tragedy*, ed. Anne Lancashire (Manchester: Manchester University Press, 1978), 4.4.42 sd.

[51]   Lancashire observes that "[t]he discovery of the tomb, for example, might have been done, highly conventionally, by the Tyrant himself, entering through the discovery area, or, more realistically, by the pulling of a curtain from before the tomb's discovery space while the Tyrant entered at 'a farther door.' ... The tomb must have been fairly large and elaborate, as it is 'richly set forth' and in Act 4, scene 4 the Lady's spirit comes from it with 'a great light' shining; and it must have had a movable top or side" (55).

Webster's play creates a kind of sacrality around the Duchess's absence from the stage through a false resurrection and the pointed lack of a body in the tomb, and in so doing it follows both the liturgical drama, which turns on the revelation of the empty grave clothes, and Luke 24, which pointedly avoids depicting the resurrection.

The Second Maiden's Tragedy, by contrast, prompts its audience to confront the superstitious, potentially ridiculous aspects of a theatrical resurrection by emphasizing the presence rather than absence of the resurrected body. As Anne Lancashire notes, the Lady's line, "[b]ehold, I'm gone; / My body taken up" makes direct reference to the angel's declaration, and thus her character collapses the role of the messenger angel and the role of the martyr (4.4.61-2). Like Christ, she appears twice after her death, and her second appearance in the final scene of the play is doubly fascinating because it calls for the body and the spirit to be represented simultaneously on stage. If *The Duchess of Malfi* stages the absence of the body, this scene depicts two bodies, one spiritual and one corporeal, both played by boy actors wearing similar costumes and on stage at the same time, a doubling effect that calls attention to the limits of the medium. The result is precisely the opposite of "*non est hic*," a scene that exposes the theatricality of the miracle rather than its transcendent mystery.[52]

The Second Maiden's Tragedy ultimately reflects a sense of uneasiness about the potential for idolatry associated with the Lady's body and distances itself from the Catholic tradition by creating an anti-realistic stage image, while in *The Duchess of Malfi* there is no direct reference to Christ's resurrection, but rather an appropriation of the emotional power associated with "*non est hic*." Despite their very different approaches to representing a resurrection, however, it is possible that the King's Men may have been banking on the resonance between the two plays, as well as that between Webster's play and the Catholic resurrection tradition. Both scripts call attention to a missing body in ways that reference the material technology inherited from the guild-sponsored dramas, but the earlier play makes much more pointed allusions to the biblical event and calls for the Lady's spirit to appear on stage along with her corpse. By pointing out the material similarities between the effects used to heighten the experience of the resurrection in the cycle plays and those used to intensify a similar event in the public theater, this chapter seeks to undermine the assumption that seventeenth-century players and playwrights were exclusively interested in presenting a parody of the biblical miracle, in part by drawing a contrast between plays such as *The Duchess of*

---

[52]   Both of these plays were first performed immediately after the company's acquisition of the Blackfriars playhouse, and while the Globe itself would have been relatively dark during a winter performance, the hall playhouse might have provided the best setting for these staged resurrections. On the other hand, as Andrew Gurr has pointed out, the lack of special effects at the Globe were balanced by the "vastly greater crowds" and "the packed mass" of playgoers, which "could generate a higher intensity of audience reaction" (*Playgoing in Shakespeare's London*, 47).

Malfi and those such as *The Second Maiden's Tragedy* whose overt references to Catholic tradition work to separate the public playing companies from an existing religious discourse.

Shakespearean Revivals

In performing acts of resurrection, the commercial playing companies were not dealing with a new set of representational problems, but they were solving them through both "quotation and invention." The players could not help but be influenced by the vitality of the theatrical traditions surrounding the tomb property, but they were also responding to the particular historical moment in which they were working. Ever sensitive to the richness as well as the constraints of his medium, Shakespeare employed a wide variety of resurrections in his plays, and once we begin to pay attention to them within the context of a set of conventions inherited from the cycle plays, and from his contemporaries, it becomes evident that he had been experimenting with this set of material technologies throughout his career as a playwright. In other words, though Shakespeare cannot be said to have "borrowed" from *The Duchess of Malfi* in composing *The Winter's Tale,* since his play pre-dates it, I am arguing that Shakespeare, like Webster, was reconfiguring an existing set of theatrical and religious conventions, and moreover that he seems to have done so quite deliberately over a period of many years. Several of the plays that precede *The Winter's Tale*—*Romeo and Juliet* (1596), *Much Ado About Nothing* (1598), and *Pericles* (1608)—also make creative use of tomb properties, and thus provide an immediate context for the self-conscious appropriation of the resurrection tradition in the later work.

Strictly speaking, the material technology that the London playing companies inherited from the cycle plays was the business of having an actor step or leap out of a coffin-like object. The tomb scene in *Romeo and Juliet* thus departs from other on-stage resurrections because it does not call for Juliet to rise from her tomb. Instead, the play sets her resurrection—the moment in which the sleeping potion wears off and she "stirs" (5.3.147)—in her family monument, where she lies in full sight on her bier.[53] The force of this scene derives from the ironic juxtaposition of Juliet's fake death, her revival, and her actual death: she is brought back to life from a false suicide only to die in earnest. Here the contrast between what might have been, had this been a comedy, and what actually happens is made all the more striking by the fact that the scene takes place in a tomb. Through the appearance of Romeo just before Juliet's reawakening, the play flirts with a comic

---

[53] The stage directions are difficult to interpret, but we do know that at one point Romeo opens the tomb and enters it: the dialogue refers to a "mattock and wrenching iron" (5.3.22). On the other hand, Juliet's bier was probably represented by nothing more elaborate than a plinth.

ending, just as some comedies gesture toward a tragic ending before producing the necessary resurrection.

Among this latter category of plays is *Much Ado About Nothing*, in which Hero's wedding is broken off and immediately followed by her funeral. Her death is then carefully orchestrated by the friar, who urges her to "die to live" and prompts her father to maintain the fiction by performing "all rites / That appertain unto a burial" (4.1.253, 207-8). The friar's hope is that the enactment of Hero's death, and the lively presence of her ghost, will help Claudio on the path to repentance. "Th' idea of her life," he reasons, "shall sweetly creep / Into his study of imagination, / And every lovely organ of her life / Shall come apparell'd in more precious habit, / More moving, delicate, and full of life," than when she lived in fact (224-8). The song sung at Hero's funeral also hints at the possibility of her return, calling upon the surrounding graves to "yawn and yield your dead," until Hero has been properly laid to rest (5.3.19). The setting of this scene is the family mausoleum, but unlike *Romeo and Juliet* this play does not show Hero's body, for she is awake and breathing in her father's house. Playgoers are thus able to enjoy the irony of Claudio performing his penance in front of an empty tomb.

Although it uses a different kind of stage property, one that underscores Shakespeare's unconventional relationship to the generic tradition I have been describing, *Much Ado About Nothing* clearly relies on its audience's awareness of the material technologies associated with staging the resurrection. This comedy deploys thematic elements that run throughout many of these scripts: it exhibits the potentially disastrous effects of male jealousy, but also the potential for love to triumph over death. In this sense, *Much Ado About Nothing* prefigures the treatment of the resurrection motif in *The Winter's Tale*. Claudio's devotions, and his promise to maintain them nightly, echo the repentance that Leontes performs after his wife's death. Both Hero and Hermione survive because they have allies who are able to convert their husbands' jealousy into repentance, mediators who understand that this transformation can only take place in the absence of the beloved. And like *Much Ado About Nothing*, in which the only substitute for the dead Hero is the live Hero disguised as another woman, *The Winter's Tale* flirts with the idea of a replacement wife when Leontes promises Paulina that he will never marry again unless his new bride is identical to Hermione herself.

The endings of the two plays are also strikingly similar in the way they frame the act of resurrection. In both plays, the lost wife is produced only moments before the final lines are spoken, and in each instance on-stage witnesses are prevented from reflecting on what has just transpired. The friar's promise that he will "qualify" the amazement of the spectators by telling them "largely of fair Hero's death" after the festivities have ended clearly prefigures Leontes's assertion that the events of those sixteen lost years will be described in a more "leisurely" fashion at a later time (5.4.67, 69, 5.3.152). If we look too carefully, these plays suggest, we may begin to question the efficacy of such a neat resolution. Therefore, the friar urges us, "[l]et wonder seem familiar," for the resurrection of the dead is both impossible and absolutely central to narratives informed by the Christian tradition (5.4.70).

Like *The Winter's Tale*, *Much Ado About Nothing* uses the resurrection motif to perform the victory of love over human mortality, but as the plays' attenuated endings suggest, both are simultaneously shadowed by death and loss. When Hero removes her veil and announces that, "[o]ne Hero died defiled, but I do live, / And surely as I live, I am a maid," she plants the idea in the audience's mind that the Hero who "died defiled" can never be fully resurrected (5.4.63-4). Rather than undermining the play's impact, however, these darker overtones demonstrate the powerful connection between its fictional reversals and the tragicomic quality of the biblical narrative that stands behind it.

Unlike other Shakespearean plays that employ the resurrection motif, *Pericles* does call for a character to physically emerge from her tomb. Traveling in a ship wracked by storms, Pericles is forced to throw his wife, whom he believes to be dead, overboard in a rich coffin. It appears he has acted too soon, however, for immediately after she washes up on shore, Thaisa is "brought back to life" by a magician named Cerimon, who narrates her revival for the audience: "Nature awakes, / A warmth [breathes] out of her. ... See how she gins to blow / Into life's flower again" (3.2.92-4). Like Paulina's speech in Act 5, scene 3 of *The Winter's Tale*, Cerimon's words are performative, for as he describes her resurrection, the audience sees it unfolding before their eyes. As in *The Winter's Tale*, the meeting between husband and wife is preceded by the meeting between the father and his daughter, a girl who resembles his wife as she looked at the time of her supposed death. Another parallel lies in the setting of these final reunions: Thaisa is eventually discovered in the temple of Diana, a community of vestal virgins that echoes the sanctity of Paulina's "chapel." The entire operation is much more believable than the one in *The Winter's Tale*, however; Cerimon claims no special powers, but rather blames those who pronounced her dead too soon.

The many resemblances between the two plays suggest that *Pericles* is the natural precursor of *The Winter's Tale*, but it differs fundamentally from the later play in presenting an ending untroubled by the possibility of loss. *Pericles* leaves no doubt as to how its protagonists have spent their time since they were separated, whereas *The Winter's Tale* never fully explains where Hermione has been for the past sixteen years. The means by which Paulina has resurrected her remains something of a mystery, both to the characters and to the audience, while Thaisa's recovery is easily explained. The only characters who die in *Pericles* are its malefactors, whereas the otherwise happy ending of *The Winter's Tale* is clouded by the absence of Mamillius, the innocent son who will never be returned to his mother. In other words, *The Winter's Tale* challenges the notion that everything that has been lost can be recovered and resists giving its audience full satisfaction. By allowing the moment of resurrection to be tinged with a sense of sadness, both *The Winter's Tale* and *Much Ado About Nothing* tacitly admit that their resurrections do not represent a complete solution to the problems of death and loss.

One other element that sets *Pericles* apart from the plays discussed earlier is its staging of the resurrection, which is still firmly anchored in the use of the tomb property. By contrast, *The Winter's Tale* eschews the stage business of having the actor emerge from a tomb or coffin, thus avoiding the problem of having to make the material technology appear realistic. A coffin-style prop appears not only in *Pericles* but in a series of plays produced by the King's Men in 1608, 1611, 1618, 1631, and 1637, indicating that the company probably owned one or more. But *The Winter's Tale* ingeniously reworks existing conventions without using a tomb property, providing a new solution to the representational challenge of staging a character's resurrection. Thus it directly and self-consciously references the phenomenon Anthony Dawson describes as the strategic translation of religious affect into the secular theater.

Throughout Act 5, *The Winter's Tale* prepares its audience for a dramatic triumph in which Paulina presents a statue of the long-dead Hermione to her grieving husband and daughter. But in contrast to the sense of possibility that characterizes Paulina's pronouncements in the final scene, her speeches in Act 5, scene 1 use the trope of resurrection to relate events that can never take place. She describes Perdita's recovery, for example, as an event "as monstrous to our human reason, / As my *Antigonus* to break his grave, / And come again to me" (5.1.41-3). Later in the same scene, when the lords are urging Leontes to marry again for the sake of his kingdom, Paulina protests that no woman could fill Hermione's shoes: "one worse, / And better us'd, would make her sainted spirit / Again possess her corpse, and on this Stage / (Where we offenders now) appear soul-vex't, / And begin, 'Why to me—?'" (56-60). Paulina paints a picture of Hermione's ghost as a resurrected spirit both insubstantial and corporeal. She goes on to speak further on the ghost's behalf, telling Leontes that "[w]ere I the ghost that walk'd, I'ld bid you mark / Her eye, and tell me for what dull part in't / You chose her" (63-5). And when a messenger describes Perdita, whose identity has not yet been revealed, as a "peerless piece of earth," more lovely than any other member of the female sex, Paulina chides him for neglecting to mention the beauty of the dead queen. Lamenting man's infidelity, she calls on Hermione directly, remarking that her "[g]rave," and her memory, have been forced to give way to the superficiality of "what's seen now" (94, 97-8). Paulina's goal is the same as that of Leonato in *Much Ado About Nothing*, to test the fidelity of the would-be husband. Like the earlier play, this one entertains the idea of having Hermione emerge from her tomb but withholds the physical property from the final scene, simultaneously revealing that the absent tomb was empty all along. As Leontes himself observes, he has "said many / A prayer" at a grave that never had a body in it at all (5.3.140-41).

In establishing the terms under which it will enact Hermione's resurrection, the play directs audience members to a familiar set of conventions by referencing the trope of the false resurrection, a device that can be traced back to plays such as *Romeo and Juliet*. The dialogue between the gentlemen in Act 5, scene 2 signals Shakespeare's knowledge of the existing stage tradition, preparing the playgoer for the spectacle of Hermione's statue coming to life by providing a tantalizing series of clues about the royal drama being played off stage. The story of Perdita's return is a kind of resurrection motif in and of itself, and the stories told about her by the gentlemen echo the events of other tragicomedies, especially *Pericles*.

When Pericles is reunited with his daughter, he sees Thaisa in her; similarly, Leontes is immediately attracted to Perdita because of her resemblance to his young bride. The likeness is so striking, in fact, that Paulina is forced to chide the king for having "too much youth" in his eye (224). If, however, it is possible to read this scene as a reference to the long-awaited moment of resurrection, it is only because the language of the previous scene is so consumed with grave-breaking. Although they are physically absent from the final act, graves are everywhere in the dialogue, and the affective technology associated with the opening of the tomb plays a vital part in the performance of Hermione's resurrection.

In the end, *The Winter's Tale* does provide audience members with a reawakening, though it is not the one they have been expecting. As both fictional bystanders and paying customers stand in awe of the image, she tells them, "I like your silence, it the more shows off / Your wonder" (5.3.21-2). No one can be silent, however, when the statue moves and becomes living flesh. The satisfaction audience members experience during this moment is enhanced by the fact that they, like the on-stage spectators, have believed Hermione to be dead since the end of Act 3. Consequently, they are as surprised as the rest of the characters when the play concludes with a comic ending involving reunions and marriages. At the same time, the play presents a barrier to the audience's straightforward enjoyment of the performance, as the characters return again and again to the question of whether Paulina's incantations are "lawful" spells or dangerous works of witchcraft. Thus, the pleasurable tension in the scene is heightened by the suggestion that something not quite lawful might be taking place. The script purposefully calls attention to the unorthodox aspects of the miracle, which might easily have been associated with necromancy and superstition in the charged atmosphere of Jacobean London.

The overt references to religion in Act 5, scene 3 reveal a range of potential problems surrounding the introduction of Hermione's statue. On the one hand, by making the statue come to life Paulina risks being accused of practicing black magic, and she must reassure her audience that her "spell" is as lawful as Hermione's "holy" actions (104-5). On the other hand, Hermione's image has the potential to provoke idolatry even before it begins to move. The setting of the play is technically a pagan one, but the statue is housed in what Paulina calls a "chapel," a term that might have led audience members to see the connection between this object and the statues of saints outlawed by Protestant reformers (86). *The Winter's Tale* admits this possible connection when Hermione's daughter Perdita kneels to the statue and asks its blessing. But Leontes's mixed response to his wife's reawakening is perhaps the best indicator of the characters' capacity to alternate between delight and caution. When Hermione embraces him, he cries out, "[o]h, she's warm! / If this be magic, let it be an art / Lawful as eating" (109-11). He is both transported with amazement that a stone image has become warm as flesh and anxious about the source of the miracle.

Why, then, does the play invite the specter of idolatry by performing the animation of Hermione's statue, engaging openly with England's Catholic traditions? The answer is that the traditions the play is most interested in are theatrical traditions, not Catholic ones *per se*. The act of placing a statue in a chapel does connect the scene to specific kinds of worship outlawed by the reformers, but because Hermione's statue moves it also recalls the set of staging conventions that were already a vital part of the playing company's repertory and also featured prominently in *The Second Maiden's Tragedy* and *The Duchess of Malfi*. When we consider that the play is invoking a set of practices that are both religious and theatrical, we can better understand why self-consciousness, anxiety, and wonder go hand in hand in its resolution. *The Winter's Tale* anticipates the criticisms of those Protestants who frowned on any direct visual reference to the resurrection of Christ, while at the same time appropriating the power of the spectacular dramatic moment in which the one who was "lost" is found again. This moment is even more successful in eliciting an emotional response from its audience precisely because it is never fully explained, and because, like the biblically inspired resurrections depicted in the cycle plays, it provokes both pathos and joy. At the same time, *The Winter's Tale* insistently calls attention to the artfulness of the theatrical resurrection, thus distancing the scene from the religious context originally associated with the tomb property. In the words of Stanley Cavell, "religion is Shakespeare's pervasive, hence, invisible business"—invisible because the play never actually stages a resurrection in which a body rises out of a grave, pervasive because the interplay between absence and presence established by the biblical narrative is at the heart of Hermione's reawakening.[54]

When the statue is made or revealed to be living flesh, the audience sees a synthesis of artificial and natural forms that is unique to the theater and, the play asserts, superior to all other arts, including the craft of sculpture. Early references to the sculptor Giulio Romano accordingly focus on the slippage between the object and its referent: "He so near to Hermione hath done Hermione that they say one would speak to her and stand in hope of answer" (5.2.99-100). Leontes's first observation is that the statue has his wife's "natural posture," and he is immediately compelled to address it directly, affirming that "[t]hou art Hermione" (23, 25). When the king observes the wrinkles on the image, Paulina reminds him that the carver has purposefully aged his subject; this is naturalism, she asserts, not idealized beauty. Prompted to ask her blessing, Perdita kneels to kiss the statue's hand, and Leontes begs a touch from its lips. In both cases, Paulina begs them to refrain, pointing out that the "oily painting" is still wet on the stone (83). Like Perdita in Act 4, who hopes that Florizel would never worship a painting simply because it looked like her, Paulina is reminding the characters, and the audience, not to treat an object like a person.

But the statue is in fact a body, recognizable as God's creation rather than man's idolatry. The theater uses human bodies as well as artificial forms, and thus, like grafting, it is "an art / Which does mend Nature," using natural means to represent the natural world (4.4.95-6). Earlier, in Act 2, Paulina presents the

---

[54]   *Disowning Knowledge in Six Plays of Shakespeare* (Cambridge: Cambridge University Press, 1987), 218.

infant Perdita to Leontes as a work of art, a copy of the mother. As Robert Egan points out, she credits "good goddess Nature" for the likeness between the two because at this stage of the play art and nature are in harmony (2.3.103). When she gives Hermione back to him at the end of Act 5, however, she must work to make the king believe in "nature's work of art," thus restoring his world to "its original harmony with the order of nature."[55] In the final scene, the equilibrium is reestablished, and the audience is made aware that Paulina's natural magic is rooted in the human body itself, the body of a boy actor. By focusing on an art form within the theatrical fiction, *The Winter's Tale* draws attention to the materiality of the statue, only to assert that the actor's body, characterized by its innate potential for transformation—the capacity for motion and breath that Huston Diehl calls "aliveness"—is far more remarkable.[56] The point is not to shock the audience by the sudden appearance of a body, for Hermione has been on the stage all along, but rather to reveal the actor's natural body beneath the artificial trappings of the statue.

When Paulina at last shows Leontes and Perdita the statue of Hermione, the tomb property is displaced by a new form of theatrical resurrection: the actor, feigning death and then feigning life again, supplies the beginning and the end of the mystery. Thus, while acknowledging its roots in the religious theater, with all its tantalizing references to resurrections—"I'll fill your grave up," says Paulina, as she urges Hermione to leave death behind (5.3.101)—Shakespeare's play ultimately discards the physical remnant of the Catholic tradition as unnecessary, as if indicating to antitheatricalists that they cannot accuse him of any lingering attachment to the outlawed cycle plays. Forestalling any critique linking Hermione's statue with idolatry, *The Winter's Tale* thus shifts the ground underneath the generic convention, suggesting that the dramatic potential of the actor's body makes the physical tomb superfluous. The absence of the tomb property ultimately clarifies the nature of the play's investment in Catholic dramas of resurrection, an interest that consistently privileges living practices over dead objects.

In his own account of *The Winter's Tale*, Michael O'Connell suggests that Shakespeare's text demonstrates the drama's self-conscious response to the antitheatricalists' attacks against idolatry in the theater. For O'Connell, this play is the culmination of a gradual process whereby post-Reformation playwrights adapted their own art to the demands of a new ideology that was deeply suspicious of images by asserting a supreme confidence in "what is seen" on the stage.[57] Like O'Connell, I interpret *The Winter's Tale* as a highly self-conscious affirmation of the theater, but I suggest that although it marks the height of Shakespeare's experimentation with this particular trope it does not represent the last appearance of the material technology on the public stage. On the contrary, it was succeeded

---

[55] Robert Egan, *Drama Within Drama: Shakespeare's Sense of His Art in* King Lear, The Winter's Tale *and* The Tempest (New York: Columbia University Press, 1975), 64-6.

[56] Diehl, "'Strike All That Look Upon With Marvel,'" 27.

[57] O'Connell, *The Idolatrous Eye*, 138.

by a 1637 revision, William Berkeley's *The Lost Lady*, which contains all the stock features of the plays discussed above—including the tomb property—and was performed by the King's Men at the Blackfriars playhouse.

Berkeley's tragicomedy presents all the generic conventions associated with the tomb property while pushing them to the very limits of believability. A virtuous lady, thought to be dead, is mourned by her lover, who visits her tomb daily. As it turns out, the dead body belongs not to her but to her treacherous maid, and she returns to visit her lover disguised as an Egyptian sorceress. She also appears, however, as her own ghost, and misleads him into believing that the sorceress is responsible for her murder. Her lover dutifully poisons the Egyptian, only to find—when wiping off her black face paint—that she is in fact the lady herself. In a completely unjustified but necessary plot twist, the poison turns out not to be deadly poison and the lady quickly revives. Is it possible that this play was inspired by the absent tomb in Shakespeare's resurrection? If so, such a claim would be bolstered by the fact that *The Winter's Tale* has so much in common with the other texts discussed in this chapter. Shakespeare's play, like Webster's, accentuates the affective power of the moment of resurrection by avoiding a direct reference to dramatizations of the biblical narrative. Unlike the tomb scene in *The Duchess of Malfi*, however, the dead woman's body becomes the visual and thematic focus of the final scene in *The Winter's Tale*. If Webster plays up the affective nature of the Duchess's resurrection by drawing attention to the empty tomb, Shakespeare shifts the ground underneath the generic convention by suggesting that the dramatic potential of the actor's body makes the physical tomb superfluous. For its part, Berkeley's play pushes this conclusion even further by combining the roles of Hermione and Paulina and introducing a further threat—not only that the lady may be dead and gone, but that we might not recognize her when she reappears. Its success as a piece of theater, even more so than Shakespeare's play, depends on the audience's ability to recognize its sophisticated engagement with the Catholic resurrection tradition.

By focusing on the source of the emotional impact in these scenes of resurrection, I have argued that it was the material difference between the tomb properties that gave audience members access to the emerging structures of feeling associated with the tomb, including the interplay between presence and absence. The plays discussed in this chapter, and others that straddle the line between sincerity and satire, demonstrate that the use of tomb properties in the London theaters was not a simple case of appropriation, but rather a complex set of negotiations, building off one another and fueled by the demands of the repertory theater. All the public theater plays that employ tomb properties and the material technology associated with them present evidence of the theater's sophisticated reworking of earlier dramatic precedents, and the robust structure of feeling surrounding this particular convention is demonstrated by the frequency with which the companies used tomb properties to create scenes of resurrection. What is most striking about *The Winter's Tale* and *The Duchess of Malfi*, however, is their ability to tap into this tradition without directly importing the material technology. The methods of appropriation used in these two plays rely on the audience's familiarity with the existing generic convention, established first in the guild-sponsored drama. Their departure from the material aspects of this tradition ironically allows these plays to take greater advantage of the emotional power inherent in staging the resurrection.

A careful study of this continuing dramatic tradition provides further evidence for the importance of breaking down the artificial boundary separating the "medieval" and "early modern" periods, but the affective similarities between the public theater tragedies discussed here and the cycle dramas performed during the late Middle Ages also allow us to tackle the barrier that has been set up between "sacred" and "secular" forms of cultural production. This distinction, which Lawrence Clopper has shown to be alien to pre-Reformation performance, also falls short when used to describe the possible impact of an on-stage resurrection in the public theater. The fact that plays as different as *The Lost Lady*, *The Duchess of Malfi*, and *The Winter's Tale* can appropriate the most engaging aspects of the resurrection confounds any attempt to conclude that this appropriation was always done in the spirit of parody. Simultaneously, the contradictory responses to these characters' ghostly presence disprove the assumption that the plays' staged resurrections are "sacred" in any straightforward sense of the term. I have argued that these plays cannot be construed as purely satirical or entirely secular, but neither can we read their appropriation of biblical themes as a wholesale return to the experience of pre-Reformation theater. In this sense, they allow us to reflect on the diversity of religious experience and religious belief during the early seventeenth century, but more importantly on the public theater's sophisticated recontextualization of a powerful material technology.

Chapter 2

The Trappings of Ceremony:
Setting the Table and Other
Theatrical Practices

Thursday last the players of the Fortune were fined 1,000 pound for setting up an altar, a bason, and two candlesticks, and bowing down before it upon the stage, and although they allege it was an old play revived, and an altar to the heathen gods, yet it was apparent that this play was revived on purpose in contempt of the ceremonies of the church.

—Edmond Rossingham to Viscount Conway, 8 May 1639[1]

For they having gotten a new old Play, called *The Cardinalls conspiracie* whom they brought upon the *stage* in as great *state* as they could, with *Altars, Images, Crosses, Crucifixes,* and the like, to set forth his pomp and pride. But wofull was the sight to see how in the middest of all their *mirth,* the Pursevants came and seazed upon the poore Cardinall, and all his Consorts, and carryed them away. And when they were questioned for it, in the High Commission Court, they pleaded *Ignorance,* and told the Archbishop, *that they tooke those examples of their Altars, Images,* and the like, *from Heathen Authors.* This did somewhat asswage his anger, that they did not bring him on the Stage: But yet they were fined for it, and after a *little Imprisonment* gat their *liberty.* And having nothing left them but a few old Swords and Bucklers, they fell to Act the *Valiant Scot,* which they Played five dayes with great applause, which vext the Bishops worse than the other, insomuch, as they were forbidden Playing it any more; and some of them prohibited ever Playing againe.

—*Vox borealis or the northern discoverie,* 1640[2]

In Chapter 1, I examined a set of material technologies that were part of a lengthy theatrical tradition and were subsequently modified by the public playing companies in response to tensions surrounding the representation of the resurrection in post-Reformation England. I drew mainly on accounts of the guild-sponsored drama to describe the physical characteristics of this technology, given the paucity of evidence surrounding the tomb properties used in early modern performances.

---

[1]   Mary Anne Everett Green, ed., *Calendar of State Papers, Domestic Series, of the reigns of Edward VI, Mary, Elizabeth and James I,* 1639 (London: Longman, Brown, Green, Longmans & Roberts, 1856), 140-41.

[2]   *Vox borealis, or the northern discoverie: by way of dialogue between Jamie and Willie* ([London or Edinburgh]: Margery Mar-Prelat, 1641), B2r-v.

This chapter likewise focuses on a material technology with Catholic origins, but in this case we have at least one extraordinarily detailed account of what the staging actually looked like. The suppression of *The Cardinal's Conspiracy* may have struck a harsh blow to the Fortune company, but contemporary observers of the play's performance have provided us with a valuable record of contemporary stage practices. In contrast to the general dearth of theatrical accounts from the period, here we have an embarrassment of riches: two narratives, one of which expands upon and embellishes the other.[3]

Admittedly, neither author purports to have been in the audience at the Fortune, but their knowledge of the production testifies to its infamy; both accounts make it clear that what was most upsetting about the play, as far as the authorities were concerned, was its implicit critique of certain traditional objects and ceremonies that had begun appearing in parish churches under the influence of Archbishop William Laud. Laud was appointed Archbishop of Canterbury in 1633, but his program of re-sanctifying the altar and other church furnishings began as early as 1617. In contrast to strict Calvinists, who had banned nearly all the material elements of Christian worship, Laud followed in the footsteps of moderates such as John Hooker and Lancelot Andrewes, who viewed ceremonies not as idolatrous in and of themselves but as appropriate manifestations of piety, if properly expressed.[4] Modern scholars tend to associate the controversial elements of early modern plays with residual elements of Catholic practice, but with *The Cardinal's Conspiracy* the company was poking fun at a set of recent innovations in church practice perpetrated by citizens who considered themselves godly Protestants. Thus, although it is true that the production was apparently suppressed because it challenged official state policy, in 1639 there were many Londoners who opposed official policy precisely because it tolerated a more "popish" form of Protestant worship. In some aristocratic households the mass continued to be performed as it was before the Reformation, while in many parishes the laity and clergy created a kind of compromise between the Protestant emphasis on the word of God and their own attachment to traditional objects. And this ongoing popular interest in

---

[3]   According to Andrew Gurr, "[t]he company had evaded the censor by using an old play, and applied it to a current cause for anger in the city. The intention was to feed popular hatred of Romanism" (*Playgoing in Shakespeare's London*, 191).

[4]   Laud is often associated with the movement known as Arminianism, which challenged various points of Calvinist doctrine including predestination. Patrick Collinson describes the Arminianism of the 1630s as follows: "under the mastership of William Beale, the chapel of St. John's College Cambridge, a place not noted for ignorance and illiteracy, was 'dressed up after a new fashion'. It had an altar frontal depicting the deposition from the Cross and large gilt-framed pictures around the walls portraying the life of Christ 'from his conception to his ascension', with a large crucifix behind the altar which was surmounted with a canopy painted with angels and a 'sun with great light beams and a dove in the midst'. By this time the vicar of Sturry, near Canterbury, a man 'famously noted for a forward agent in superstitious and popish innovations', had a large painted crucifix framed and hanging in his parlour. Such were the aesthetics of English Arminianism" (120).

finding a middle ground not entirely devoid of the material aspects of worship in turn fueled the theater's exploration of the altar's ritual function.

In the early years of the seventeenth century, the communion ceremony was the site of a debate over what constituted proper devotion. Catholic recusants defined the terms of their own religious practice within, or in spite of the parameters set out by the reformers, while many anti-Calvinists, Laud among them, found shades of gray between the two extremes of the Protestant communion table and the Catholic altar. The terminology of the altar figured prominently in Protestant attacks on the mass, evoking both the misguided bloodlust of biblical idolaters and the misconception the reformers believed to be at the heart of English Catholicism. References to the Christian altar were not excised from the Book of Common Prayer until 1552, but according to many Protestants, the label "altar" mistakenly associated the service at the heart of Christian worship with an actual sacrifice. The preferred term for the reformers was "holy table" or "God's board," signifying that the object was the site of a commemorative act, a commonly-shared meal. From the perspective of church officials, therefore, it was essential to differentiate between the terms "altar" and "table," just as it was essential to remove the other traces of Catholic "superstition" from the visible church.

On a physical level, Catholic altars were different from communion tables because they were made of stone and were permanently affixed to the floor in the east end of the church. They were marked with consecration crosses, and relics were embedded in them to sanctify them as the holiest places in the church. The communion table, on the other hand, was made of wood and contained no saints' relics. In terms of their relationship to the architecture of the church, the table was to be placed lengthwise, so as to accommodate the maximum number of communicants, while the altar was placed flush against the east wall, facing away from the congregation. Originally abolished by Edward's ministers, who issued an injunction that "all shrines, covering of shrines, all tables, candlesticks, trindles or rolls of wax, pictures, paintings, and all other monuments of feigned miracles" be made "utterly extinct," altars were rebuilt under Mary as part of a short-lived return to state-sponsored Catholicism, then abolished again by Elizabeth, whose 1559 Articles specified that every stone altar be replaced by a wooden communion table that could be moved into the middle of the chancel during the time of the service in order to facilitate the taking of the sacrament by the entire congregation.[5] As with other aspects of the ongoing theological debate, the 1559 statute provided a compromise between traditionalists and strict Protestants by indicating that, between services, the table should stand where the altar did, and that it should be moved into the lower end of the chancel for communion. In practice, however, the letter of the law was rarely followed, and individual parishes seldom moved their tables from place to place within the church. James's canons of 1604, published just after he took the throne, follow nearly every point of the 1559 articles, and

---

[5]   Walter Howard Frere, ed., *Visitation Articles and Injunctions of the Period of the Reformation*, vol. 2 (London, New York: Longmans, Green & Co, 1910), 126.

the slippage between the altar and the table continued to provoke debates among both theologians and everyday churchgoers throughout the sixteenth and early seventeenth centuries.

Perhaps the most important practical difference between the altar and the table lay in how the two objects were treated, but the iconoclasts' attacks on Catholic altars were rarely successful in perpetuating this distinction. Within the traditional rituals of the English church, it was customary to sanctify the altar with relics and to re-sanctify it before each performance of the mass. After each Easter service, in particular, "the altars of the church were ritually stripped of all their coverings and ornaments, while a series of responses from the Passion narratives and the prophets were sung. As each altar was stripped, the priest intoned a collect of the saint to whom it was dedicated. Each of the altars then had water and wine poured on it and was washed, using a broom of sharp twigs."[6] This process protected the sacred implements of the altar, which would then be stored by the churchwardens in a locked chest (if they could afford one), but it also clearly defined the boundaries between ritual observance and daily life. Inspired by this process of cleaning and re-sacralizing the altar, parishioners with Catholic sympathies quickly became adept at rebuilding the church furnishings that had been destroyed or defaced by the reformers. When Mary succeeded to the throne, officials in one London parish immediately set about reclaiming their altar from the parish kitchen. The wardens' account reads: "payed for nayles to mende the kytchyn when yt was broken downe for the alter stone / payed to the felos that helped up the stone of the alter."[7]

Although many of the faithful were lucky enough to be able to reclaim their altar stones, in 1556 Bishop Bonner warned that they should not set up "any gravestone taken from the burial, or other unseemly place," suggesting that less wealthy parishes were attempting to make do with the materials they had at hand.[8] Margaret Aston writes that "many were told to 'enquire of the altar stones,' to find out 'where the altar stones became,' and to return a certificate about it." "It was one thing," she observes, "to dig an altar stone out of the highway (as was done at Smarden in Kent), another to recoup it from the fireplace of master Harper, or Master Norton of Norwood, who had built the high altar stones from Sutton Valence and Hartlip into their chimneys."[9] In the case of Sherborne, the churchwardens spent ten shillings and sixpence on the rebuilding of the altar during the first six months of Mary's reign, and an additional seven shillings on new vestments and altar cloths. The furniture of the altar, including a gilt crucifix and candlesticks, cost them almost twelve pounds, and another two pounds nine shillings for the labor. This expenditure was equivalent to the sum of the parish's expenses for

---

[6]   Duffy, 28.

[7]   Christopher Haigh, *The English Reformation Revised* (Cambridge: Cambridge University Press, 1987), 206-7.

[8]   Aston, 385.

[9]   Ibid., 286.

an entire year.[10] The actions of such parishioners were predicated on a belief that with the right accompaniments and the blessing of a priest, a gravestone could be successfully transformed into an altar. In response, Elizabethan Protestants attempted to reverse the Catholic practice of sanctifying the altar by commanding that altar stones be converted "to some common use" in order to demonstrate their lack of holiness. Occasionally, parishioners complained about such abuses, like the one committed by Christopher Sampford of Halberton, who took the altar stone into his kitchen and threw "filthy waters upon it." Ironically, despite Sampford's attempt to demystify the altar, his neighbors continued to describe it as "sanctified" even when it was being stored in the kitchen.[11] Thus English Catholics and others with a more traditional view of the mass were able to believe that, under more favorable conditions, they could successfully restore their altar stones to the center of their communal practice.

As the accounts of the Fortune performance suggest, the controversial status of altars during this period can be attributed in large part to the objects associated with them, and in many parishes the reformers attacked these accoutrements rather than the altar stones themselves. In some local churches crosses and crucifixes were eschewed altogether, while in others objects such as altar frontals were converted to new purposes by having superstitious signs and letters removed from them. The churchwardens of St. Margaret's in Ludlow, for example, paid a seamstress two shillings in 1569 "for the taking out of the sign of the cross out of the altar cloth" in an effort to make it more like an ordinary table covering.[12] Although there were important material distinctions between stone altars and wooden communion tables, the implements placed on them were easily reconfigured, and it was through these objects that certain elements of traditional Catholic practice, including a more reverent attitude toward the altar or table, were reincorporated into English churches. Eventually, a type of communion table that would have been forbidden under Elizabeth—one with rich frontals, elegant candlesticks, and even the occasional cross—became more or less acceptable under James, and almost commonplace under Charles, thanks to the influence of Laud and his supporters. As early as 1617, Laud, who was then Dean of Gloucester, demanded that the communion tables be placed altarwise in the east end of the nave so as to reassert their sacred function, which had been compromised by the practice of

---

[10]   Haigh, *English Reformations*, 209. Grindal's injunctions for 1571 specified that all altars should be "pulled down to the ground, and the altar stones defaced and bestowed to some common use: and rood lofts altered. The materials to be sold to the use of the church" (Edward Cardwell, ed., *Documentary Annals of the Reformed Church of England, Being a Collection of Injunctions, Declarations, Orders, Articles of Inquiry, &c. from the Year 1546 to the Year 1716, with Notes Historical and Explanatory*, vol. 1 [Oxford: University Press, 1839], 336).

[11]   Whiting, 40.

[12]   Aston, 332.

using the table "as a convenient place to throw a coat or set a lunch."[13] Laud's fear was that the altar would be used for many purposes "until there was no difference between the Lord's table and that in any man's kitchen," a possibility that became more pronounced when churchwardens were forced to stow their altar stones in profane hiding places.[14]

Although most of the altar stones in parish churches had been destroyed by the time Laud came to power, he shared with English recusants the strong desire to preserve traditional ritual objects from desecration, and when he and other prelates began to add crosses, tapers of virgin wax, and silk cloths to their communion tables, their critics saw this as recreating the atmosphere of the Catholic mass. In the visitation articles from the 1620s, parishioners who chose to rail in and elevate their communion tables were frequently accused of referring to them as "altars." For those with more traditional sympathies, the term represented a continuous set of practices dating from the early Christian church and continuing through the Elizabethan and Jacobean periods. For their opponents, the word implied both a dangerous innovation and a return to pagan superstition. In 1628, Peter Smart published a sermon highlighting the offenses of the anti-Calvinist minister John Cosins, using the language of domestic abuse:

> For they despising the plaine simplicity and modest attire of that grave matron Christs holy spouse, have turned her officers all out of doores, with all her household stuffe, her tables, her cuppes, her bookes, her communions: the very names of her ministers, and such like words used by the holy Ghost throughout the new Testament. Instead whereof the words *Priest*, and *Altar* are taken up by them, because without *Priest* and *Sacrifice* there is no use of an *altar*, and without all three *Priest*, *Sacrifice* and *Altar*, there canne be no masse. But the *masse* comming in brings in with it an inundation of Ceremonies, Crosses and Crucifixes, Chalices, Images, Copes, Candlestickes, Tapers and basons and a thousand such trinkets which attend upon the *masse*.[15]

Although Smart's critique refers to an extreme case, the words he uses are illuminating in and of themselves. He describes the reformed church as a violated matron, pure and unadorned in nature, whose "household" objects have been

---

[13]   As early as 1617, Laud, who was then Dean of Gloucester, demanded that the communion tables be placed altarwise in the east end of the nave, a location more appropriate to its sacred function. "The table was used as a convenient place to throw a coat or set a lunch.... After 1617, scattered parishes imitated Laud's arrangement and adopted the program that would bring with it striking changes in the liturgy; this in turn would affect the physical appearance of churches in the direction of allowing more images" (Phillips, 155).

[14]   Charles Carlton, *Archbishop William Laud* (London: Routledge & Kegan Paul, 1987), 96.

[15]   *The Vanitie & Downe-Fall of Superstitious Popish Ceremonies* (London: Heyres of Robert Charteris, 1628), 8.

rejected in favor of whorish trumpery. By replacing the minister with a priest and the table with an altar, men such as Cosins, Smart argues, cannot help but recreate the mass. Importantly, it is the changes in terminology that lead to the proliferation of the "trinkets," which in turn transform the communion into a Catholic ceremony. Smart's text is thus a tribute to the power of labels, but it also testifies to the difficulty Protestants faced as they attempted to prevent tables, cups, and books from being supplanted by "Crosses and Crucifixes, Chalices, Images, Copes, Candlesticks, Tapers and basons." The danger which became more apparent than ever in the 1620s and 30s was that any kind of ceremonial object could usher in an idolatrous attitude toward the eucharist.

It was under these conditions that *The Cardinal's Conspiracy* was revived on the public stage, suggesting that the players knew full well it would resonate with the "innovations" advocated by men such as Laud and Cosins. Unfortunately, the script has been lost, and we do not know when it was first performed or how pagan its setting actually was, but the disparities between the two narratives quoted at the head of this chapter provide some suggestive clues. Perhaps the most obvious difference is that while Rossingham describes the offending stage properties as "an altar, a bason, and two candlesticks," objects that might indeed have been associated with heathen religion, the author of *Vox Borealis* maintains that they were explicitly Catholic: "*Altars, Images, Crosses, Crucifixes*, and the like." Furthermore, whereas the later account specifies that the objects were intended to demonstrate the cardinal's pomp and pride—and perhaps, by implication, Laud's—Rossingham's letter suggests that the players were able to invoke a sense of scorn for Laudian policies despite the use of pagan accouterments. Indeed, the overlap between pagan and Christian stage properties was not without precedent, for in 1634, "Cromes a Broker" was committed to the Marshalsea "for lending a church Robe with the name of Jesus upon it to ye players in Salisbury Court to present a Flamen a priest of the Heathens."[16] Other documents from the period similarly testify to the practice of converting church vestments into players' costumes, but this example is unusual in that an identifiably Christian garment was associated with a pagan priest, a juxtaposition that underscored the reformers' claims that Catholicism was nothing more than pagan idolatry resurrected. Moreover, if the cardinal in the 1639 production was indeed modeled on Laud, the players were drawing an even more shocking analogy between a modern Protestant divine and a pagan necromancer. Here the reappropriation of a robe from a reformed church might have suggested that the elements of the new Protestantism were, no less than Roman Catholicism, susceptible to abuse.

Rossingham's account is particularly intriguing because it suggests that the censors were more anxious about the implications of certain stage settings than whether individual properties resembled Christian implements, but the *Vox Borealis* description refers to stage objects that directly evoked current religious

---

[16] N. W. Bawcutt, *The Control and Censorship of Caroline Drama: The Records of Sir Henry Herbert, Master of the Revels 1623-73* (Oxford: Clarendon Press, 1996), 191.

controversies. By pointing to the things that were at the heart of Christian ritual, this text contradicts its own claim that the players were drawing "*from Heathen Authors.*" And just as it exaggerates the extent of the literal connection between actual church furnishings and the stage objects used by the Fortune company, so it extends the conditions of their punishment. Some, its author claims, were imprisoned, and forbidden from playing again. Most poignantly, it describes how the archbishop literally took away the actors' property, their investment, leaving them with nothing but a bare table stripped of its ornaments. The altar consisted in what was put on it, and in order to indicate that the property in question was an altar rather than a banqueting table the players had to provide one or more of the following: candles, basins, cloths, images and crosses. Taking away these objects raised the question of what it was that made the altar holy, other than its practical function as the site of the communion ritual. The motives behind the suppression of the Fortune production thus were structurally similar, but not precisely identical, to those of Protestant iconoclasts. It would appear at first glance that a secular object brought on stage and made to look like an altar would only emphasize the point that anyone could make an altar and that there was nothing intrinsically sacred about the object itself, thus debunking the Catholic belief in the altar as the site of transubstantiation—but as we have seen, the process of continual transformation was central to the altar's sacred status. In this sense, then, early modern actors were mimicking the traditional practice of creating, deconstructing, and rebuilding altars, albeit for the purposes of entertainment rather than devotion. Their fictions did not rely upon the premise that the altar had been permanently debunked as a sacred object. Rather, they worked within and around the notion that convertibility was one of the altar's distinguishing features, an aspect of its sacrality that become more obvious after the Reformation rather than less so.

The Fortune production was extraordinary in its boldness but not unique in its use of an on-stage altar. Twenty-two surviving plays first performed between 1588 and 1636 explicitly call for the use of altars or ritual tables. Notably, only six, or roughly a third of these plays, have Christian settings. The low percentage of Christian altars indicates, as one might guess, that it was safer to present an altar as part of a play with a classical setting than to associate it with contemporary Catholic or Protestant practices. It is worth observing, however, that a brief flurry of plays with Christian altars were performed between 1611 and 1624.[17] By way of accounting for this trend, I would suggest that the particular type of religious toleration that characterized James's reign—a kind of lull between the extreme

---

[17]   They are: Dekker's *Match Me In London* (1611); Brewer's *The Lovesick King* (1617); Fletcher, Field, and Massinger's *The Knight of Malta* (1618); Fletcher's *The Pilgrim* (1621); Dekker's *Noble Spanish Soldier* ([Admiral's]; 1622); and Middleton's *A Game at Chess* (1624). Four of the six were first performed by the King's Men, as were many of the plays with altars during the period 1599-1642. I have listed *The Sea Voyage* as having a Christian context because its characters are European, though the sacrifice Rosellia threatens to enact reads as pagan rather than Catholic.

persecution of Catholics under Elizabeth and the drastic changes in royal policy initiated under Charles—together with the rise of Laud's project of resanctifying the churches created a space for more open references to Christian ritual in the secular theater. The early seventeenth century was marked by the consistent, but not egregious hounding of Catholics, mostly by way of monetary penalties and the seizure of goods.[18] At the same time, Laud was beginning to gain support for his program of "beautifying" English churches. In 1617, Laud first used his authority as Archbishop of Canterbury to demand that communion tables be placed altarwise in parishes such as Gloucester and Durham, signifying a return to the practice of designating a sacred space for the table apart from the rest of the congregation. It was not until the 1630s and 40s, however, that his detractors began to complain openly about the spread of high church practices and decorations in England. I do not wish to imply that the theater was involved in any kind of direct dialogue with Laud, but it is clear that the players were working to strike a balance between cashing in on the controversial nature of religious objects and avoiding the appearance of challenging current royal policies. In considering a similar set of questions about the nature of the altar and its potential for inciting idolatry, the players used the tools of their trade to their fullest advantage, playing off the structural similarities between stage altars and church altars rather than addressing the communion directly. Furthermore, their increasingly complex use of religious objects such as altars coincided with popular practices that probed and pushed the nature of the thing itself, until in many parishes the communion table came to resemble something more like the altars that had been so violently attacked under Edward and Elizabeth.

In order to avoid being accused of taking a stance in the debate over the status of the table, or of desecrating the communion service by depicting it on stage, the London playing companies tended to avoid presenting ritual objects that might be construed as Protestant. The majority of the references to "table" in Alan Dessen and Leslie Thomson's *Dictionary of Stage Directions in English Drama* refer to its use as either an eating or a writing surface, and though tables are frequently "covered," "set forth," or "prepared," this is almost never done in the manner of a religious service.[19] On the other hand, the entry for the word "altar" specifies that it was used "for various ceremonies," including funerals, sacrifices, and weddings, and that it was typically "discovered" rather than set out by the actors. Pagan sacrifices, or the threat of them, made frequent appearances on the stage, but just as often, and especially in Christian contexts, the ceremonies are social ones such as funerals and weddings. In the theater the table was more typically associated with suppers than with rituals, but it is worth noting that both tables and altars were constituted by the objects associated with them, and that without their trappings they were more or less indistinguishable, if not identical. If tapers, cloths, and

---

[18] See, for example, the 1610 Proclamation against recusants, which focuses mainly on disarmament, reproduced in   Cardwell, vol. 2, 113-20.

[19] Dessen and Thomson, 224-5.

other ritual implements were placed on it, the object in question was used as an altar; if trenchers and napkins were called for, the property was designated an eating surface.

A stage direction from Thomas Dekker's *The Noble Spanish Soldier* (1622) presents a particularly clear example of the theater's ability to put pressure on this dichotomy between "altars" and "tables." Early in the first act, the audience witnesses the play's heroine, Onaelia, alternately cursing and worshiping the king, who has cast her off after promising to marry her and make their son his heir:

> *A Table set out cover'd with blacke: two waxen Tapers: the King's Picture at one end, a Crucifix at the other,* Onaelia *walking discontentedly weeping to the Crucifix, her Mayd with her. ...*[20]

All the visual elements of this scene, which takes place in Onaelia's bedchamber, point to Catholic worship: the wax candles, which Protestants considered both extravagant and superstitious, the crucifix, and the woman weeping as she approaches the cross. Yet the primary stage property is called a table, because, practically speaking, it was precisely that. In the final scene of Dekker's play, in which the king is poisoned at supper, the same property was probably "set out" with drinking cups and plates. Onaelia's use of the table as an impromptu shrine to her former lover thus mirrors the theater's ability to adopt a single set of stage properties to a variety of purposes. The actions taken by the character within the fiction—Onaelia's transformation of her bedroom table into a shrine—point to the ease with which an ordinary communion table could be transformed back into an altar, both on stage and in the church itself. Although prop makers, actors, and playwrights were not necessarily caught up in larger mimetic or theological issues, they relied on specific material technologies that either alluded to or expanded playgoers' individual conceptions of the altar's ritual function in order to capture the imaginations of individual audience members.

If Catholics wanted to believe that the altar was immovable, a sanctified part of the church that only priests and bishops could touch, Protestants argued that it could and should be moved into the main body of the church so that all the parishioners could take communion. On the one hand, then, the theater's transformation of tables into altars and back again accorded with the reformers' understanding of the altar's lack of sacredness. On the other hand, the Catholic altar, like a stage altar, was constituted by dressing and undressing, by foregrounding rather than attempting to mask the things put upon it. Theatrical technology thus revealed a basic material reality of the Reformation—namely, that the communion table was differentiated from the altar largely by its accessories, or the absence of them. Theater practitioners during this period had an interest in the mass and its

---

[20]   *The Noble Spanish Soldier*, in *The dramatic works of Thomas Dekker*, ed. Fredson Bowers, vol. 4 (Cambridge: University Press, 1953-61), 1.2.0 sd. Subsequent references to Dekker's plays, with the exception of *The Spanish Gipsy*, refer to this edition.

ornaments precisely because their own craft was analogous to that of the priests and ministers who constructed and sanctified the altar. I am thinking here of Stephen Greenblatt's argument about the theater "emptying out" the sacraments, but I prefer to frame the relationship between the theater and the church in terms of a dialectical interchange between theatrical and religious practices.[21] The events of the Reformation had called into question the altar's function as a sacred object, allowing the players to appropriate for their own purposes the practice of revealing the ordinary surface underneath the ritual object, but they were able to do so in part because the conditions of early modern performance were well suited to that investigation. This chapter thus considers in more depth the connection between ever-evolving theatrical technologies and the reformers' attempts to distinguish between the "popish" altar and the "godly" table.

Some stage directions harp more directly than others upon the affinity between the provisional nature of stage altars and the constructed nature of church altars, and each stage property operates in a slightly different way, but all the early seventeenth-century plays examined in this chapter call attention to the "ordinary" objects behind the most holy rituals of the church, and they all inevitably draw attention to the connections between social memory and religious ritual, highlighting the fact that objects such as the altar and the communion table survived thanks to their fluctuating status. Those plays which dared to invoke Christian ritual through their use of altars were spared the wrath of the authorities, if we can trust the accounts cited above, because none of them alluded as explicitly as *The Cardinal's Conspiracy* did to current government policy. Ultimately, however, the most radical implications of early modern theatrical performances sprang from the structural similarity between the properties used on stage and the furniture of the English church. Because of the material resemblance between the technologies used to create an altar on stage and those used to create one in the church, the London playing companies were able to address current controversies surrounding the status of the central Christian ritual, the mass.

The Theatricality of the Altar

One of the most familiar attacks leveled against the players was that, like Catholic priests, they relied on mere spectacle to stimulate their audience, and in fact many of the playing companies constructed altars on stage for the purpose of creating extraordinary visual effects. The most dramatic example of this strategy is Middleton's *A Game at Chess* (1624), a play that creates a clear set of correspondences between its Spanish characters, who attempt to dazzle their English visitors with an extravagant theatrical device, and the superficial trickery of Roman Catholics in general. Like other dramas of the early seventeenth century, *A Game at Chess* carefully avoids staging the Catholic mass, but it also

---

[21]   See *Learning to Curse*, 161-83.

presents the most direct example of the use of an altar to attack popery—in this case, Spanish popery, as the play is a thinly-disguised mockery of the proposed match between Prince Charles and the Spanish Infanta. In so doing, however, the play reveals its own investment in the power of spectacle. The altar appears at the beginning of Act 5, the scene in which the White Duke and the White Knight, stand-ins for Prince Charles and the Duke of Buckingham, appear for the first time in the presence of the Black King, i.e., Philip IV. The scene is bracketed by two scenes of white triumph: Act 4, scene 5, in which the Fat Bishop is vanquished, and Act 5, scene 2, in which the Black Bishop's Pawn is betrayed by the pawn of the Black Queen. In other words, the first scene in Act 5 provides a complement to the "discovery" of the black courtiers' plots and foreshadows the defeat of the Black Knight in Act 5, scene 3. Beginning with an obsequious Latin oration delivered by the Black Bishop's Pawn, the scene dramatizes the black courtiers' attempts to impress the white ambassadors with their good intentions. After the oration is completed, the Black Knight directs his guests to "yond altar / The seat of adoration." As he speaks, an altar is "discovered" with statues and tapers on it, prompting the White Knight to mutter: "There's a taste / Of the old vessel still, the erroneous relish" (5.1.32-35).[22] The statues dance to the tune of a song that attributes their motion to the "joy" felt by their masters:

> Wonder work some strange delight
> This place was never yet without
> To welcome the faire White House Knight,
> And to bring our hopes about,
> May from the altar flames aspire,
> Those tapers set themselves afire.
> May senseless things our joys approve
> And those brazen statues move
> Quickened by some power above,
> Or what more strange, to show our love.
> (5.1.36-45)

The ability of the White Knight and the White Duke to see through this elaborate display mirrors the scenes in which the black courtiers who have been plotting against the White King and Queen are exposed as frauds.

The role played by the altar in Middleton's allegory is on one level remarkably straightforward, providing a prime example of the way theater juxtaposes Catholic theatricality with hypocrisy, but the scene ultimately deserves closer examination in relation to the rest of the play. Act 5, scene 1 is something of an anomaly, being only forty-nine lines long, and it is designed around two set pieces, the discovery

---

[22]   T. Howard-Hill gives both these lines to the White Knight, though in Q1 the line about "erroneous relish" is given to the White Duke and it does not appear at all in Q3 (169).

of the altar and the Jesuit's oration. Both of these displays are immediately derided by the White Knight and the White Duke, who by this point in the play have discovered the plot against their king. The Spanish ambassador Don Carlos Coloma had complained to the Conde-Duque Olivares that the play so "inflamed" its audience he feared an attack on his person, but I would suggest that this is not one of the scenes which would have occasioned violent anti-Spanish sentiments.[23] The play's main conflict, the threat of Spanish attack, has already been resolved by the beginning of Act 5, and this scene seems designed for the entertainment of its audience rather than to decry the evil deeds of foreign Catholics. And in terms of the sheer impact of this particular stage property, its most striking feature is not its connection to papist plots but the addition of dancing statues. The reference to "brazen" images clearly points back to Old Testament injunctions against the worship of false gods, but how exactly were the statues presented on stage: were they actors or puppets? It is possible that they were moveable mannequins resembling the ones Catholic priests were accused of using to fool unsuspecting parishioners. In 1623 Thomas Goad demanded, "[a]re not yet men living, that can remember the knauerie of Priests to make the Roodes and Images of the Churches in *England* in the dayes of Queene Mary, to goggle with their eyes, and shake their hands: yea, with wiers to bend the whole body, and many times to speake as they doe in Puppet plays, and all to get money, and deceive the ignorant people?"[24] Thus the sight of the dancing statues presented on stage in front of paying customers would have recalled not only biblical prohibitions but also some of the infamous practices of English prelates in the not-so-distant past. This type of association encourages the audience to feel superior to the members of the Black Court, but at the same time they, like the on-stage spectators, are prompted to express a sense of wonder at the sheer technical sophistication of the display.

The affinity the play constructs between the response of the on-stage spectators and the spectators at the Globe is indicated in the participle used in the stage direction: Middleton's text describes the altar as being "discovered." A handful of plays produced during this period use the phrases "an altar set out," "an altar prepared," or "attendants furnish the altar." All three of these formulations, if taken as stage directions rather than prompters' cues, suggest that the audience might have been able to watch members of the company turn a table into an altar by placing things such as prayer books, candles, and images on it. This kind of action mirrored in a general way the preparation of a Catholic altar prior to the mass.[25] By contrast, the suddenness of a "discovery" allowed the audience to experience, along with the White Knight and the White Duke, a sense of surprise, and in this

---

[23] Howard-Hill, 197.

[24] *The friers chronicle: or, The true legend of priests and monkes lieu* (London: for Robert Mylbourne, 1623), B3ᵛ.

[25] Gary Taylor argues that the statues were for Middleton "an image of Catholicism— and also probably an image, closer to home, of the re-emergent ceremonialism of the increasingly visible Arminian episcopal faction of the English church" (20).

case the unveiling of the altar would have created a considerable stir, both for the characters and for the audience. This moment is disrupted within the fiction of the play by the aside of the skeptical White Knight, who, according to Swapan Chakravorty, remains "unmoved."[26] But whatever their attitude toward Catholic idols, members of the audience were meant to be impressed with the sophistication of the company's remarkable gadgets. And although the success of the play as a whole is not predicated on any large-scale spectacle, the altar is not the only unusual stage property in *A Game at Chess*. Martin Butler points out, for example, that the sack into which the black courtiers are unceremoniously dumped at the end of the play may have resembled the one used in cycle play scripts depicting the harrowing of hell.[27] Certainly, the sack figures prominently in accounts of the performance; Don Carlos Coloma describes with outrage the scene in which "he who acted the Prince of Wales heartily beat and kicked the 'Count of Gondomar' into Hell, which consisted of a great hole and hideous figures."[28] Taking Butler's comments together with the unusual example of the dancing statues, it is possible to argue that the impact of the performances at the Globe was at least two-fold. On the one hand they reminded audiences of the knavery of Spanish Catholics, but on the other hand they were intended to "show off" a group of stage devices. Such effects, along with the air of authenticity attached to the company's acquisition of Ambassador Gondomar's chair and robe, must have contributed significantly to the financial success of the play during its nine-day run.[29]

The prominence of the dancing statues also indicates one of the many complicated ways in which theater practitioners used stage properties to explore their interest in the power of religious objects. Following M. C. Bradbrook, Chakravorty suggests that what Middleton defended from prison as "[a] harmlesse game" was a drama with "its own alienating device" embedded in it.[30] Certainly, by making dancing statues a part of the apparatus of the black court, the players were calling attention to the structural similarities between their craft and the tricks used by the priests they were so often accused of resembling. They were celebrating their own ingenuity, and this self-conscious celebration should have been, as Middleton suggested, the play's saving grace. The anonymous author of *Digitus Dei* (1624) does grant that unlike the Jesuits, who are bad actors pretending to be godly men,

---

[26] *Society and Politics in the Plays of Thomas Middleton* (Oxford: Clarendon Press, 1996), 183.

[27] *Theatre and Crisis, 1632-1642* (Cambridge: Cambridge University Press, 1984), 232.

[28] Howard-Hill, 195.

[29] In a letter dated 28 August 1624, John Wooley records the rumor that "the Players are gone to the Courte to Act the game at chesse before the Kinge, which doth much truble the spanish Ambassador." This would have been surprising because of the play's controversial subject matter, but certainly the court audience was trained to appreciate performances for their costumes and effects (ibid., 207).

[30] Chakravorty, 169.

the theater at least "professeth it selfe to be no better than it is, a Play-House."[31] This statement contradicts the assertions of critics such as William Prynne who accused the theater of having pretensions to holiness. It is also important to remember that although James was responsible for punishing the actors who committed these heinous offenses against the Spanish ambassador, no Protestant would have seen the staging of a Catholic altar as one of the "remarkable acts of sacrilege" Coloma found so distressing. In the context of a fierce anti-Catholic satire aimed at specific members of the Spanish court, it was not the presence of the altar that was most noteworthy. Rather, it was the play's celebration of its own inventiveness, analogous to that of the Black King's, which was so unusual. As Anthony Dawson writes of *Doctor Faustus*, "[t]he connection to Catholicism implies a critique of visual spectacle, but at the same time the critique is shot through with delight in the power of stage images."[32] Given the theater's interest in defending itself against attacks like Prynne's, it is surprising that the play draws an implicit comparison between the wonder of the characters and the enthusiasm of the Globe audience, who responded with such "merriment, hubbub and applause" that Coloma said he could have heard them from "many leagues away."[33]

I have argued that the playing companies were able to use altars on stage because they often presented them as part of pagan rituals and because they never specifically depicted either the mass or the Protestant communion. It is important to remember, however, that the supposed connections between the theater and the Catholic mass formed the substance of many fiery attacks, both on the church and on the stage itself. Just as the theater suffered from being compared to the false rituals of Catholicism, so the Catholic church was accused of making the mass into a game or play. More recently, the mass has been described as a commemorative drama depicting in allegorical form the events of the life of Christ. This scholarly commonplace has prompted O. B. Hardison to ask whether "the paten, chalice, sindon, sudarium, candles, and thurible [can] be considered stage properties?" His answer is yes, "[a]s long as there is clear recognition that these elements are hallowed, that they are the sacred phase of parallel elements turned to secular use on the profane stage." Hardison goes on to add, provocatively, that, "the celebration of the mass contains all elements necessary to secular performances."[34] Early modern players were very much aware of these structural similarities—as were their critics, who did not share Hardison's optimism about the likelihood of being able to separate church performances from secular ones, or any manner of performance from a sinful display of heathenish pomp. "Popish priests ... have transformed the celebrating of the Sacrament of the Lords supper into a Masse-game, and all other parts of Ecclesiastical service into theatrical sights,"

---

[31]   Scot, D3^v-4^r.

[32]   Dawson and Yachnin, 147.

[33]   Howard-Hill, 195.

[34]   *Christian Rite and Christian Drama in the Middle Ages; Essays in the Origin and Early History of Modern Drama* (Baltimore: Johns Hopkins Press, 1965), 79.

William Rainolds sneered in 1599.[35] Several decades earlier, Thomas Becon devoted two entire treatises to the theatrical elements of the mass and accused the priest of approaching his altar "as a game-player unto his stage." In this passage from the aptly named *Comparison Between the Lord's Supper and the Pope's mass*, Becon likens the priest to Roscius, the prototypical pagan actor:

> with his foolish, player-like, and mad gestures, the poor wretch writheth himself on every side, now bowing his knees, now standing right up, now crossing himself, as if he were afraid of spirits, now stopping down, now prostrating himself, now knocking on his breast, now censing, now kissing the altar, the book, and paten, now stretching out his arms, now folding his hands together, now making characters, signs, tokens, and crosses, now lifting up the bread and chalice, now holding his peace, now crying out, now saying, now singing, now breathing, now making no noise, now washing of hands, now eating, now drinking, now turning him unto the altar, now unto the people, now blessing the people either with his fingers or with an empty cup, &c.[36]

This litany of gestures gives an indication of the wide range of actions, all centered around the altar, that were available to players who wished to imitate a Catholic priest, but the broader point Becon makes here is that the mass is merely a set of hackneyed motions, no more nor less disgraceful than a stage play. On the other hand, the fear underlying this attack is that, seduced by such displays, observers might actually believe the "characters, signs, tokens" made by the priest. Similarly, the anxiety expressed by the antitheatricalists was that stage plays might actually have an impact on theatergoers. *Histrio-mastix*, first published in 1633, argued that stage plays were born from pagan idolatry and had the potential to "resuscitate, and foment it now."[37] In this account, the theater was inextricably linked to pagan idolatry as well as to more recent offenses committed by papists. Opinions such as Prynne's certainly heightened the stakes for any theater company wishing to discuss a religious subject or present a spectacular ritualistic moment, but as Huston Diehl has shown, it is less useful to associate all Protestants with antitheatricalism than to consider a wide range of potential reactions to individual plays, and to address the complexity of the questions players and playwrights were raising about the beliefs of ordinary English citizens.

Edmond Rossingham's judgment was that *The Cardinal's Conspiracy* was "revived on purpose in contempt of the ceremonies of the church"—in other words, in imitation of anti-Calvinist tendencies within English Protestantism. In this sense, then, the players would have sided with Prynne, though it is doubtful that he would have approved of using the theater to question the authority of the archbishop. By contrast, the *Vox Borealis* author suggests that what bothered its detractors

---

[35]   *Th'overthrow of Stage-playes* (London: Schilders, 1599), X3^r.
[36]   Becon, 161, 259.
[37]   Prynne, 80.

most was the financial success of public theater plays, which drew Londoners away from the church whether or not they were directly blasphemous: "they fell to Act the *Valiant Scot,* which they Played five dayes with great applause, which vext the Bishops worse than the other, insomuch, as they were forbidden Playing it any more; and some of them prohibited ever Playing againe."[38] Yet behind the larger problem of their heretical behavior toward both the government and the church, the Fortune players were tackling the basic issue of whether the altar could continue to function as a ritual object, and if so, how. *A Game at Chess* is an anti-Catholic satire that takes advantage of Protestants' hatred of altars and images, and of the recent resurgence of such objects in certain parishes, but it cannot be described simply as a response to the antitheatricalists, or as a refutation of all comparisons between the theater and the mass. Rather, the play seems to revel in its own extravagance, its ability to entertain and seduce. When the White Knight and the White Duke encounter the Black King's dancing statues, the implicit threat hanging over the scene is that they will, like the audience, be awed rather than horrified by the ingenuity of the spectacle.

Middleton's play is perhaps the most extreme example of a playing company inviting superstition into the theater in order to provoke a reaction from its audience, but what happened when an altar became linked with the concept of piety in a genuine way? The classically-inspired tragedy *Sejanus* (1604) provides one answer to this question. Produced twenty years earlier than *A Game at Chess*, Jonson's play drew from Roman history rather than contemporary events, and unlike Middleton's bold-faced allegory it employs a pagan setting, perhaps in an attempt to defuse the suggestion that its author might be satirizing the court. But the screen was apparently too thin, for according to William Drummond the members of the Privy Council accused the play's author of both "poperie and treason."[39] While Middleton and the King's Men were criticized for mocking the hypocritical machinations of Spanish papists, this play takes religion very seriously, perhaps too seriously for the stricter members of James's Protestant council.

Despite their apparent ideological differences, the fifth acts of *A Game at Chess* and *Sejanus* present a remarkable structural parallel. Both plays include a kind of revelation in which inanimate things—statues set on an altar—become miraculously animated. Thus, although this chapter deals with altars, not with statues, I want to examine *Sejanus* as a complement to Middleton's text by considering not only the stage altars in both plays, but the things that are put on them, arguing that those objects project a sense of sacrality in each scene. In *A Game at Chess,* the brazen statues are presented as part of the Black Court's "erroneous" fascination with popish tricks, but they also speak to the company's interest in promoting its own sophisticated stage technologies. The King's Men may have taken similar pains with the statue in *Sejanus*, but it is unlikely, given Jonson's famous dislike for the

---

[38] *Vox borealis, or the northern discoverie*, B2ᵛ.

[39] *Ben Jonson*, ed. C. H. Herford and Percy Simpson, vol. 1 (Oxford: Clarendon Press, 1925), 149.

prominence of Inigo Jones's visual displays, that he intended his moving statue to be the focus of his audience's "delight." Rather, this play uses the statue of Fortune to raise a complicated, but ultimately sympathetic, set of questions about the efficacy of religious ceremonies.

The statue in Jonson's play is that of the goddess Fortune, a figure whom Sejanus refers to as his protectress. She makes her first and only appearance in Act 5, when his luck has already begun to turn and his followers are preparing a sacrifice to appease her. The ritual begins with the herald's proclamation: "Be all profane far hence. Fly, fly, far off."[40] As trumpets and flutes sound, the priest—or Flamen, as Jonson calls him—"*washeth*" and then places flowering branches on the altar, calling upon Fortune to be "propitious to our vowes" (172 sd., 181). The stage direction then provides an extraordinarily detailed account of the priest's gestures:

> *the flamen takes of the honey with his finger, and tastes, then ministers to all the rest; so of the milk, in an earthen vessel, he deals about. Which done, he sprinkleth upon the altar milk, then imposeth the honey, and kindleth his gums, and after censing about the altar placeth his censer thereon, into which they put several branches of poppy, and the music ceasing, say all, All. Accept our off'ring and be pleased, great goddess.* (5.183 sd., 184)

It becomes clear that Fortune has abandoned Sejanus when, to the horror of his supporters, she "averts her face" and "turns away" (186, 185). For his part, Jonson's title character dismisses this "prodigy" as a mere trick (187). Turning on the priest, Sejanus scorns his "coz'ning ceremonies" and proclaims his own superiority by tossing "these thy wares ... Thy juggling mystery, religion" to the ground (200, 191-3). It is unclear precisely what action Jonson imagined as an accompaniment to this line, but Philip Ayres supplies the direction "*[s]weeps the altar clean*" because he cannot imagine that Sejanus would knock the statue over if it was played by a live actor (194 sd.). On the other hand, it is worth noting that Sejanus addresses Fortune directly after his outburst, commanding her to "hold thy look / Averted, till I woo thee turn again" (194-5). His purpose here is not to destroy the statue itself, but rather to humanize her by eliminating the "fumes," the "superstitious lights," and all the other "wares" of the Flamen (199). He even addresses her as "[b]ashful queen," concluding that she has turned her face away in deference to his greater power (209). The act of iconoclasm, whatever form it took on stage, is clearly designed to re-appropriate the goddess as his servant, not destroy her altogether, and ultimately he directs his anger against the Flamen and the altar rather than against the statue itself.

The material differences between Middleton's stage devices and Jonson's provide a further indication of the latter's attitude toward the altar. In *Game at Chess* the brazen statues probably resembled the puppets Catholic priests were

---

    [40] *Sejanus His Fall*, ed. Philip J. Ayres (Manchester: Manchester University Press, 1999), 5.171.

accused of using to fool unsuspecting parishioners. *Sejanus*, by contrast, seems to call for a live actor who feigns immobility only to suddenly reveal himself, as in *The Winter's Tale* (1610). Moreover, many of Jonson's historical footnotes and stage directions are devoted to those priestly wares—the earthen vessel, the honey, the milk, the censer, the spices—whereas the only other objects specified in Middleton's text are a set of tapers. These differences can be traced to Jonson's fascination with recreating the details of actual Roman rituals, but the play is also far more interested in the altar as a site of ritual sacrifice, and in the success or failure of such a sacrifice, than Middleton's.

The play's anthropological interest in ancient ritual resembles that of other texts that employ altars in pagan contexts, such as Marston's *Sophonisba* (1605), Fletcher's *Bonduca* (1613), and *The Two Noble Kinsmen* (1613). In Marston's play, the heroine sets up an altar to pray for the preservation of her chastity, and Shakespeare and Fletcher present much the same circumstance in *The Two Noble Kinsmen*, in which Emilia makes an offering to Diana, hoping to be spared the ordeal of marriage. In *Bonduca*, the heroine and her daughters gather around an altar to pray for a sign that they will have a military triumph against their persecutors. Like Sejanus's followers, Bonduca and her daughters are presented with an unlucky omen—the fire they raise sputters and dies—but Emilia receives a more ambiguous sign:

> Enter EMILIA *in white, her hair about her shoulders, [and wearing] a wheaten wreath; one in white, holding up her train, her hair stuck with flowers; one before her carrying a silver hind, in which is convey'd incense and sweet odors, which being set upon the altar [of Diana], her maids standing aloof, she sets fire to it; then they curtsy and kneel.*
>
> . . . .
>
> Here the hind vanishes under the altar and in the place ascends a rose tree, having one rose upon it.
>
> . . . .
>
> Here is heard a sudden twang of instruments, and the rose falls from the tree, *[which vanishes under the altar].* (5.1.136 sd., 162 sd., 168 sd.)

Like *Sejanus*, this text calls for historically realistic pagan implements such as wreaths, incense, flowers, and spices, and both plays may have used an actual trick altar like the one depicted in Robert Fludd's scientific treatise (Figure 2.1).[41] It is even possible that the King's Men used such an implement in *A Game at Chess*, for it certainly would have heightened the spectacular nature of the altar's discovery. In *The Two Noble Kinsmen*, however, ritual implements are presented

----

[41]   R. B. Graves explains that the flames could have been created following the model Robert Fludd proposes in his *Technical History of the Macrocosm*. Such a device "worked by emitting smoke and fire through a hole in the top of the altar that could be opened and closed by a sliding plate" (114-15).

within a secularized allegorical context. Only Jonson's play uses the altar to stage a conflict between faith and skepticism, through Sejanus's rejection of the omen of the moving statue.

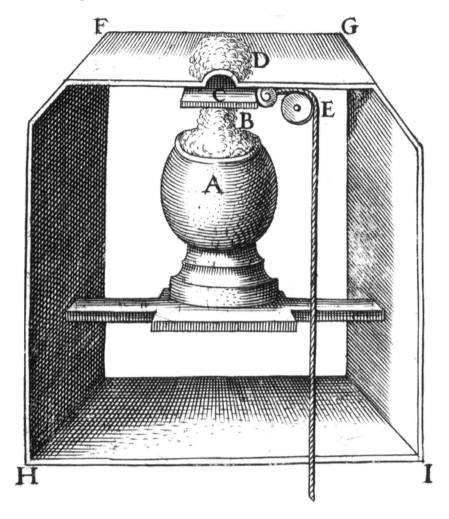

Figure 2.1   Fludd, Robert, "Trick Alter," *Technical History of the Macrocosm*, 1617-21 (vol. 2, 477). This item is reproduced by permission of The Huntington Library, San Marino, California

The presentation of Fortune has often been read as a sincere depiction of a ritual event, designed to draw attention to Sejanus's hubristic attitude toward religion. In his introduction to the Revels edition, Ayres describes the moment in which Fortune averts her face as one that "confirms her divinity for an audience at the same time as it (paradoxically) converts her most devoted worshipper into her chief contemner." Gary Taylor draws a similar conclusion, but he sees a clearer reference in the play to debates within the reformed church of England: "In *Sejanus* a moment of reverent (Catholic) affect is superseded by a moment of contemptuous (Protestant) affect, but the contempt of a contemptible character only reinforces the reverence of spectators."[42] It seems clear that the play is casting a negative light on Sejanus's unbelief, and his act of iconoclasm does resemble the behavior of the sixteenth-century reformers. I would suggest, however, that it is not merely the statue the play is interested in rescuing from Protestant skepticism. *Sejanus* is concerned with re-sanctifying the altar itself, together with the objects that designate it as holy. The scene recalls, for instance, Eamon Duffy's description of the purification ceremonies used in the pre-Reformation church. Although Jonson's Flamen cleanses himself, rather than the altar, in this scene, the "reverence" with which he instructs the others to place their garlands on it, and the subsequent sprinkling and censing of it, establish the altar as a sacred thing that must be treated with respect.

The custom in pre-Reformation England was to remove the ornaments from the altar as soon as the liturgy was over, so that in a sense the altar only existed during the service. In a kind of inversion of the iconoclastic attacks described above, the altar was stripped, bathed, and re-clothed almost as if it were a human body. Similarly, the statue is not the only object being animated in Jonson's play, which uses the power of the theater over inanimate things to dramatize the mystery of ritual itself and the power of the altar's transformation into the site of ritual sacrifice. Insofar as *Sejanus* draws attention to the magical quality of the altar it is easy to see why the Privy Council found this play "popish." The gestures of the Flamen, however historically accurate, project the same attitude toward inanimate objects that Protestants found so offensive in the performance of the mass. Nicholas Ridley's 1576 injunctions for the district of Canterbury, for example, enquire as to whether the minister "do wear any cope in your parish church or chapel ... or use at the ministration thereof any gestures, rites, ceremonies, not appointed by the Book of Common Prayer, as crossing or breathing over the sacramental bread and wine, or shewing the same to the people to be worshipped and adored, or any such like, or use any oil and chrism, tapers, spattle, or any other popish ceremony?" William Tyndale likewise deplores the "nodding, becking, and mowing" of the priest who "playeth out the part" of Christ's passion.[43] And Becon, the most expansive critic of the mass, provides a litany of priests' theatrical gestures: "their duckings and loutings, their turnings and returnings, their gaspings and gapings, their kneelings and crouchings, their whinings and starings, their mockings and mowings, their crossings and knockings, their kissings and lickings, their noddings

[42]   Ayres, 13; Taylor, 23.

[43]   *Articles to be enquired of, within the prouince of Canterburie* (London: [H. Denham], 1576), A4ʳ; Jonas A. Barish, *The Antitheatrical Prejudice* (Berkeley: University of California Press, 1981), 160.

and nosings, their washings and weepings."[44] Seen within the context of such critiques, the Flamen's washing and censing and sprinkling would surely have registered as Catholic, and thus the play's survival depended upon Jonson's ability to successfully displace his own interest in ceremony onto a pagan context.

But the play's sympathetic treatment of religious ritual is more than a thinly-veiled reaction against Protestant polemics. *Sejanus* also speaks to the survival of the mass in London, and in cities all over England in the years immediately preceding and following the death of Elizabeth I. If, under James and his son Charles, the boundaries between the Protestant and Catholic communion were beginning to blur, Elizabeth's reign seems to have been characterized by the persistent attempt on behalf of English recusants and their expatriate allies to perform the mass as a specifically Catholic event. In 1591, James Clayton, a resident of Carlisle, confessed that he had "[h]eard mass in the house of Tailor, a grocer, in Fleet Street" with five or six other people. The previous year, John Gondsalvus de Lima, a Portuguese priest, was arraigned for holding a mass at the home of the French ambassador in London, and in 1593 a priest named Cornelius was arrested along with several of his colleagues for holding mass in Dorset.[45] One of England's most famous aristocratic recusants, who died in 1608, built a chapel with a stone altar in her own house, to which she invited local people who wished to receive the Catholic communion. According to her biographer, the Viscountess Montague sometimes received "60 communicants at a time" with more than 120 in the congregation.[46] These examples indicate that English citizens, particularly those with means, continued to have access to Catholic altars and Catholic communion ceremonies throughout the sixteenth century. Thus, by framing Sejanus as an iconoclast and by lingering over the priest's reverent gestures toward the altar, Jonson creates a theatrical environment that allows playgoers to contemplate the positive aspects of ritual, while simultaneously alluding to the fact that altars continued to play a vital role in the religious culture of early modern England.

Policing the Boundaries

Like *A Game at Chess*, Jonson's play employs a spectacular device that references the structural similarities between stage altars and church altars. It differs from Middleton's play, however, in providing a space for sympathetic playgoers to consider the consequences of Protestant iconoclasm. In the second half of this chapter, I turn to two plays that prompt positive rather than negative responses to the staging of an altar and ultimately express an interest in the communal quality of ritual practice. The first of these is Fletcher, Field, and Massinger's *The Knight*

---

[44]   Becon, 385-6.
[45]   Green 1591, 324; ibid. 1593, 356.
[46]   A. C. Southern, *Elizabethan Recusant Prose, 1559-1582* (London: Sands, 1950), 43.

of Malta (1618), which presents the altar as the site of rituals that can sustain communities and their value systems, and deflects the potential controversy surrounding its depiction of this Catholic object by transposing its characters to an island in the Mediterranean. Notably, the play was first performed during a period when the anti-Calvinist reforms that were to become especially prominent in the 1630s—those reforms that marked a shift away from the position that all material images, objects, and sacraments were dangerous incitements to idolatry—were first envisioned and implemented. Fletcher, Field, and Massinger's tragicomedy poses some of the same questions the anti-Calvinists did about the use of sacred objects, especially the communion table, and eventually it arrives at the same answers, though it avoids the potential threat of imitating the mass by using the material technology of the altar to represent a set of rituals which are only tangentially related to the communion.

In *The Knight of Malta* powerful Christian symbols appear at every turn, literally propping up the society's values—which are realized in the strict moral code of The Order of St. John of Jerusalem, otherwise known as the Knights of Malta. This organization, which had both a military and a religious focus and was sponsored by the Catholic church in Rome, was first established in Malta in 1529. It also had an English branch, or langue, that Parliament abolished in 1540 when its members refused to deny their allegiance to the pope. Yet this play, performed eighty years later for a public audience in London, is fully at ease with its own depiction of the knights' Catholic objects, specifically the cross and the altar, and it closes by bringing both items together in a paraphrase of two of the ceremonies actually used by the members of the Order: the ritual of induction, and the ritual by which a knight who had violated its laws was disrobed and expelled. The play's action is framed by the history of the Order itself, and it focuses on the problem of determining the symbolic meaning of religious symbols from an anthropological standpoint. On the one hand, then, the ceremonies represented in this play ostensibly mimic those of the Order of St. John, but they also advance a case for the social importance of Christian ritual more generally. Upon closer examination, the religious objects in *The Knight of Malta* read not as Catholic but as generically Christian, and they are used to raise questions about the function of rituals that were still vitally important to a wide variety of believers in post-Reformation England.

The Order of St. John was an international organization made up of representatives from different countries who dedicated their lives to protecting Christian interests in the Mediterranean. They were most famous for successfully defending the island of Malta against the Turks in 1565, a victory openly celebrated by English officials; on the eve of the battle, public prayers were said in Salisbury for their safe deliverance, and upon hearing news of their victory Archbishop Parker offered a formal thanksgiving. Queen Elizabeth wanted to take advantage of the knights' military accomplishments, but she was also responsible for the death or expulsion of all but two of its members living in England at the time, many of whom had been previously arrested for harboring priests or espousing papist sympathies, and her contradictory attitude reflects the knights' uneven history in post-Reformation England. After Mary's brief attempt to revive the English langue, its members were selectively punished instead of being formally disbanded. While some private citizens may have only known about the Knights of Malta through royal proclamations and injunctions, others had access to accounts of the order as it existed in its heyday, including its titles, rituals, and military triumphs. In the early seventeenth century Richard Knolles (1603) was still recounting the glorious battle of 1565, while George Sandys (1615; second edition 1621) and William Lithgow (1614; second edition 1632) were recording with ethnographic enthusiasm the ongoing ceremonial life of the Order in Malta. Augmenting the stories of official sanctions, these accounts provided the authors of *The Knight of Malta* with a rich set of details about the nature of the knights' religious rituals and the objects that anchored them.[47]

Drawing most directly from the accounts of Sandys and Lithgow, *The Knight of Malta* addresses the social function behind the ceremonial use of the altar and the cross. In the play sacred objects are presented as the material markers of social identity, but unlike many of the objects I discuss in Chapter 3, the cross in this play does not circulate from person to person. Rather, it remains stable even as it registers drastic alterations in characters who are no longer virtuous. The cross of the Order, which the knights wore pinned to their garments over the heart, was a token of personal faith in the face of foreign threats. Throughout the course of the play, this cross functions as the marker of a knight's membership in the brotherhood and an embodiment of the abstract virtues that will outlive him and his personal fame. The removal of the cross indicates the degradation of the knight who is no longer worthy of wearing it, but the object itself maintains its sacred status and can be transferred to another member of the Order.

In a similar fashion, the altar appears in the play as a public means of registering a knight's faith, and its value is fixed by institutional structures and customs within a particular ritual space. Because the play focuses on the important role these objects perform in sustaining the community of knights, it manages to successfully promote the efficacy of the rituals that occur around them—the induction of the hero, Miranda, into the Order, and the banishment of Mountferrat—which are used to punctuate its moralistic ending. In this depiction of these objects and the social values attached to them, it is possible to discern a positive attitude toward the rituals and customs that were missing from most English parishes in the early seventeenth century. These powerful material objects and the practices built around them stand in dramatic contrast to the relatively sparse apparatus of the reformed church, and they point to the ongoing struggles between Calvinists and other Protestants, including Laud, who were exploring the possibility of a return

---

[47]   Sandys and Lithgow both specify that the newly made knight should attend mass immediately after being invested, but the play carefully avoids this aspect of the ceremony.

to the ceremonies that had held parish communities together in pre-Reformation England.

Like many altar properties in seventeenth-century drama, the one in Fletcher, Field, and Massinger's play is suddenly "discovered" halfway through Act 5, scene 2—"*An altar discovered, with Tapers, and a book on it. The two Bishops stand on each side of it;* Mountferrat *as the Song is singing ascends up the altar*" (5.2.198 sd.)— and, as in *A Game at Chess*, the timing presumably served to heighten the sense of pomp. Though the process of constructing the device is not described in the text, the scene does contain a rich account of the rituals surrounding it. To begin with, the initial stage direction lists the objects that are to be placed on the altar, namely, a book and a set of tapers. Secondly, the direction specifies that the altar is to be placed on an elevated platform. Thirdly, characters designated as bishops are called for to oversee the ceremony. Fourthly, the music of a choir, perhaps a chorus of minor characters, accompanies both the disrobing of the villain Mountferrat and the induction of the hero Miranda. As Marianne Brock suggests, some of these details can be traced back to the statutes of the order, printed in Rome in 1586, which call for an altar with a book on it to be the focus of the induction ceremony. These statutes also specify that the newly-made knight should kiss both the missal and the altar as a sign of his devotion.[48] The amount of detail surrounding the altar's ritual function in *The Knight of Malta* is relatively atypical, though the play does resemble *Sejanus* in having both an anthropological interest in religion and a sympathetic attitude toward more traditional church practice. In addition to imitating the ceremonies of the Order as it existed in the Mediterranean in the seventeenth century Miranda refers to "the bench of Saints above / Whose succour I implore t'enhable me," and vows to live chastely as a member of the Order (5.2.240-41). One of the implications of his speech is that even virtuous knights need saints, just as they need crosses to register their membership in the Order and ceremonies to hold them together as a community. The play also introduces the knights' monastic lifestyle without employing the pejorative terms that typically characterize depictions of nuns and monks in early modern drama.

George Sandys's account of his travels in the eastern Mediterranean is similarly preoccupied with the social function of ritual, and it provides a likely source for the playwrights' interpretation of the induction ceremony:

> The ceremonies used in knighting, are these. First, carrying in his hand a taper of white waxe, he kneeleth before the Altar, clothed in a long loose garment, and desireth the Order of the Ordinarie. ... Then is he girt with a belt, and thrice strooke on the shoulders with his sword . ... Which done two Knights do put on his spurres .... And so goes he to masse with the tapir in his hand; the workes of pietie, hospitalitie, and redemption of Captives, being commended unto him.[49]

---

[48] *The Knight of Malta* (Bryn Mawr, 1944), xlix.
[49] *A relation of a journey begun an: Dom: 1610* (London: [Field], 1615), X1r.

Although many of the ritual elements used in the scene are also included here—the taper, the altar, the spurs, and the sword—this account differs slightly from the play script. According to Sandys, the celebrant carries a single taper of wax, but the play calls for two tapers to be placed on the altar. He also reports that the newly-made knight should kneel in front of the altar, while in the play the only gesture that is called for is an ascent to the altar, which sits on a raised platform. The lines of the song suggest that Miranda, too, is meant to go up to the altar: "*As this flame mounts, so mount thy zeale; thy glory / Rise past the Stars, and fix in Heaven thy story*" (235-6). In fact, the scene is built around the parallel between the two central figures, one of whom is receiving the cross of the Order while the other is being stripped of it; both symbolically and literally, Miranda rises as Mountferrat falls from grace. A much older text, William Durandus's *Symbolism of Church Ornaments*, suggests a similar link between the steps to a church's high altar and the spiritual ascent of the virtuous man. "By these steps," Durandus wrote in 1286, "the ascent of virtues is sufficiently made manifest, by which we go up to the Altar, that is, to Christ."[50] The elevation of the altar had long been part of Catholic tradition, but it also became an important aspect of anti-Calvinist reforms directed at protecting the communion table from profanation.

Like the contemporary narratives on which it is based, the play text foregrounds the altar and its implements in describing the ceremony of inducting a new knight into the Order, but ultimately it trades kneeling for rising, creating an elevated playing space above the level of the stage where the altar and the bishops are set. So while *The Knight of Malta* spares Miranda the charge of idolatry that might be associated with kneeling in front of an altar, especially one with a Catholic missal on it, the play simultaneously articulates a different set of issues about the sanctity of the altar; it can be read alongside the debates between mainstream Calvinists and those, like Lancelot Andrewes and William Laud, who held more sympathetic views about the benefits of elaborate church ceremonies. The term "table" replaced the word "altar" in the reformed prayer book printed in 1552, and under Elizabeth the communion table was referred to as the "Lord's Board" or "God's board"—anything but an altar. Although Laud himself maintained that he wanted to enforce a uniform mode of Protestant practice, not a return to Catholicism, he and his followers were often accused of resurrecting the word "altar" as well as its trappings by advocating that the table be elevated, placed flush against the east wall of the church, and railed in to prevent any improper use of its surface.[51]

---

[50]   *The Symbolism of Churches and Church Ornaments, a Translation of the First Book of the Rationale Divinorum Officiorum* (Leeds: T. W. Green, 1843), 76.

[51]   According to Alexandra Walsham, "not only did Laud hate papists with a passion, initiating a series of sharp proclamations against them and taking stringent measures against pilgrims to the shrine of St Winifred at Holywell in Wales in 1637-8; but, as Keith Lindley has shown, the fines nonconforming Catholics paid to the Exchequer were an important source of revenue" ("The parochial roots of Laudianism revisited," 646).

Laud was not able to promote the elevation and railing in of tables systematically until 1633, when he became Archbishop of Canterbury, but during the early seventeenth century concerns about exposing the communion table to "common" usage were shared by strict Protestants and anti-Calvinists alike. William Prynne was particularly anxious about the possibility that "schoolmasters will teach their boys to write upon this table, and the boys will lay their hats, satchels and books upon it, and in their master's absence sit upon the same."[52] Officials such as Archbishop George Abbot likewise complained that local parishioners tended to treat the communion table like an ordinary piece of wood. His articles for Gloucester, issued in 1612 and echoed in many later visitations, directly ask whether the communion table is "so used out of time of divine service, as is not agreeable to the holy use of it; as by sitting on it, throwing hats upon it, writing on it, or is it abused to other prophaner uses?"[53] Although he and Abbot shared a mutual concern about the treatment of the communion table, Laud's proposals for amending this situation ran contrary to the idea of making the table accessible to all communicants, for parishioners would now have to kneel at the rail to receive communion. Ceremonies, Laud proclaimed, "are the hedge that fence the substance of religion from all the indignities which profaneness and sacrilege too commonly put upon it," thus providing a thinly veiled metaphor for the physical changes he wished to make to English churches, which included placing a rail around the communion table to keep out children and stray dogs.[54] He and other anti-Calvinists claimed that rails were an "ancient" part of church furniture, but to many Protestants the business of elevating and railing in the table was merely the first step in provoking naïve believers to worship both it and the host. Although the stage directions in *The Knight of Malta* do not call for any gestures that might be construed as superstitious, the emphasis on ascending to the altar evoked Laudian-era attempts to re-sanctify the communion table, making it more like an altar again.

If we accept the premise that the altar in the induction scene was placed on an elevated platform resembling those in some seventeenth-century churches, and that both Miranda and Mountferrat are meant to ascend it, we should then consider what type of platform it was and how it was constructed. The previous scene, in which Miranda's chastity is tested and proved by the virtuous Oriana, contains a stage direction that reads: "*Altar ready, / Tapers & / booke*" (5.1.45). Fredson Bowers, editor of Beaumont and Fletcher's collected works, dismisses this as a prompter's cue and relegates it to a footnote.[55] For his part, Peter Mullany takes it quite seriously, glossing the scene as follows: "Before an altar, set with

---

[52] Aston, 370.

[53] Kenneth Fincham, ed., *Visitation Articles and Injunctions of the Early Stuart Church*, vol. 1 (Woodbridge, Suffolk [England]: Boydell Press, 1994), 100.

[54] Peter White, "The via media in the early Stuart Church" in *The Early Stuart Church, 1603-1642*, ed. Kenneth Fincham (Stanford: Stanford University Press), 211-30, 228.

[55] Bowers, vol. 8, 440.

tapers and a book, Miranda tells Oriana of his love for her."[56] This reading seems unfounded, however, as neither character acknowledges the property. It is likely that such a platform would take several minutes to assemble, for the gap between this anticipatory stage direction and the one in Act 5, scene 2 is about 325 lines. But although the stage direction is unclear about how this piece of stage furniture might be made, there is a likely antecedent for the altar platform within the play itself. In Act 2, scene 5, Oriana is put on a scaffold—the script calls for "*Scaffold set out and the staires*"—and it is here that she prepares for her execution, as two knights, her champion and her accuser, battle for her honor, which has been undermined by Mountferrat's rumors. When the governor, her brother Valetta, instructs her to "go up" it, she responds, "[t]hus I ascend; neerer I hope to heaven" (2.5.0, 24-5). The same platform, and the same set of steps, might have served for both scenes. The thematic connection between Miranda's virtuous ascent and Oriana's is further emphasized by the language of the play's final act. During the induction ceremony, Miranda's hortatory song compares his burning zeal to a holy fire. Similarly, when Miranda begs Oriana to "regard / The torturing fires of my affections," she responds, "[m]y flames, *Miranda*, rise as high as thine," and she urges him to "[t]hink on the legend which we two shall breed / Continuing as we are, for chastest dames / And boldest Souldiers to peruse and read" (5.1.68-9, 73, 93-5). Her "legend" and his "story" are the subject matter of the play, and the scaffold that raises them both up is the mechanism by which the play frames the centrality of religious ritual in the Maltese society. Further, the visual echo between Oriana's scaffold and the altar emphasizes its function as a device for marking the all-important boundary between the sacred and the profane.

Although the 1610s have neither the immediacy of the early 1600s, in which Jonson could still invoke the ferociousness of Elizabethan iconoclasm, nor the political valence of Middleton's *A Game at Chess*, produced in the immediate aftermath of the proposed Spanish match, the altar was by no means absent from the lives and imaginations of Londoners during the period in which *The Knight of Malta* was first performed. I have suggested that the play's elevation of the altar, which concretizes the society's moral standards and defines the parameters of its community, is structurally similar to Laud's elevated communion table, but the first several decades of the seventeenth century were also a time when altars themselves were made available to a wide variety of English citizens, as they had been in the 1590s. In 1615, Bishop James wrote to Archbishop Abbot that he had information from a Polish surgeon, "a pretended Catholic, and much courted by the priests, who ... have given him an altar, devotional books, and beads, &c."[57]

---

[56]   "The Knights of Malta in Renaissance Drama," *Neuphilologische Mitteilungen: Bulletin de la Societe Neophilologique/Bulletin of the Modern Language Society*, vol. 74 (1973): 297-310, 306.

[57]   Green 1615, 301. There is an important material difference here between the altar given to the Polish surgeon, presumably a small portable altar (the priests take it out of a chest that also contains books and beads), not a large stone altar. Such objects were

This surgeon had also attended mass with these priests and took down the names of those in attendance. There were hundreds of recusants in London who had access to altars and to the ceremony of the mass, especially in the homes of foreign ambassadors.[58] This practice of mass-going became so common that in 1621 the House of Commons issued a petition to the king, urging him to "banish recusants from London during their sittings, to restrain them to within five miles of their residences, to take away their arms, to prevent their hearing mass at ambassadors' houses, and to allow no Jesuit priest in prison to go abroad, or to say masses."[59] To their consternation, James replied that all these laws already existed and therefore did not need to be restated in a formal proclamation.

Unwilling to offend Catholic sympathizers, James tended to rule by omission, and during the early years of his reign recusants continued to congregate to celebrate the mass, not just in Lancashire or Northumberland but in London as well. James himself had strong Calvinist leanings; like his Archbishop of Canterbury, George Abbot, he approved of kneeling in receiving the sacrament, while emphasizing that the ceremony was a "a commemoration only of a sacrifice." In 1618, however, Laud's mentor George Buckeridge addressed a sermon to the king in which he publicly defended the practice of "outward prostration" before the communion table. Buckeridge acknowledged the importance of "inward devotion," without which all gestures are no better than "the stage playing of a fast, or a prayer, or a Maundie," but he also stressed the absolute necessity of bodily gestures as tokens of proper adoration.[60] As king of Scotland, James had criticized the English for maintaining a set of services that were still "too much like the mass," but as king of England he constantly endeavored to mediate between various factions, and in 1603 Robert Cecil expressed his concern that, thanks to the king's leniency, "the priests go openly about the country, the city and private houses saying Mass."[61]

---

important aspects of the ritual lives of English recusants, who had to be ready to pack up their gear at a moment's notice to avoid detection and carry them from place to place.

[58]   Secretary Conway to Walter Balcanquall, Master of the Savoy, 1626: "Information being given that there is a place within the Savoy where mass is usually said, with much resort of people, he is to cause the priest to be apprehended, and to seize upon the popish books and massing stuff" (ibid. 1626, 252).

[59]   Ibid. 1621, 224. The sentiment was echoed by the *Petition of the House of Commons to the King, 1624*: "considering the mischief done by the seductions of Papists, their unwonted concourse about London, and flocking to mass at ambassadors' houses, the preparations for invasion in Spain, and danger from a Catholic party in the kingdom, &c., all Jesuits and seminary priests may be banished by proclamation, all recusants disarmed, all licences for their repair to London withdrawn, resort to mass forbidden ... and generally all laws put into execution against them. ..." (ibid. 1624, 206).

[60]   *A sermon preached before His Maiestie at Whitehall, March 22. 1617, being Passion-Sunday, touching prostration, and kneeling in the worship of God* (London: Bill, 1618), T3ʳ.

[61]   George Yule, "James VI and I: furnishing the churches in his two kingdoms," in *Religion, culture and society in early modern Britain*, eds Anthony Fletcher and Peter Roberts

In 1623, more than sixty persons who had been attending mass in the French ambassador's house in Blackfriars were killed when it suddenly collapsed, and in 1626 Secretary Conway was still complaining that members of the city's recusant population were regularly resorting to a house in the Savoy to receive the Catholic communion.[62] In addition to the wide disparities in adherence to the laws and injunctions governing communion tables, some altars were never demolished, some were rebuilt, and some were newly made specifically for recusant churches and private chapels.

In the wake of the Reformation, English parishioners were forced to define their own forms of community, but many found that religious objects and rituals were by far the most effective means of doing so. Bishop Lancelot Andrewes's private chapel, which set the standard for those who favored more sacramental furnishings, featured "a holy table covered with an embroidered carpet, candlesticks, sacred vessels, incense, copes and in time, images."[63] On a less grandiose scale, members of other English parishes were simultaneously acquiring more elaborate plate for their tables and putting wooden rails around them.[64] As churches recovered financially from the shock of the Edwardian and Elizabethan reforms, communion tables were outfitted with more expensive cushions, cloths, and candlesticks, provoking some, including John Cosins, to behavior that horrified their Calvinist counterparts. Cosins's actions, as documented by Peter Smart, represent the extreme manifestation of anti-Calvinist attitudes, but he was not the only English Protestant who held a reverent view of the communion table and its implements. Pauline Croft argues that Robert Cecil, who complained about James's tolerance for papists, simultaneously had a strong interest in "sacrament-centered worship." His home at Salisbury was gorgeously gilded and decorated with pictures of Christ and the Virgin Mary, and Croft also suggests that Cecil shared a sacramental aesthetic with Richard Niele, who was responsible for refitting Westminster between 1605 and 1610 with furnishings that included a

(New York: Cambridge University Press, 1994), 182-208, 186, 183.

[62]   Green 1626, 252.
[63]   Phillips, 154.
[64]   My own examination of London churchwardens' accounts in the Metropolitan Archives bears out the basic premise that communion table accessories (along with pulpit cloths and cushions) were becoming more elaborate in the 1620s and 1630s. St. Alban Wood Street, for example, owned two communion cups, a plate, and a "table cloth" in 1584, while by 1625 their stock was augmented by a silver pot for wine, a black leather case for the pot, cushions, a brass candlestick, and twenty-seven small wooden candlesticks (MS 7673/1, 1^{r-v}, 115^{r-v}). In 1631, St. Alphage London Wall possessed two communion cups and covers, with cases, four flagons of pewter with plates, a plate for the bread, a brass branch with twelve sockets and a box to put them in, and three small branches, a damask table cloth, two napkins, one new damask table cloth, and a green table cloth (MS 1432/4, 1r).

high altar "with rich gold and velvet hangings."[65] The early seventeenth century was a period in which recusant behavior was tacitly tolerated, but it was also a period in which greater numbers of Protestants were expressing an interest in restoring the material elements of traditional religious ceremonies. By the 1620s, the spread of high-church sympathies, fueled by the attempts of men such as Laud and Buckeridge to re-sanctify the communion table, forced the king to abandon his policy of toleration, and the latter years of his reign would be spent trying to stamp out such sensibilities without offending powerful Catholics, including the foreign ambassadors living in London.

Within this climate of controversy surrounding the "proper" ritual use of the communion table, *The Knight of Malta* presented its audience with a set of on-stage ceremonies that defied standard Protestant tropes linking altars with idolatry. Like the altar in the home of the French ambassador, the one in this play forms the center of a tightly knit community of believers and serves as an anchor for the values espoused by that community. The paired ceremonies of induction and banishment in the final scene establish the altar as the keystone of Malta's moral code and the tool with which its boundaries are enforced. The play's depiction of the Order of St. John was undoubtedly meant to pique audience members' curiosity, and thus its use of the word "altar" is in one sense purely anthropological. But the induction scene may also have resonated with the desire of English recusants and some English Protestants to rescue the holy table from the threat of profanation and restore certain traditional aspects of the mass.

Ritual Objects, Social Objects

The Knight of Malta creates a kind of double displacement: presenting its characters as part of an international religious organization rather than an English one and eliminating any specific reference to the communion from its depiction of the induction ceremony. In so doing, the play manages to focus on the socially anchored aspects of traditional Catholicism while displaying a set of rituals that was less familiar, and thus less problematic, than the mass itself. Other Jacobean plays with Christian contexts likewise rely on the principle of displacement, but they present less complicated solutions to the problem of staging religious ritual. Dekker's *Match Me in London* (1611) calls for two friars to "set out" an altar for the marriage ceremony of an Italian tyrant, thereby framing the scene as a satiric attack on the mass, while Massinger's *The Pilgrim* (1621) calls for an altar to be "prepar'd" for a reconciliation scene that is construed as more secular than sacred.[66] Brewer's *The Lovesick King* (1617) provides a more perplexing example of this kind of staging practice, going so far as to present an altar as part of the

---

[65]   "The Religion of Robert Cecil," *The Historical Journal* 34, no. 4 (December 1991): 773-96, 796.

[66]   Dessen and Thomson, 5.

furniture of a nunnery. When hostile troops attack the building, the nuns gather to pray for a miracle: "*Alarm. A great Cry within. Enter Abbot bearing a Cross, Cartesmunda with two Tapers burning, which she placeth on the Altar, two or three Nuns following.*"[67] The play's surprisingly positive attitude toward the nuns and their altar is the result of a dramatic strategy that valorizes religious chastity by emphasizing the threats made against it. A set of monastic behaviors becomes virtuous rather than superstitious when characters are placed in a position of having to defend themselves and their value system from a hostile attack. As I explain in Chapter 3, a similar dynamic is often at work in plays that use crosses and crucifixes as stage properties: those who wear them are frequently female characters under threat of sexual aggression or Christians facing violence at the hands of nonbelievers.

Ford's *The Broken Heart* (1630), first staged in the converted monastery at Blackfriars, also foregrounds female chastity and plays off Jacobean texts such as *The Lovesick King* by combining elements of several different ceremonies into one remarkable ritual—a scene which, as Lisa Hopkins has noted, seems to contain several overt references to Catholic practice. If *The Knight of Malta* represents religious ritual as a means of policing communal boundaries, this play stages one exemplary ritual as the celebration of the social values that have been perverted during the course of the play. During the final moments of *The Broken Heart*, its heroine Calantha stages her own funeral in order to avoid an unwanted marriage. She then sanctifies her decision by declaring her religious faith, which is manifested in an on-stage altar property. I agree with Hopkins that, despite its pagan setting, the specific objects and gestures used in this scene are inextricably tied to Christianity. I would add, however, that rather than voicing "an appeal for a return to Catholic rites," the play offers a more subtle commentary on recent history, for, as the members of the so-called Laudian movement were aware, a return to Catholicism was not the only option for English Protestants who saw a role for traditional ceremonies in their lives.[68] Like *The Knight of Malta*, Ford's play coincides and engages with anti-Calvinist "innovations."

The Broken Heart culminates in a spectacle that blends together a coronation, a marriage, and a funeral, but it also affords Calantha the opportunity to dictate her last will and testament. In the previous scene, she famously shows no emotion when messengers tell her that her father the king, his favorite Ithocles, and her friend Penthea have all died, but in this scene she reveals that Ithocles was also her betrothed. She announces their marriage by putting a ring on the finger of his dead body, delivers her instructions for how the kingdom is to be ruled, and finally succumbs to heartbreak. The attention to detail that characterizes the scene's

---

[67]   Anthony Brewer, *The love-sick king, an English tragical history with the life and death of Cartesmunda, the fair nun of Winchester* (London: n.p., 1655), A3ᵛ.

[68]   *John Ford's Political Theater* (Manchester: Manchester University Press, 1994), 171.

initial stage direction indicates the extent of the play's investment in Calantha's ceremony:

> *An altar covered with white, two lights of virgin wax; during which music of recorders. Enter four bearing* Ithocles *on a hearse, or in a chair, in a rich robe, and a crown on his head; place him on one side of the altar. After him enter* Calantha *in a white robe and crown'd. ...*Calantha *goes and kneels before the altar; the rest stand off, the women kneeling behind. Cease recorders during her devotions. Soft music.* Calantha *and the rest rise, doing obeisance to the altar.*[69]

In several ways, this passage presents a more elaborate version of moments in other early modern dramas that depict the altar as the center of a social ritual—the end result of this extensive visual display is, after all, Calantha's "marriage"—but the ceremony in *The Broken Heart* is more explicitly coded as Catholic than the rituals in any of the Jacobean plays described above. The fact that the tapers are described as being made of "virgin wax" signals to the reader of the quarto if not to the audience that these are both expensive and deeply symbolic ornaments. The use of wax candles, especially in the daytime, horrified strict Protestants, who complained about the wastefulness of the practice throughout the early years of James's reign.[70] Moreover, unlike Miranda, Calantha actually kneels before the altar, and she and her maids make "*obeisance*" to it; it is possible that the actors might even have kissed the property. The presence of Ithocles's dead body, and the suggestion than Calantha is soon to follow him, also enhances the idea of the altar as the site of sacrifice. As Eamon Duffy notes, "the burning of candles round a corpse was an act with profound resonances."[71] Candles that had been blessed could be used to keep devils at bay, but more generally they symbolized the light of salvation; they were often burned in memory of the dead by relatives and by chantry clergy. Finally, the white cloth covering the altar, which provides a visual echo of Calantha's white costume, marks it as pure and holy, while simultaneously indicating that this ritual object, like the dead body of Ithocles, plays an active role in the scene.

Although the stage direction in Act 5, scene 3 is the first to actually specify the physical presence of the altar, its weighty symbolic value is established early on in the play. The image of the altar is initially used to emphasize the virtues associated with Spartan piety when the king announces that, in honor of his army's victory, "our humility / Shall bend before their altars, and perfume / Their temples with abundant sacrifice" (1.2.1-3). Having established the symbolic connection between altars and humility, the play shifts its interest in religious piety to Penthea, a young

---

[69]   *The Broken Heart*, ed. Donald K. Anderson (Lincoln: University of Nebraska Press, 1968), 5.3.0 sd.

[70]   David Dendy, *The use of lights in Christian Worship* (London: S.P.C.K, 1959), 159.

[71]   Duffy, 361.

wife who eventually starves herself to death because she cannot overcome her husband's jealousy or fend off the attentions of Orgilus, the man to whom she was originally betrothed. Immediately before Penthea's death, her husband Bassanes bemoans the wrongs he has done her, promising to "redeem" his "sacrilege" against her honor. "Humility," he swears, "shall pour before the deities / I have incens'd, a largess of more patience / Than their displeased altars can require" (4.2.34-7). Orgilus, too, draws a comparison between virginity, Penthea's virtue, and the altar, but he does so within the context of urging her to remember her vows to him, vows "[a]s sweetly scented as the incense smoking / The holiest altars (2.3.30-31). She responds by reminding him that her virginity was stolen when she was forced to marry Bassanes, and that she must now break her former promise in order to avoid bringing Orgilus further shame.

Throughout the first four acts of the play, references to religion and piety bring this distorted connection between Penthea's chastity and her willingness to accept her fate to the forefront of the audience's attention. With her death, Penthea's status as a faithful spouse is at last secured, but before she dies she teaches her friend Calantha how to preserve her own virginity. Here, as in *The Knight of Malta* and *The Lovesick King*, religion is represented as a mechanism for defending chastity, and altars are positioned as the bulwarks of virtue. In Act 3, scene 5, Penthea models for Calantha the ritual of the virgin bequest, asking her to "take that trouble on 'ee to dispose / Such legacies as I bequeath impartially" (3.5.37-8). These legacies are, respectively, her youth, her honor, and her brother Ithocles. A crucial aspect of Penthea's martyrdom is that although her brother deprived her of her happiness with Orgilus by forcing her to marry Bassanes, she pleads his cause with Calantha as part of settling her debts to heaven, and in the end, Calantha adopts this seemingly fanciful template in her own death scene when she gives herself to Ithocles and her kingdom to her would-be lover.

After crowning Ithocles and setting up his body near the altar, Calantha turns to Nearchus, prince of Argos, and instructs him to carry out her will. She frames her requests as "articles" to their marriage, but Bassanes immediately picks up on her intention: "This is a testament; / It sounds not like conditions on a marriage" (5.3.53-4). Unlike Penthea's fanciful bequests, which serve as a prologue to her "gift" of Ithocles, these conditions are practical and political: she instructs Nearchus about the pensions and "preferments" that he, as king, should bestow on the most loyal Spartans, and only after making these conditions clear does she turn to what she calls her "neglected husband" (57-8). Placing a ring upon the corpse's finger, she fulfills her father's own "last bequest," and as she seals their union with a kiss she gives her last instruction: "command the voices / Which wait at th'altar, now to sing the song / I fitted for my end" (65, 78-80). The song declares the joys of youth to be ephemeral but asserts that love "*reigns in death*" despite the ravages of time (93). Although its trappings are Catholic trappings, there is nothing shocking or perverse about this ritual within the context of the play; rather, it is the culmination of the various claims *The Broken Heart* makes about religion, virginity, and honor, all of which center around the symbolic status of the altar. Furthermore, the text's striking combination of marriage, coronation, funeral, and testament exalts all four social rituals, and the altar at the center of them, by demonstrating that they can be used to help Calantha break the cycle of revenge and loss that characterizes the first four acts of the play.

The strikingly overt references to Christian practice in *The Broken Heart* represent the culmination of a subtler trend of bringing altars on stage under the cover of foreign or pagan rituals. The first performance of Ford's play also falls near the end of a period in which anti-Calvinist "innovations" were viewed with measured tolerance by the authorities. In December of 1640, a year after the performance of *The Cardinal's Conspiracy* at the Fortune, thousands of Londoners signed a petition and presented it to the House of Commons. The reactionary nature of this document indicates the extent to which more elaborate church furnishings had gained popularity in London during the 1620s and 30s. Its authors complained that there were an increasing number of papists in the capitol, leading to "[t]he turning of the Communion Table altarwise, setting images, crucifixes and conceits over them, and tapers and books upon them, and bowing or adoring to, or before, them ... which is a plain device to usher in the Mass."[72] One year later, a group of irate parishioners from St. Giles-in-the-Fields, also in London, accused their fellow churchgoers of setting up altars "with all manner of superstitious altar-furniture, crosses, crucifixes, candles, candlesticks, etc." to the detriment of godly worship. In the parish of All Hallows Barking the citizens drafted a letter to Laud himself, complaining that "Now there is a new font erected, over which certain carved images and a cross are placed, and also our communion table is removed out of its ancient accustomed place, and certain images placed over the rail which stands about the table, all which, as we conceive, tends much to the dishonour of God, and is very offensive to us parishioners, and also perilous. We have desired our doctor [Edward Layfield, Laud's nephew] that the images might be taken down, yet he refuses so to do." Finally, in 1643, an ordinance was passed in both houses of parliament "directing the demolition of altars, altar-rails, and chancel steps, and the removal of crucifixes, crosses, and images and picture of the Trinity, Virgin and saints."[73] Almost one hundred years after the Reformation first took hold in England, Protestant officials were still struggling to enforce the standards laid out by Edwardian and Elizabethan reformers.

As the 1640s wore on, there were numerous violent clashes between those who favored more elaborate church furnishings and those who opposed them, but the practical issues Laud and his opponents were addressing—what the communion table should look like, what should be put on it, and where it should be placed within the church—presented problems for church officials and churchgoers since Elizabeth first attempted to establish a uniform mode of worship in 1559. By 1644, Laud was ordering "divers crucifixes to be set up in churches over the communion-table, in his chapel at Lambeth, at Whitehall, and at the university

---

[72] Phillips, 176-7.
[73] Ibid., 172; Aston, 76.

at Oxford, of which he was Chancellor." The archbishop defended himself against his detractors by asserting that he was merely revealing the continuity of Christian practice: "all such Rites as had been practised in the Church of Rome, and not abolished, nor disclaimed by any Doctrine, Law or Canon of the first Reformers, were to continue in the same state in which they found them." "And is it not to be thought," he continued, "that Queen Elizabeth and King James would have endured [such rituals] in their time in their own chapel, had they been introductions for Popery?" For many English citizens, this was precisely the point. Elizabeth had famously refused to give up the cross in her private chapel, and therefore why should they uproot their own customs and destroy their own church furnishings? In protesting his innocence, however, Laud glossed over the fact that the cross in Elizabeth's private chapel had caused great consternation among her ministers during the early years of her reign and was eventually replaced by a less controversial tapestry of the crucifixion.[74] It is unclear, and perhaps irrelevant, whether Elizabeth and James were for or against Catholic practice *per se*; as monarchs, they were responsible for trying to forge a consistent form of public devotion. The drama reminds us that their articles and injunctions could never completely cancel out the variety of popular responses to the material aspects of the communion, the ceremony that served as the focal point of Christian worship.

Of all the plays discussed in this chapter, Middleton's allegorical comedy celebrating the failure of the Spanish match would seem to be the most topical. But although *A Game at Chess* bears the most direct political relevance, it is far less interested than *The Broken Heart* in posing questions about the nature of post-Reformation worship. The later play, which emerged during a time of tremendous fractiousness rather than one of national self-congratulation, is also in some ways far more radical in that it takes the social and affective aspects of religion seriously. The larger question that framed all the seemingly inconsequential quarrels about whether the site of the communion should be called an altar or a table, whether it should be placed flush against or perpendicular to the east wall of the church, was the question of how to maintain the holiness of church sacraments. Of the seven sacraments celebrated by Catholicism, the reformers acknowledged only two: baptism and communion. As a result, court preachers such as Andrewes and Buckeridge placed extraordinary emphasis on the eucharist, to the discomfiture of their Calvinist colleagues. The question, then, was how to keep the service sacred without resorting to popish gestures or to the elaborate purification rituals Jonson references in *Sejanus*. In Ford's play, Calantha relies upon the sanctified materiality of her altar, using kneeling and other gestures of "obeisance" to communicate the sincerity of the words she is about to utter. Her actions are not in and of themselves sacramental—although the body of her dead husband does take on eucharistic overtones when she places it next to the altar—yet all the ceremonial objects and gestures described in the initial stage direction are necessary to make her pronouncements efficacious. This scene combines worship,

[74]   Phillips, 177; Aston, 307-14.

testament, marriage, and funeral, integrating social rites with religious ones and revealing the inextricability of religious gestures from the most solemn aspects of secular life.

In reading plays such as Ford's alongside historical accounts of religious controversy in the period, I have attempted to account for the potential impact of altar properties on the public stage, specifically addressing the process by which a group of actors transformed an ordinary table, one that might have been used as a writing desk in a previous scene, into an altar. As with any consideration of early modern performance, these kinds of readings must ultimately acknowledge the diversity of audience response, which in turn reflected but was not determined by the diversity of religious beliefs in the period. Laud's aim was to resist the de-sacralization of the altar, and he would presumably have been displeased by the idea that players were turning their tables into altars on stage. Just as anti-Calvinists disliked the idea that an altar might become a place for schoolboys to set their hats, they would have been uncomfortable with the notion that the gestures of the mass could be imitated as part of a secular entertainment It is possible that some strict Protestants would have sided with Laud on this issue, agreeing that it was profane and sacrilegious to put religious objects on stage, even though they disdained the trappings of the Catholic altar and firmly opposed the anti-Calvinists' goal of beautifying and re-sacralizing the furnishings of the English church. A third group of readers and playgoers, however, were not professionally invested in the placement of the communion table. Their reactions, while informed by their understanding of appropriate religious practice, would also have been more readily influenced by theatrical conventions: the spectacular aspects of *A Game at Chess* or the communal values attached to the altar in *The Knight of Malta*. For the benefit of such spectators, the drama assigned its altar properties a wide range of social and theatrical meanings, informed and facilitated by the fluctuating status of the communion table in post-Reformation religious practice.

Members of the church hierarchy, most notably Archbishop Laud, are the easiest to trace in the historical record, and they serve as useful touchstones for an exploration of early seventeenth-century attitudes toward the communion table. I have attempted to follow historians such as Pauline Croft, however, in acknowledging the complex emotional responses of individual believers to widely publicized debates about "proper" Christian worship. In the case of plays that employ altars, the range of popular attitudes toward the communion table and the constant slippage that existed between the godly table and the idolatrous altar afforded the London playing companies a perfect opportunity to explore the boundaries of their own stagecraft. Theater practitioners were aware that there was no exact uniformity in English worship, but they were also addressing the structural connection between church altars, which were constantly being taken apart and rebuilt, stripped and re-outfitted, and stage altars, which were continually adapted to fit the needs of the players from one scene to the next. The variety of opinions about what constituted "God's board" provided actors with both the matter and the license for their depiction of altars on stage, while their own theatrical technologies supplied the conditions under which they could explore the complex social resonance of both the altar and the table.

Chapter 3
Persistence and Adaptation:
Staging the Cross at Home and Abroad[1]

Given the theater's ability to reorient controversial subjects—and objects—within various fictional contexts, it is not altogether surprising that tombs and altars appeared as properties on the London stage. In using tombs as stage properties, the public theater left aspects of the Catholic tradition behind in order to convey the affective power of the resurrection as a theatrical event, and most plays that staged rituals using altars displaced them onto foreign or pagan settings, avoiding any direct reference to the communion even while playing up the slippage between Protestant and Catholic ceremonial forms. But despite the flexibility the theater demonstrated in treating religious matters, the presence of crucifixes and crosses on the post-Reformation stage is quite surprising. Unlike altars, crosses were unmistakably Christian, and no object was more directly associated with Catholicism than the crucifix, which included the *corpus* of the suffering Christ and thus, according to the reformers, necessarily prompted inappropriate acts of worship. In the minds of English Protestants, the potential for idolatry inherent in large wooden crucifixes, metal altar crosses, and pictures of the crucifix was so dangerous that, by association, even the sign of the cross was viewed with suspicion.[2]

Yet even though they sought to eliminate objects that featured the anthropomorphized image of God, only the strictest Protestants were willing to forego the cross altogether. "From mee, no Pulpit, nor misgrounded law, / Nor scandall taken, shall this Crosse withdraw," John Donne protests in his homage to the cross as an omnipresent, nonsectarian emblem of faith.[3] He maintains that the loss of the thing itself is as bad as another crucifixion, and he concludes that "[n]o Crosse is so extreme, as to have none" (ll. 14). For Donne, the cross is an anchor of his faith and a seal of his membership in God's family; he sees it everywhere he looks, from the shape of a seagull's wings to the outline of a ship's mast. This poem makes clear the contradiction involved in eliminating the cross: how could

---

[1] Parts of this chapter are reprinted with permission from *Studies in English Literature 1500–1900* 47, No. 2 (Spring, 2007): 473-90.

[2] There is some overlap between the two terms during the early modern period, but because of the important material differences between the crucifix, which included the figure of Christ, and the cross, which did not, I use the word "crucifix" only when the primary document names the more controversial object, namely, the cross plus the *corpus*.

[3] "The Crosse," in *The Divine Poems*, ed. Helen Gardner (Oxford: Clarendon Press, 1959), ll. 9-10.

any representation of Christ's passion be unlawful when the crucifixion is the focus of Christian history? The reformers were thus forced to strike a series of compromises organized around the materiality of this controversial image. They could not hope to eliminate all forms of the cross from popular religious practice, and so they admitted that the sign itself might be *adiaphora*, a thing indifferent. At the same time, they banned particular types of crosses that they believed were especially likely to incite idolatrous thoughts.

In Chapter 1, I dealt primarily with theatrical adaptation, the transformation of a liturgical convention into a more flexible set of dramatic ones; here, I examine a group of objects that were already being adapted outside the theater. The sheer number and variety of forms of the cross that existed in post-Reformation England provide a particularly striking example of the way items associated with Catholic superstition were reshaped and re-imagined. Chapter 2 also dealt with Catholic objects that were adapted to suit the times, but the crucial difference between altars and crosses is that while altars were replaced by a new kind of liturgical object, the crosses that survived in sixteenth- and seventeenth-century England were most often non-ceremonial. Insofar as they ultimately pointed back to the visual image of Christ's crucifixion, they still remained highly charged, but they were not necessarily controversial. The cross was recognizable, for instance, as the emblem on St. George's shield and it appeared opposite King Henry VIII himself on the royal seal.[4] In this heraldic context, the cross stood for England's military might or, by extension, the triumph of Christianity over all infidels; here the association with the struggle against Islam tended to counteract any association with Catholic superstition. The military context associated with these crosses was crucial, but so was their materiality, for they were two-dimensional and did not feature the image of Christ. Furthermore, unlike freestanding structures such as altar crosses and roods, these crosses were attached to the body, and could not be worshiped as statues of saints were. This profusion of nonliturgical crosses that prompted theater practitioners to experiment with the kinds of crosses they brought on stage, resulting in a series of conventions I describe as an "affective technology" because they tend to reference private rather than ritual worship and because their meaning is often determined by the context in which they are represented as well as by their specific materiality. Thus the perceived contrast between the outlawed object and the permissible sign or remembrance of the crucifixion helps us to account for the existence of such properties in early modern drama.

Given the standard narratives that have been constructed about Reformation-era iconoclasm, it is surprising that a large number of crosses could still be found in England in the sixteenth and seventeenth centuries. In fact, when we count all the various materializations of the object, crosses were remarkably prevalent in the public theater. This trend can be more readily understood when we consider that many of them were small properties held in the hand or worn on the body and that they often appeared in secular rather than ritual contexts. Accordingly, this chapter

---

[4]   Phillips, 90.

shifts the focus away from the large liturgical objects discussed in the first half of the book in order to tackle the theater's interest in the materiality of religious practice on the level of personal devotion. Before going on to discuss the presence of these individualized tokens of faith on the public stage, I want to explore in greater detail the various material manifestations of the cross as well as the statutes that attempted to control the use of these potentially controversial items.

The Materiality of the Cross

In order to be able to experiment with various kinds of crosses and crucifixes within fictionalized settings, theater practitioners had to be able to parse the material distinctions between them. According to the *Oxford English Dictionary*, seven separate meanings for the word "cross" were operative during this period, ranging from the physical object that figures prominently in biblical history to an immaterial sign. One of the first definitions refers to the "particular wooden structure" on which Christ was martyred, while other definitions include "a model or figure of a cross as a religious emblem," "a representation or delineation of a cross on any surface ... used as a sacred mark, symbol, badge," "a staff surmounted by the figure of a cross," "a monument in the form of a cross," and "the sign of the cross made with the right hand." The *OED* also provides a definition associated with international military conflict: "the ensign and symbol of Christianity, esp. when opposed to other religions" (2, 5, 4a, 6, 7a, 3a, 8). Although all these objects and signs were still theoretically available to the individual believer in post-Reformation England, only a few were broadly accepted. Among them was the sign of the cross made with the hand, which, despite some objections on the part of strict Protestants, continued to be used in baptism ceremonies, as specified by the order of service in the 1559 Book of Common Prayer. The acceptability of the cross as a sign, symbol, or remembrance of the crucifixion continued to be the subject of debate throughout Elizabeth's reign and well into James's, but the image of the cross never disappeared entirely from the minds of their subjects.

The main issues at stake when considering the materiality of crosses are their size, dimensionality, and figuration—in other words, whether the cross included the body of Christ and could thus be called a crucifix. On one end of the spectrum were large wooden roods, the centerpiece of the medieval liturgy and among the first objects to be destroyed by the reformers in the 1530s and 40s. The problem with roods was threefold: they were large, publicly displayed objects of veneration, they were three-dimensional, and they featured the physical body of Christ. On the other end of the spectrum was the cross of St. George, which appeared as a regular feature of the players' costumes in local parish pageants even after other kinds of crosses had been banned. There were, of course, several other types of material crosses in between these two extremes, and the playing companies were very much aware of these less controversial objects when considering the challenge of staging religious objects and symbols that evoked the crucifixion.

Generally speaking, small crosses were less offensive than large ones because they were not a formal part of the Catholic liturgy. At the same time, however, the small cross posed its own particular threat. Along with books, rosaries, *agnus deis*, and portable altars, small crosses could circulate easily and were used to promote the Catholic faith throughout the sixteenth century. Following her excommunication by the pope in 1570, Elizabeth's parliament passed an act that prohibited the bringing in of "any token or tokens, thing or things, called by the name of an *Agnus Dei*, or any crosses, pictures, beads or suchlike vain and superstitious things from the bishop or see of Rome."[5] And yet the problem of smuggling persisted. Writing from Venice in 1580, Christopher Hodgson informs his contact in England that he is sending "1,000 grains, five gilded crosses, the pardon whereof the bearer will tell you, and three *Agnus Deis*. I have sent you all I could get."[6] Nor were English Protestants entirely unfamiliar with such objects. An elaborate fold-out diagram from Bernard Garter's *A newyeares gifte* (1579) provides a key to the different types of Catholic "merchandize"—including portable altars, hallowed grains, rosary beads, crucifixes, and various relics or charms—available during this period, all of them small enough to go undetected (Figure 3.1).[7] On one level, these items were construed as dangerous signs of disloyalty to the queen, but their most frightening quality was their ability to proliferate in secret and thus breed new generations of recusants in English parishes.

In other words, things such as small crosses made of wood or metal provided evidence of the clandestine trade that was keeping English recusant communities alive. To their dismay, ecclesiastical officials often missed these remnants of popery in their visitations, for unlike altars, statues, and church plate, rosaries and crosses could be easily hidden about the body. In a letter dated 1591, Henry Scrope reports to Lord Burghley that he had searched the packs of several itinerant priests and found "a surplice, wax candles (which I suppose have been hallowed), three pairs of beads with crosses fixed to them, and one Popish manual."[8]

---

[5]   Cardwell vol. 1, 363-6. In 1577, indulgences were granted by the Pope to those "having beads, coronals, crosses, &c, e.g. anyone having one of the blessed grains in his beads" (Green 1577, 528).

[6]   Green 1580, 4.

[7]   The author introduces his diagram with verses that begin: "Their trinkets here I bring unto thy showe / As if it were into a Market place" (Bernard Garter, *A newyeares gifte, dedicated to the Popes Holinesse* [Bynneman: London, 1579], H1ᵛ).

[8]   Green 1591, 325.

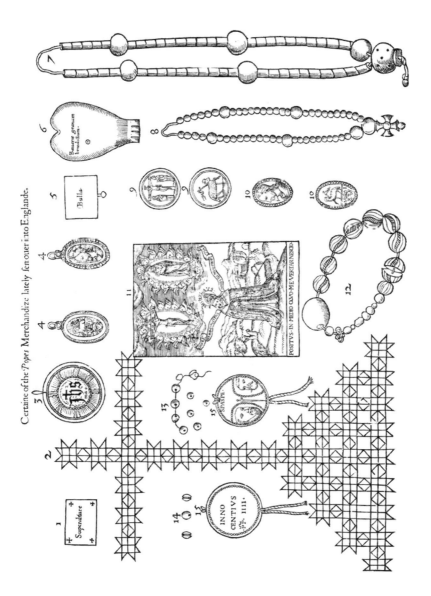

Figure 3.1 "Popish merchandise," *A newyeares gift*, 1579 (H1^v–2^r). By permission of the Folger Shakespeare Library

Thirty years later, John Sweet, S.J. was found with a bag full of "superstitious things" in his possession, and when authorities searched the houses in Exeter where he had been staying they found "many crucifixes, Popish books, *Agnus Deis*, grayves, beads and other superstitious relics."[9] Such objects were proof of the priest's intention to administer the mass and his attempt to provide the faithful with individual objects of devotion they could use in his absence.

The question of dimensionality was in some ways more straightforward than that of size: simply put, a two-dimensional cross was much more likely to be acceptable to moderate Protestants, although in more fervent parishes the image of the cross was unacceptable in any form, particularly in the fabric of the church itself. The churchwardens of St. Laurence Ludlow, for example, paid a local woman two shillings to unstitch a cross from their altar cloth upon Elizabeth's ascension in 1559.[10] But for the most part, two-dimensional crosses were less provocative than objects that resembled statues. By the same logic, both altar crosses and roods were problematic because they were prominent objects of adoration in the pre-Reformation church: one was elevated on the altar while the other loomed over the congregation from its place on the rood screen. These qualities made three-dimensional images the main target of iconoclasts, especially during the first wave of attacks in the 1540s.

In contrast to freestanding objects that could be worshiped, narrative images of the crucifixion were widely accepted, even by the author of the Elizabethan *Homilies* (1563), one of the most influential attacks on idolatry. "Men are not so ready," the homilist admits, "to worship a picture on a wall, or in a window, as an embossed and gilt image." Moreover, narrative images with several figures were also preferable to static icons: "a process of a story, painted with the gestures and actions of many persons, and commonly the sum of the story written withal, hath another use in it, than one dumb idol or image standing by itself." Susan Brigden's *London and the Reformation* ends with the story of Richard Alington, a citizen who had always received "ineffable, peculiar and special comfort by a picture of the cross and Christ nailed thereunto" and who drew a sketch of the crucifixion on

---

    [9]   Marie Rowlands, *English Catholics of Parish and Town, 1558-1778* (London: Catholic Record Society, 1998), 53. Tessa Watt alludes to the connection between popular entertainment, print culture, and the trade in Catholic relics when she points out that a "Derbyshire piper was caught selling beads, crucifixes and books in Nottinghamshire in 1616" (178). In 1633, authorities in Plymouth captured John Jenkyn of Penzance and found upon his person "diverse crucifixes, pictures, and other superstitious things, with two or three popish books" (McClain, 193).

    [10]   Thomas Wright, ed., *Churchwardens' Accounts of the Town of Ludlow, in Shropshire* (New York: AMS, 1968), 137-40. By contrast, the Marian bishops complained that many churches, having suffered the loss of their roods under Edward, suspected that Mary's reign might not last, and they replaced them temporarily with painted cloths rather than proper freestanding images (Phillips, 109).

his will of 1561.[11] Alington was not alone in his attachment to this kind of image, however, and woodcuts of the crucifixion continued to be produced and tolerated well into the seventeenth century. The crucifixion was a perfectly ordinary subject for practicing needlework, along with "unicorns, peacocks, flowers, and abstract designs."[12] Even the Earl of Leicester, whom historians have described as a staunch Protestant, owned a painting of "Christ taken from the cross," though he wisely kept it at his home in Essex rather than at Kenilworth, where the queen might see it.[13]

Anticipating the Elizabethan *Homilies*, Thomas Cranmer attempted to rescue the crucifix from the charge of superstition by taking a cue from the traditional defense of images as didactic tools. "The Image of our Saviour," he reasons, is "as an open book," and that image "hangeth on the cross in the rood, or is painted in cloths, walls or windows, to the intent that beside the examples of virtues which we may learn in Christ we may be also many ways provoked to remember his painful and cruel passion."[14] By comparing the static image of the crucifix to a narrative of the crucifixion and arguing that they serve the same function, Cranmer was attempting to elide the material differences between crucifixes, stained glass windows, and books. The fact remained, however, that iconoclasts typically attacked crucifixes first, and although in some cases the terms "cross" and "crucifix" were used interchangeably, there is evidence that very clear distinctions were drawn between them. Pre-Reformation churchwardens' accounts routinely specify whether their crosses had "crucifixes" on them, and whether the figures of Mary and John were also attached. In subsequent inventories, the same churchwardens would assure Elizabeth's officials that all their images, including their crucifixes, had been sold, defaced, or burnt. But the persistence of such objects in individual homes and private chapels forced Protestant pamphleteers to continually insist that "throughoute all England, there should be neyther crosse nor crucifixe left."[15]

Although the crucifix was widely dismissed by Protestants as an incitement to idolatry, akin to statues of saints, legislation explicitly banning the use of crucifixes was slow in coming. At the convocation of the clergy in 1536, Latimer specified that in addition to the images of saints, crucifixes should be "put out" of every church.[16] To his dismay, however, the Ten Articles published in 1538 distinguished between the idolatrous worship of images and their proper use "as laymen's books to remind us of heavenly things." These injunctions did not explicitly outlaw the

---

[11]   *Certain sermons or homilies appointed to be read in churches in the time of Queen Elizabeth* (London: n.p., 1687), 178; Brigden, 630.

[12]   Watt, 137.

[13]   Susan Foister, "Paintings and other works of art in sixteenth-century English inventories," *Burlington Magazine* CXXIII (May 1981): 273-82, 274.

[14]   John Edmund Cox, ed., *The Works of Thomas Cranmer*, vol. 2 (Cambridge: Printed at the University Press, 1844), 101.

[15]   Diehl, *Staging Reform, Reforming the Stage*, 20.

[16]   David Wilkins, *Concilia Magnae Britanniae Et Hiberniae*, vol. 3 (Bruxelles: Culture et Civilisation, 1964), 805.

crucifix, and they even permitted practices such as creeping to the cross on Good Friday; indeed most Henrician reformers, unlike Latimer, were not yet ready to dismiss crosses and crucifixes altogether. The process of removing crosses from churches accelerated upon Edward's ascension, however. In 1547, his ministers began to take inventory of all the parish churches in England, and four years later the government ordered the seizure of all the remaining "gold and silver plate, jewels, vestments and church furniture" that had survived in English churches.[17] The seizure was motivated partly by a desire to pay off state debts, but this action also served as an admission that the crown and its ministers could not, in fact, prevent the abuse of images except by removing them altogether.

Despite the violence of the Edwardian iconoclasm, there continued to be a gap between the government's willingness to see crucifixes destroyed and its readiness to declare them intrinsically idolatrous. Instead, the Edwardian articles of 1547 attempted to qualify the nature of image abuse, stating that, "to the extent that all superstition and hypocrisy crept into divers men's hearts may vanish away, they shall not set forth or extol the dignity of any images, relics or miracles."[18] Once again no specific mention is made of crosses or crucifixes, and this same language was repeated even more cautiously in Elizabeth's 1559 Articles of Uniformity. Margaret Aston reads the 1559 Articles as a moderated version of the earlier law, arguing that the description of "appropriate" church furnishings was ambiguous and that the focus on abuse was closer to that of the Henrician articles.[19] As a result, later visitation articles, such as Archbishop Grindal's in 1571, insisted that worshipers not "superstitiously make upon themselves the sign of the cross ... nor rest at any cross in carrying any corpse to burying, nor to leave any crosses of wood there."[20] It is worth noting that Grindal mentions three very different types of crosses here: the sign of the cross, a market or roadside cross, and a small wooden cross used as a memorial. The vagueness of the Edwardian and Elizabethan statutes made room for waves of popular iconoclasm, which the queen then attempted to control, but it also left room for these types of nonceremonial crosses to proliferate, eventually facilitating the survival and the gradual return of some of Catholicism's material trappings under James and Charles.

To emphasize the persistent materiality of the cross in post-Reformation England is not to claim that there were no objections to its presence. During the early years of the Henrician reformation, for example, William Turner expressed his outrage over the fact that it was still acceptable to light candles in front of a crucifix. In his 1543 pamphlet, *The huntyng and fynding of the Romishe foxe*, he complained bitterly that although the crucifix was an idol, it continued to be tolerated because it was an image of God rather than the picture of a saint.

---

[17]   Charles Lloyd, ed., *Formularies of Faith, Put Forth by Authority During the Reign of Henry VIII* (Oxford: At the Clarendon Press, 1825), 13-14; Phillips, 97-8.

[18]   Cardwell, vol. 1, 210-12.

[19]   Aston, 299.

[20]   Cardwell, vol. 1, 337.

In a letter to Heinrich Bullinger dated 1542, Richard Hilles confirmed that "[t]he year but one before I left England, the public orders of the king were sent to the bishops and to the principal laity in every parish, that by reason of the superstition of the common people they were not to permit any wax candles to be burned or placed before images in the churches, except only before the crucifix, and at the festival of Easter, before the sepulchre of Christ."[21] Referring to Elizabeth's own stubbornness around the issue, Thomas Sampson wrote to Peter Martyr in 1580 that "[t]he altars are indeed removed, and images also throughout the kingdom; the crucifix and candles are retained at court alone." Edwin Sandys reported that on her ascension Elizabeth ordered that "the image of Christ crucified, together with Mary and John, should be placed, as heretofore, in some conspicuous part of the church, where they might more readily be seen by all the people," and it was not until 1561 that explicit orders were given for the removal of all crucifixes. In 1566 officials in Lincolnshire were busy burning all remaining roods, and in 1571 the visitation articles were still calling for the removal of "crosses, candlesticks, holy-water stocks, or fat images, and all other relics and monuments of superstition and idolatry" from the churches in York.[22]

Simply put, the crucifix represented everything the reformers disliked most about Catholicism: as a representation of the son of God, the crucifix flouted the second commandment against making graven images, and as a large, freestanding structure with lifelike qualities it tempted naïve believers to respond emotionally to it. Some large roods even functioned like puppets, moving in response to pilgrims with hand gestures or tears of blood. Traditional Catholic practice involved everything from creeping to the cross to the kissing of small crucifixes, behaviors that, according to Protestants, encouraged the faithful to see these objects as somehow alive. According to William Charke, crucifixes have the power "to snare the heart of a carnall man, bewitching it with so great glistering of the painted harlot," and the Elizabethan homilist announces that because of their seductive qualities the practice of venerating images is in constant danger of being resurrected whenever popish objects are present.[23] The very "seeking out of Images," the homilist writes, "is the beginning of Whoredom." By taking them out of their "lurking corners" and displaying them in the light of day, idol-makers tempt both men and women to "spiritual Fornication." The fear expressed by Protestant iconoclasts, particularly in the 1580s and 90s, was that devotional objects were being harbored in private households and would soon begin to "creep" back into parish churches, as they did during the Marian restoration. This was the "tragedy" ecclesiastical visitors were struggling to avert by eliminating crosses from homes as well as from churches.[24]

---

[21]   Aston, 245, 229.

[22]   Ibid., 312-13; Frere, vol. 3, 108-9.

[23]   William Charke, *An answere to a seditious pamphlet lately cast abroade by a Iesuite with a discouerie of that blasphemous sect* (London: Barker, 1580), B1ᵛ.

[24]   *Certain sermons or homilies*, 182, 260, 213.

The reformers' task was further complicated by an initial reluctance to meddle in the private lives of English citizens. The problem, as stated by the homilist, was that images kept in the home would eventually make their way into the public eye: "First, men used privately stories painted in tables, cloths, and walls. Afterward gross and embossed images privately in their own houses. Then afterwards, pictures first, and after them, embossed images began to creep into churches, learned and godly men ever speaking against them."[25] But the early iconoclasts reversed this process, attacking first the objects that had crept into the churches, and it was not until the latter decades of the sixteenth century that Elizabeth began to authorize the purging of individual households. Tessa Watt notes that "[p]ictures of the passion, the virgin Mary and saints remained perfectly acceptable in private houses" throughout the early years of Elizabeth's reign. Even the fervent iconoclast William Perkins was willing to concede that paintings of biblical subjects were not objectionable as long as they were kept in what he called "private places."[26] Admittedly, these objects were viewed more favorably because they served a narrative function, but there was no guarantee they might not be "abused," or worshiped, by their owners.

Crucifixes and other elements of pre-Reformation church furniture experienced a brief revival in the 1620s and 30s thanks to the advocacy of Archbishop William Laud, Queen Henrietta Maria, and a host of individual clerics, but even in 1580 Thomas Sampson was incorrect in stating that all crucifixes except the queen's had been successfully eliminated. Patrick Collinson, for instance, describes a 1584 raid on a Catholic household in Salisbury that turned up "twelve printed superstitious pictures … and one crucifix."[27] Many sixteenth-century parishioners took crucifixes from their churches into their homes to save them from destruction, and prominent aristocratic recusants continued to use and circulate various sorts of crucifixes throughout the early 1600s.[28] The Vaux family of Harrowden Hall in Northampton, for instance, owned not one but two altar crucifixes for their private use in 1600, and in 1624 an altar crucifix was discovered during a search of Lady Vaux's home at Stanley Grange. The members of this particular family, many of whom ended up in prison for harboring priests, were among the class of wealthy Catholics who had access to a variety of different crosses. The objects listed in a 1605 family inventory include: "Item a cross full of relics that was Mrs. Anne's grandmother's. Item a gold crucifix bigger than that full of relics. Item a cross of gold without a crucifix that hath little crystals." The first of these crosses was probably a jeweled cross, worn about the neck, the second possibly a freestanding devotional object, and the third an altar cross. This last item may even have been

---

[25]   Ibid., 180.

[26]   Watt, 134, 185-6.

[27]   Collinson, 118.

[28]   For example, the Archdeacon's court in Oxfordshire records the existence of "vestments, crucifixes, bells and cloths galore in the hands of locals" in 1584 (J. J. Scarisbrick, *The Reformation and the English People* [Oxford: Blackwell, 1984], 141).

the same one that appeared in a 1612 inventory as "one cross of gold given to his Lordship when he was very young," worth no less than 300 pounds.[29] Like the churchwardens' accounts, these documents carefully specify which objects have or are crucifixes, but for the Vaux family the subject of figuration was important only insofar as it determined how each cross could be used. The altar crosses helped them recreate the traditional experience of the mass, while the small crucifixes served as the focus of private devotion. Each of these items, however, was also clearly designated as a material link between family members. The larger items were an essential element of the family's ritual practices, and they were kept from generation to generation, but so, too, were small objects, like the cross belonging to "Mrs. Anne's grandmother."

Documents such as the 1605 Vaux inventory reinforce some of the key differences between material crosses, but such texts also provide clues about how these differences played out in various social contexts. Similarly, post-Reformation attitudes toward the cross ranged from devout worship to disgust. At one extreme were individuals such as Roger Martyn, whose story I will return to later in the chapter. Driven by his personal attachment to the broken crucifix from his parish church, Martyn rescued the object and kept it in his own home, hopeful that one day his children would be able to worship it in public. Thus, despite the fact that Elizabeth managed to establish some uniformity of Protestant practice in England, the crucifix remained a vital part of Martyn's life history and his children's future. His affection for the crucifix, which he recorded in a diary sometime around the end of Elizabeth's reign, stands in dramatic contrast to the story of William Malden, whose autobiographical account was appended to Foxe's *Actes and Monuments* (1563).[30] Malden's personalized narrative of Protestant history does resemble Martyn's journal, however, in that it too brings the debate about the crucifix closer to home.

Malden first converted to the reformed faith in 1538 when he began reading the Bible with a group of other men in his hometown of Chelmsford. He and his father's apprentice bought an English version of the New Testament and kept it hidden in their bedstraw. From the Bible and the primer Malden progressed to reading a polemical work on the mass, which taught him that worshiping the crucifix was "plaine idolatry, and playnely againste the commandement of God." One night he repeated this argument to his mother, chiding her for being one of those foolish persons who knocked their breasts and knelt before the crucifix in procession. His mother promptly shifted the discussion away from the crucifix as an object of civic pride, reminding him that the idol he was attacking had played a role in his childhood and was inextricably linked to his own body: "Wilte not thou worshippe the crosse? And it was about the when thou were cristened, and must be layed on the when thou art dead." For Malden's mother, the crucifix and the

---

[29]   Godfrey Anstruther, *Vaux of Harrowden: A Recusant Family* (Newport, Mon: R. H. Johns, 1953), 406, 461.

[30]   John Gough Nichols, *Narrative of the Days of the Reformation* (Westminster: Printed for the Camden Society, 1859), 348-51, 349.

ceremonies associated with it dictated not only public worship but also the private life cycle of an individual believer. Malden was unconvinced, however, and he repeated his charge to his father later that same night, urging him to abandon that "graven image." His enraged father gave him a thorough whipping for his disrespect, but the blows he received—a mirror of the martyrdom experienced by Foxe's more famous converts—only made him rejoice that he was "betten for Christ's sake."[31] While Roger Martyn disobeyed the authority of Elizabeth's ministers to preserve a crucifix for his children, Malden's disparaging remarks about the crucifix caused a permanent rift in his family, ultimately prompting him to reject his parents' authority.

Although it takes place several decades before the performances of the public theater plays I address here, Malden's story is instructive in that it demonstrates the personal impact of the Reformation, complicating the broader narratives that represent crucifixes as synonymous with Catholic idolatry. As J. J. Scarisbrick, Eamon Duffy, and Lisa McClain have shown, individual narratives of recusant resistance teach us to question the effectiveness of the reformers' efforts to stamp out Catholic practice in England. Similarly, by associating the crucifix with the home, the family, and the body of the individual believer, the theater was able to effectively create complex emotional portraits of the faith systems associated with this "Catholic" object. Even Malden's narrative, in which he describes himself as a victim of his parents' blind attachment to Catholicism, represents his mother's adherence to the crucifix as an expression of her natural desire to preserve her family's traditions. According to Thomas Sampson and others, Elizabeth herself was initially loathe to remove the crucifix from her private chapel. Her reluctance would not necessarily have surprised her contemporaries, and her refusal to remove the crucifix can be construed as a matter of individual choice. But it could also be read as a form of resistance that posed a much larger problem for her Protestant ministers. As a three-dimensional part of her altar furniture, Elizabeth's crucifix was a potential object of idolatrous adoration as well as a beloved personal possession, and her subjects might take her recalcitrance as a sign that they, too, could ignore the prohibitions against idol worship.

The implications of this ongoing uncertainty about the degree to which a cross was an idol can be seen in the remarks of Bishop Jewel. In 1560 he mockingly described the foolishness of his opponents, who demanded that "either the crosses of silver and tin, which we have everywhere broken in pieces, must be restored, or our bishoprics relinquished." Here Jewel attempts to dismiss the Catholics' defense of "their little cross" as trifling, but he and his allies were equally invested in the outcome of the debate, during which the crucifix in the queen's chapel suffered several attacks at the hands of those who shared her ministers' concerns. Bishop Parkhurst was able to gloat in 1562 that "[t]he crucifix and candlesticks in the queen's chapel are broken in pieces, and, as some one has brought word, reduced to ashes. A good riddance to such a cross as that! It has continued there too long already,

---

[31]   Ibid., 349-50.

to the great grief of the godly, and the cherishing of I know not what expectations to the papists."[32] In his letter, which acknowledges the danger inherent in Catholic objects, Parkhurst specifies that this particular cross was especially offensive, both because it stood on the altar and because it fueled the hopes of English recusants. In the end, Elizabeth reputedly agreed to a compromise: she would abandon this element of her chapel furniture if the bishops would agree to let her replace it with an altar tapestry that depicted the crucifixion. This substitution of the static, three-dimensional object for the two-dimensional narrative representation once again underscores the fact that the reformers, who ostensibly eschewed all outward ornaments in favor of the immaterial word of God, were of necessity concerned with the particular materiality of the cross. Although they had clarified the reasons for their dislike of the crucifix, the reformers had not managed to overcome the persistent physicality of the cross itself. And because even the gesture of making the cross with one's hand could be construed as representational, this materiality continued to be a debatable topic—not only in churches and in private homes but also in the theater.

Theatrical Negotiations

I have been suggesting that because of the adaptability of crosses and crucifixes outside the theater, their affective value was also flexible inside the theater, but one group of stage crosses could only be construed as overtly negative, namely, the ones that appeared in traditional ceremonial contexts. In *The History of the Life and Death of Thomas Lord Cromwell* (1600), for instance, a crucifix is used to underscore the play's depiction of the Catholic traitors who nearly halted the Reformation. Bishop Gardiner uses a small hand-held crucifix in this play to bless the men he has hired to accuse Cromwell of treason, promising them that their deed will earn them a place in heaven. "Kneel down," he commands, "and I will here absolve you both; / This Crucifix I lay upon your heads, / And sprinckle Holy-water on your browes."[33] Given that this event takes place during what Protestants referred to as the dark days of popery in England, the audience is immediately prompted to question the force of Gardiner's absolution and recognize that the crucifix and the holy water are superficial tokens used to cover up his lack of inner faith. Presumably, playgoers would be encouraged to draw similar conclusions from scenes in other plays that represent the practice of swearing on crosses, as when Lorenzo urges Pedringano to "[s]wear on this cross, that what thou say'st is true" in Kyd's *The Spanish Tragedy* (1587) or, more obviously, when the Duke of Anjou swears "by this cross" that he and his men will kill as many Huguenots

---

[32]   Aston, 311, 13. Eight months later the queen conceded only that the candles not be lit before the crucifix.

[33]   *The true chronicle historie of the whole life and death of Thomas Lord Cromwell* (London: [Read], 1602), F1ʳ.

"as we can come near" in Marlowe's *The Massacre at Paris* (1593).[34] In its own way, each of these plays makes a familiar set of references to Catholic superficiality.

In some cases, these negative allusions to papist rituals are intensified through association with the power structures of the Catholic hierarchy. In one of the few Shakespearean stage directions to directly reference the material elements of religious practice, *Henry VIII* (1613) introduces a processional cross as a feature of the ceremonies immediately preceding Katherine's trial. In this scene, the attributes of the bishops and the cardinals, which include "*two priests, bearing each a silver cross*," are displayed for the audience's benefit as well as for the queen's (2.4.0 sd.). And though the play's depiction of these figures is not explicitly satirical, the pompousness of the procession encourages spectators to see Katherine as the victim of a Catholic hierarchy consisting entirely of men. John Webster provides a similar juxtaposition between ceremonial trappings and the abuse of power in *The Duchess of Malfi* (1614). Immediately before the Duchess's banishment, her brother the Cardinal gives up his "*cross, hat, robes, and ring*" at the shrine of Our Lady of Loreto in order to take up his battle gear before formally exiling the Duchess and her family (3.4.7 sd.). The bewilderment of the onstage bystanders, who are expecting a reunion rather than a banishment, mirrors and enhances the audience's own reaction to the spectacle of the Duchess's suffering. In each of these dramatizations of the early modern Catholic aristocracy, the cross denotes superstition and corruption because of its association with traditional ceremony and the church hierarchy.

Although it is not surprising that several of the plays that use crucifix or cross properties frame them as emblems of Catholic superstition, I maintain that they provide the exception rather than rule. The remainder of the plays discussed in this chapter place crosses in fictional contexts that downplay the potential for idolatry and allow them to be viewed more sympathetically. One of these theatrical displacements, alluded to above, involved using the cross as an emblem of the Christian struggle against pagan or Muslim enemies in order to flatten out the distinction between proper Protestant doctrine and false Catholic devotion. Ironically, the Protestant martyrologist John Foxe provides one of the clearest articulations of this strategy. His relation of the story of Constantine helps explain the tradition of using the cross as a weapon against the enemies of the Christian faith while reminding his readers about the distinctions between the cross as symbol and the cross as material object. In his description of Constantine's military triumphs, Foxe describes a vision that appeared to the future emperor one night as he marched toward Rome:

---

[34]   *The Spanish Tragedy*, ed. David M. Bevington (Manchester: Manchester University Press, 1996), 2.2.87; *Dido Queen of Carthage and The Massacre at Paris*, ed. H. J. Oliver (London: Methuen, 1968), 5.5.51-2.

casting up his eyes many times to heaven, in the south part, about the going down of the sun, [he] saw great brightness in heaven, appearing in the similitude of a cross, giving this inscription, *In hoc vince*, that is, 'In this overcome'. … Behold in the night season in his sleep, Christ appeared to him with the sign of the same cross which he had seen before, bidding him to make the figuration thereof, and to carry it in his wars before him, and so should he have the victory … . [The cross] was given to him of God, not to induce any superstitious worship or opinion of the cross … but only to bear the meaning of another thing, that is, to be an admonition to him to seek and inspire to the knowledge of [Christ]. … The day following this vision, Constantine caused a cross after the same figuration to be made of gold and precious stone, and to be borne before him instead of his standard.[35]

In this passage Constantine does exactly the opposite of what he is commanded to do: he takes the "sign of the cross," a remembrance of Christ and an ensign under which he is instructed to conquer his enemies, and turns it into a "standard," a staff with a jeweled cross on it. In other words, the future ruler of the Christian world creates a material thing capable of inciting "superstitious worship." And yet, as Foxe notes, it was through this sign that Constantine established the peace of the church that was to last until the days of Wycliffe. On the basis of Foxe's apparent lack of concern about Constantine's "figuration … made of gold and precious stone" we are prompted to conclude that the problem of the crucifix was a uniquely post-Reformation one: only now, when papists have begun to misuse the image of the cross, are material crosses becoming inherently problematic.

Foxe goes on to describe how, upon entering the city, Constantine holds the cross in his right hand and tells the citizens of Rome that it is the "true token of fortitude" through which he has freed them from the tyrant.[36] In other words, Constantine presents his cross as a sign of Christian military might rather than an object of devotion, an adjustment many Elizabethans would later make in their celebrations of St. George. The attempt to recover the cross from its papist associations and reorient it around the idea of Christian victory can also be seen in a small jeweled cross owned by Anne of Denmark that was inscribed with the words: "*In hoc signo vinces.*"[37] Even the baptism service in the 1559 *Book of Common Prayer* appropriates this kind of military language in the words the priest uses to describe the cross: a "token that hereafter [the child] shal not be ashamed to confesse the faith of Christ crucified, and manfully to fight under his banner against sinne, the worlde and the devyll, and to continue Christes faithful suliour

---

[35]   *Actes and Monuments of These Latter and Perillous Dayes* (Imprinted at London: Iohn Day, 1563), 103.

[36]   Ibid., 104.

[37]   Diana Scarisbrick, *Jewellry in Britain 1066-1837* (Wilby: Michael Russell, 1994), 129.

and servant unto his lives ende."[38] Perhaps it was because of this kind of language, which commanded the newly christened soul to act as a soldier in the defense of his or her faith, that the use of the sign of the cross in baptism was tolerated by so many Protestants.

As he relates Constantine's vision and his early victories for Christianity, Foxe envisions a scenario in which the cross slips easily back and forth between an immaterial sign and a material thing under the rubric of building a Christian empire, but his disregard for object-focused worship is made more explicit in his narratives of sixteenth-century Protestant martyrdom. The frivolity of Catholic objects is most evident in the story of Jan Hus, whose tormentors dress him up in church vestments and put a chalice in his hand only to strip him of all these ornaments as a sign of his degradation. The process is meant to be humiliating, but in Foxe's view all these external signs of the Catholic church are ungodly, and the act of having them removed constitutes the preface to a good death. Thus, when they take the chalice away from him, Hus correctly responds by praying that God will not "take away the Chalice of his redemption," the immaterial proof of his salvation.[39] On one level, the difference between these passages is clear: Constantine's cross, however blatantly material, is a sign of his triumph over the enemies of God. By contrast, the popish vestments, crosses, and chalices with which his accusers attempt to torment Hus are all the recognizable trappings of English papistry, and, in Foxe's view, Hus is right to cast them off in favor of the immaterial signs of his true faith. But apart from this obvious opposition, what is intriguing about the suggestion in both these narratives, Constantine's and Hus's, is that although it is important to reject the material trappings of Catholicism, even a large, jeweled cross can function as a true emblem of Christianity when presented in the right context—for instance, in the framework of the uncorrupted, primitive church. The context in which the cross appeared was almost as important as its materiality, and for this reason the theater often distanced its cross properties from the charge of superstition or idolatry by removing them to foreign or pre-Christian contexts.

In the previous chapter, I argued that plays such as *The Knight of Malta* (1618) employed altars in scenes that highlight the ongoing metamorphosis of English church interiors after the Reformation and pointed to the social impact of these changes. The material process of creating such objects, and the prominent role they play in several early modern scripts, suggests that there was an ongoing interest in these and other objects formerly associated with the Catholic church.

---

[38]   *The Booke of common praier* (London: Jugge and Cawode, 1559), 275. The order of service called for the priest to "make a Crosse upon the Childes forehead," but also to carefully explain its significance as a sign of the child's fidelity to Christ. This practice was still being enforced by the visitation articles for London and of the ten dioceses in 1605 and in Norwich in 1619 (Fincham, *Visitation Articles and Injunctions of the Early Stuart Church*, vol. 1, 8, 28, 158).

[39]   Foxe, *Actes and Monuments*, 623.

Further, I suggested that *The Knight of Malta* was able to draw upon that interest, temporarily dodging the controversial association between Catholic altars and idolatry, by placing its altar on the island of Malta. Here I hope to demonstrate that the play's foreign setting also allows it to introduce the cross worn by the knights on their outer garment as one of its main visual and symbolic features. The intimate connection between the body of the knight and his cross prevents it from registering as an emblem of superstition, especially because the cross is a sign of his enmity toward the Muslims he has promised to defeat.

The historical Knights of Malta swore to live chaste and defeat the enemies of Christianity, and the cross they wore on their cloaks indicated their dedication to both these virtues. Accordingly, one of the primary questions raised by Fletcher, Field, and Massinger's play is whether the cross can continue to function as a symbol of Christian faith after a knight has abandoned his vow of chastity. In the first few lines of the play, the villainous French knight Mountferrat swears by "the honour of this Christian crosse, / (In blood of Infidels so often dyde)" that he will gain Oriana's favor, by force or trickery if necessary (1.1.19-20). Throughout the play, his former glory as a defender of Malta is contrasted to the baseness of his lust and the dishonorable nature of his plots to win her love. Dramatically speaking, the cross presents the perfect opportunity for thematizing the kind of hypocrisy typically associated with unscrupulous Catholics. A small object pinned to the knight's black cloak, the cross could be misappropriated as easily as any other piece of clothing worn about the body. Mountferrat himself openly admits to the audience that he wears his cross to cover his misdeeds, just as "Churchmen so wear Cassoks" (1.1.161). But although the crosses in *Knight of Malta* indicate that the sign itself, once materialized, always has the potential to be separated from its wearer, this separation is never an indication of a change in the status of the cross: rather it is an indication that the wearer himself has become degraded. In other words, the play interrogates the status of the individual believer, not the outward sign of his faith. Although the stability of the cross may appear to be threatened by its association with characters such as Mountferrat, its value is firmly anchored in the rules and strictures of the Order itself.

As a symbol of Christian military might, the cross of Malta had its own complex history off stage. Elizabeth's government disparaged the Order's affiliation with the Catholic hierarchy in Rome, but nonetheless it lauded their military victories against the Turks. Furthermore, when considering the original performance of the play, it is hard not to see the Maltese cross as analogous to the cross of St. George. Although one stood for English national identity and the other symbolized an international alliance of Catholic knights, they both emblematized the Christian struggle against foreign "others." In this particular context, the cross was still an important part of militaristic imagery, as indicated by *The Marchants auiso* (1589). The verso of this work's title page contains an image of Constantine's fiery cross, alongside the words "*In hoc signo vinces*"—the phrase that appears both in Foxe and on Anne of Denmark's jeweled cross—and the image appears again at the head of the section containing "certain godly sentences" of moral advice. Individual parishes reinforced the sense of national pride associated with such representations by continuing to stage pageants dedicated to Saint George. The records from Norwich in 1549, for instance, call for "a coote Armour of white dammaske with a cros of redde dammaske. ... Item a Iackette of fustyan with a redde crosse." In 1621 the soldiers in the Chester pageant were still being outfitted "each man with a white Iacket St Georges crose on ther red breeches" and "white stockens red gardters" to go with it.[40] In Heywood and Rowley's *Fortune by Land and Sea* (1609), a friendly ship is identified by its sails, which bear the cross as an emblem of St. George. Although playgoers would undoubtedly have known the difference between the stylized appearance of the Maltese cross and their own St. George's badge, the cross worn on a shield or on an actor's body would have been recognizable to them as the sign separating Christians from the foreign infidels they fought against abroad.

The Knights of Malta themselves were familiar to many English readers through contemporary prose narratives. George Sandys, one of the most thorough observers of the Order, has relatively little to say on the subject of the cross, but he specifies that each knight had two of them: one was worn, like an official seal, on "ribands about their necks," while the other was attached to their cloaks in the form of "large white crosses set thereinto on the shoulder, of fine linen."[41] He also notes that during wartime the knight would change his white cross for a red one. William Lithgow's *Total Discourse* (1614) provides a particularly illuminating description of the handling of the cross during the induction ceremony and suggests that the cross used in *The Knight of Malta*'s final scene might have been as prominent as the altar:

> the Chappell clarke, a Priest of the order, receiving [the newly appointed knight] with divers ceremonies, taketh a blacke Cloak in his hand, and shewing him the white crosse that is fixed thereon, demandeth if he doth not beleeve that to be the signe of the Crosse, whereon *Jesus Christ* was crucified for our sinnes, he confesseth it, kissing the Crosse: After which, his receiver putteth the crosse of the Cloake upon the heart and left side of the new made Knight, saying: Receive this signe in the name of the Trinity. ... This done he knitteth the Cordon of the Cloake about him saying; Receive this yoake of our Lord that is sweet, and light, and thou shalt find rest for thy soule.[42]

---

[40]   David Galloway, ed., *Norwich 1540-1642* (Toronto: University of Toronto Press, 1984), 27; Clopper, *Chester*, 339. Such pageants also included banners with crosses on them. A closer dramatic precedent for the staging of *The Knight of Malta* can be found in *The Spanish Tragedy* (1587), in which Hieronimo instructs Balthazar to outfit himself like a knight of Rhodes for his play within a play.

[41]   Sandys, X1[v].

[42]   *A most delectable, and true discourse, of an admired and painefull peregrination* (London: Okes, 1614), Ddd[r-v].

This ceremonial process is duplicated almost to the letter during the induction of Miranda, the play's hero and Mountferrat's anti-type. During his induction into the Order, the bishop shows Miranda the cross and asks him, "[b]uildst thou thy faith on this?" to which Miranda replies, "[o]n him that di'd / On such a sacred figure, for our sins." The bishop then makes a display of pinning it to his left side, over his heart, "for / Thy encrease of faith, Christian defence, and service / To th'poor" (5.2.254-8). It is clear that Miranda knows his cues, which are inspired by accounts such as Lithgow's, but the script also goes out of its way to identify the cross as a remembrance of Christ's suffering, not an image of him.

To underscore the point, the playwrights provide an additional explanation of the cross's meaning. "With thy right hand protect, preserve it whole," the bishop urges Miranda, "[f]or if thou fighting 'gainst heavens enemies / Shalt fly away, abandoning the crosse / The Ensigne of thy holy Generall, / With shame thou justly shalt be robb'd of it, / Chas'd from our company, and cut away / As an infectious putrified limb" (260-66). In an attempt to assure its audience that there is nothing superstitious about this cross, the play emphasizes the cross's status as a sign of loyalty, not just to Christ but also to his earthly wars. Like the spurs and the sword, the knight's cross is a marker of his responsibility to the military order that was inextricably tied to religious rituals and objects. But as the bishop reminds Miranda, the cross can be taken away from him just as it was taken away from Mountferrat, and if he "abandons" it, he will be cut off from the body of the Order like a useless limb. The play indicates that it is the fragility of the knight's body, not the materiality of the cross, which poses a threat to social stability. Throughout Th*e Knight of Malta* the cross itself remains intact as a symbol of Christian virtue precisely because it is detachable from the human body.

The contrast between the dematerialized cross and the unstable male body is reinforced by Miranda's encounter with a non-Christian woman. When the governor of Malta, who is also Oriana's brother, tells Miranda that he must continue to live chaste, he gives him a probationer's robe, one with a smaller or different colored cross, "to keepe waking / Your noble spirits; and to breed ye pious" until he is ready to join the Order (3.1.202-3). The prominence of the novice's cross on his garment is foregrounded when Miranda nearly succumbs to his desire for his beautiful Muslim captive, Lucinda. The meeting between the two characters begins innocently as a kind of catechism on the subject of the Christian faith. In response to her questions, Miranda teaches Lucinda about the meaning of his cross, calling it "[t]rue sign of holinesse, / The badge of all his Souldiers that professe [God]" (3.4.25-6). When he changes the subject, however, and threatens to take advantage of her position as his captive by forcing her to yield her chastity, she uses his own words to rebuke his lack of Christian virtue. She directs his attention away from herself, recalling him to the meaning of the "remembrance" he wears on his body, warning him that if he touches her, "[e]ven in the act, ile make that crosse, and curse ye" (3.4.141, 149). Although she is not a Christian, Lucinda understands the proper function of the cross and threatens to appropriate its power as a talisman to ward off his advances. In the end, she triumphs over the weaker nature of her would-be ravisher, pointing out the significance of his cross and highlighting its status as an immaterial sign of virtue that must be immediately separated from any man whose bodily lust would corrupt it. Although Miranda later claims that he was merely testing Lucinda's virtue, the lingering question posed by this scene is whether he is truly ready to wear the cross and whether his inner virtues match his outward deeds.

The Knight of Malta draws an implicit contrast here between Lucinda, who later converts to Christianity, and Mountferrat's lascivious mistress, Abdella. At first glance, the differences between these two women appear to underscore the opposition between Miranda and Mountferrat; Mountferrat loses his cross because, despite his military valor, he cannot contain his desire for Miranda's beloved, Oriana, while Miranda eventually accepts her marriage to another man. Controlling his own passionate feelings, he pledges to uphold the rules of the Order and forego the pleasures of matrimony. But the play also suggests that perhaps Mountferrat has merely been unlucky in encountering a woman who encourages his vices. Mountferrat's sin, after all, is not cowardice but love, and the play hints at the fact that Miranda—who, like his rival, is in love with Oriana—has only narrowly escaped the same temptation. As the governor of Malta prepares to strip Mountferrat of his cross, he explains that despite his deeds on the battlefield, the Frenchman has become "[u]nworthy of that worthy signe thou wear'st" and is thus "unworthy our society." As Valetta points out, the cross has become Mountferrat's "burthen, not thy prop" (5.2.205, 213, 220). Like Lucinda's rebuke, this pronouncement is a warning to Miranda of what could happen to him if he gives in to his physical desires. Thus, although Miranda and Mountferrat are construed as opposites in the play's final ceremony, in which one is inducted and the other expelled from the Order, the play also indicates through this juxtaposition that any knight could easily become unworthy of the sacred object he has vowed to uphold and protect. In Malta, it is the knight himself—not the symbol of Christian virtue—which is expendable, and ultimately the play bears out the idea that the knight is nothing without the badge of his salvation.

A contemporary anecdote concerning an Italian man who lost his cross at a bathhouse underscores the important role crosses played in marking the individual identities of Christians living abroad. Upon entering the bathhouse, the man attaches a straw cross to his shoulder, hoping to preserve his sense of selfhood among the sea of naked bodies, only to have it stolen from him by another bather, who proclaims: "Now I am you: begone, you are dead!"[43] For this Christian, the cross constitutes and is equated with his own life—without it he is indistinguishable from any other person in the public baths. The story suggests that many Europeans living abroad shared his fear of losing their identities, and while the society of knights depicted in *The Knight of Malta* seems to afford its members protection from such threats, the play suggests that even within this community of the faithful one can easily slip and be exposed as a fraud, a nobody. In the very first scene of the play,

---

[43]   Neill, *Issues of Death*, 8-9.

Mountferrat picks up a cross, not recognizing it as his own until he compares his bare cloak with those of the other knights in the room. "White innocent signe," he exclaims, "that do'st abhorre to dwell / So neere the dim thoughts of this troubled breast, / And grace these graceless projects of my heart" (1.1.156-8). Having lost the one thing that secured his identity as a Christian knight, Mountferrat must subsequently be cut off from the Order like a "putrefied limb."

As an object attached to the body, the cross signifies the knight's membership in the Order and can be removed as his status changes, in order to preserve the stability of the emblem itself. Thus, for all its fascination with the ceremonies of the Order, *The Knight of Malta* adopts a distinctly post-Reformation attitude toward the cross: to secure its viability as the immaterial sign of Christian virtue, it must be removed from the material body of the knight at the first sign of his impurity. Even when the cross is described as a large, freestanding object, hanging in the governor's hall, it is associated with the protection of chastity rather than with adoration or worship. In this sense the play participates in a broader dramatic tradition in which the cross, stitched onto a costume or worn around the neck, registered not as Catholic but simply as Christian, reminding its audience of the plight of Europeans living in predominantly Muslim territories. When brandished by Christian exiles in the Mediterranean or the Levant, the cross registered as a positive sign of adherence to the true faith, a kind of international alliance rooted in values such as chastity that were supposedly practiced only by Westerners.

There is an important difference between plays in which individuals prove their virtue when isolated from their fellow Christians and *The Knight of Malta*, in which a community must sustain itself by enforcing conformity among its members, who are Christians of various nationalities. The characters in *The Knight of Malta*—Frenchmen, Italians, and other Europeans—wrestle with each other over who among them is worthy to wear the cross, and at no point in the play is the idea of a Turkish attack presented as an imminent threat. At the same time, many of the plays that tell stories of crusaders or pilgrims traveling alone in predominantly Muslim territories emphasize the same features of the cross highlighted in *The Knight of Malta*: its proximity to the body, the idea of its immateriality as a sign of virtue, and its talismanic qualities. In Heywood's *The Four Prentices of London* (1594), for instance, the cross is used to identify a Christian knight who has been separated from his company. Eustace, one of the play's title characters, tells his long-lost sister that although he is "an exile from the Christian Campe / Yet in my heart I weare the Crosse of Christ."[44] Through this pronouncement he confirms his rightful place among the Christians by pointing out his enduring attachment to the cross. Importantly, Eustace identifies himself not by his garments but by his inner virtues. By asserting that he wears the cross "in his heart" he goes one step further than Miranda and the other knights of Malta, demonstrating a wholly dematerialized attitude toward what would otherwise be a mere ornament of faith.

---

[44] *The foure prentises of London with the conquest of Jerusalem* (London: Okes, 1632), H3ʳ.

Yet there would have been a notable tension between Eustace's statements and the reality of the theatrical production, for it is likely that the other characters wore crosses on their garments as well as "in their hearts." The play acknowledges the interplay between the cross's materiality and the immaterial values associated with it by assigning special powers to the physical object, and like *The Knight of Malta*, *The Four Prentices of London* confirms that power by demonstrating that even infidels can recognize it. "There is some vertue in the Crosse they weare," a Muslim soldier marvels. "It makes them strong as Lyons, swift as Roes" (K4ʳ). Once again, however, this is part of the rhetoric of the dialogue, not the action of the play, in which the cross is simply a sign worn on a costume, as in the St. George pageants. Thus the text participates in a long popular tradition of using the cross in a nationalist context as a material object with abstract virtues attached to it.

Rowley's *A Shoemaker a Gentleman* (1608) sets its imperiled Christians in Roman Britain, but it bears many of the same features as the plays set in Jerusalem or the Mediterranean. In this text, an angel honors the devotions of a loyal Christian virgin by using "the sign that holy Christians wear, / When in the field their standards they up-rear / Against the foes of heaven" to transform the fountain in her courtyard into a spring with miraculous healing powers.[45] But the transformation is not described as unprecedented; rather, the Angel's words are there to reference actual saints' lives and to place the virtuous Winifred within this line of narrative conventions and within the dramatic tradition of depicting Christian soldiers. Later, when her confessor Amphiabell converts a Roman lord, he urges him to "[w]ear but this emblem of a Christian, / Not as a thing material / To avail you, but for the strengthening of your memory" (2.2.26-8). In Rowley's play, the cross is doubly displaced from the context of Catholic superstition: first by being given talismanic powers associated with the war against the infidels and second by stressing its immaterial status as a remembrance rather than an idol. Moreover, the cross is not assigned a particular visual prominence within the theatrical production. On this point *A Shoemaker a Gentleman* diverges from *The Knight of Malta*. Due to its foreign setting and the rhetorical distance it establishes between the corruptible body and the incorruptible cross, the later play gives the object a more active role in the dramatic action.

Revisiting the knights of Malta three years after the first performance of the play he co-authored with Fletcher and Field, Massinger composed another tragicomedy about the Order in which the characters of Mountferrat and Miranda are fused into a single knight. Bertoldo, another knight of the Order, is ostensibly the hero of *The Maid of Honour* (1621), but when he travels abroad and is temporarily seduced by a foreign princess it becomes clear that his true beloved, Camiola, is the play's moral center. Unlike Miranda, Bertoldo falls in love with a Muslim woman who does not rebuke him for violating his vow of chastity. In fact, her sexual aggression is reminiscent of Abdella in *The Knight of Malta* and, like Mountferrat, Bertoldo

---

[45]   *A Shoemaker, a Gentleman*, ed. Trudi Laura Darby (New York: Routledge, 2003), 1.3.103-5.

is soon stripped of his cross as a result of his behavior. He is forgiven, however, when he realizes his mistake, repents, and returns to Camiola. In a less ceremonial re-working of the final scene from the earlier play, she urges him to "resume your order" and continue "fighting / Bravely against the enemies of our faith," before his fellow knight restores "*the white crosse*" to his breast. In general, this play is less concerned than the earlier one with affirming the status of the cross as a marker of the knight's Christian identity because its focus is the chastity of the Christian woman. Unlike Oriana, who obeys her brother's command to marry, Camiola becomes a nun, changing her mirror for a "holy booke" and her jewels for beads.[46] But although the emphasis has shifted, both texts are clearly flirting with a positive outlook on Catholic institutions such as Camiola's nunnery and the Order of the Knights of Malta, while ensuring that the cross itself remains a sign of nonsectarian Christian faith, framed by the Protestant language of immateriality. Crucially, that dematerialized virtue is dramatized through its association with Christian bodies, and it is these bodies that are the focus of the audience's sympathy.

Although Elizabeth herself acknowledged the important role the Knights of Malta and other foreign Catholics played in the struggle against the Turks, within the borders of Protestant England the spread of popery was a greater threat than that of Muslim invasion, and every materialization of the cross was potentially controversial. Thus plays with English settings are generally more cautious—or outright polemical—in their use of crosses and crucifixes. There are also a handful of texts that provide chronological rather than geographic separation between their characters and their audience members while shifting their focus to England. In what follows I consider yet another dramatic strategy, one that, like the majority of the plays discussed in this chapter, centers on the body of the individual believer. Broadly speaking, the plays that depict mythical episodes from England's remote past follow *The Knight of Malta* in associating the cross with the defense of female chastity.

In Chettle and Munday's *The Death of Robert Earl of Huntington* (1598), the cross is presented sympathetically, but from a deeply nostalgic point of view that creates the necessary distance between audience members and the Catholic characters on stage. The England depicted in this play is a green world full of jovial friars and mythical heroes, so it is not particularly shocking when, on his deathbed, Robert calls for his "beades and Primer" and instructs his friends to lay "[u]pon my brest the crosse." These ornaments are acceptable tokens of his faith rather than signs of popery, and the play passes over this speech without any hint that we are to read his behavior as superstitious. More strikingly, Robert's beloved Matilda becomes a kind of virgin saint after his death, taking shelter in an abbey after the king attempts to compromise her virtue. When the monks and nuns turn against her, urging her to give up her chastity, she bravely "*[d]rawes a Crucifix*" to ward them off. "In his name that did suffer for my sinne, / And by this blessed signe, I conjure you," she cries, thinking that they have metamorphosed

---

46   Philip Massinger, *The maid of honour* (London: I. B., 1632), L4ᵛ.

into demons: "Avoide yee fiends, and cease to trouble mee."[47] As in *The Knight of Malta*, the symbol of the cross functions in this play as a magical talisman, but here the symbol is dramatically materialized in a hand-held crucifix that is rendered acceptable because of chronological rather than geographical distance.

Another very material cross appears in Anthony Brewer's *The Lovesick King* (1617), described on its title page as an *"English tragical history."* The tragedy begins when the abbey of St. Swithin is attacked by soldiers and its inhabitants are threatened with rape. Their attempts to protect themselves are first described indirectly, as observers watch the aged abbot climb the walls "with his holy Cross / between his hands" to plead for mercy (A1ᵛ). When the walls are breached, the audience is given a glimpse of the frantic ceremonial preparations: "Alarm. *A great Cry within. Enter Abbot bearing a Cross, Cartesmunda with two Tapers burning, which she placeth on the Altar, two or three Nuns following"* (A2ᵛ)· As in Chettle and Munday's play, the nunnery is represented here as the fort of chastity, and surprisingly, the characters' genuine devotion is indicated by an altar, a processional cross, and a pair of tapers. This blatant reference to English Catholicism is understandable only when we consider that the setting of the play is England's distant past, rather than its recent trials. Additionally, the nuns are positioned as virgins under attack; like the cross itself, the members of this Catholic institution were seen as less threatening in such circumstances.

Generally speaking, then, these plays successfully reference the mysterious powers associated with the cross because their characters are part of a nostalgic picture of a defunct religion. There is another principle at work here, however. Simply put, it is easier to stress the virtues associated with the cross when it is attached to characters who are weak and defenseless. Dekker and Massinger's *The Virgin Martyr* (1620), which similarly displaces its religious objects into early Christian history, provides a striking example of this particular tactic. This play presents the cross sympathetically by associating it with a virtuous martyr rather than a head of state; specifically, the cross is connected to Dorothea, a Christian who is persecuted and eventually killed for her beliefs by the governor of Cesaerea.[48] In one sense, then, the cross property in this play stands in clear contrast to the pagan idols Dorothea abhors, but in another sense it is the most unusual materialization of the cross in all the surviving play scripts. After Dorothea's death, she sends

---

[47]   *The death of Robert, Earle of Huntington Otherwise called Robin Hood of merrie Sherwodde* (London: [Bradock], 1601), D1ᵛ, K2ᵛ.

[48]   As Alexander Leggatt has argued, "the Christians defying pagan Rome can be seen as Protestants defying Catholic Rome" (*Jacobean Public Theater* [London: Routledge, 1992], 62). Leggatt complicates this rather broad observation by speculating that when Dorothea is tied to a pillar and beaten before her decapitation, the audience may be prompted to think of a crucifixion. There is no particular evidence in the text for this intriguing conclusion, although Leggatt's reasoning supports Huston Diehl's argument that Protestant martyrdom was a vital part of the theater, just as theatricality was a vital part of Foxe's depictions of Protestant martyrdom.

a basket of flowers and fruit from heaven to convert her former tormentor, Theophilus. In addition to the miraculous food, he finds a *"crosse of Flowers"* at the bottom of the basket and promptly uses it to repel a demon (5.1.138). These bizarre events can be partially explained by the fact that *The Virgin Martyr* was put on at the Red Bull, where the presence of demons, angels, and crosses would come as no surprise to regular playgoers, but I would argue that this text also follows a larger tradition of altering the materiality of the cross to avoid the charge of treason or superstition. By presenting a cross of flowers, a property with no real life counterpart, the playwrights take this strategy a step further than the plays which displace the cross into foreign contexts and/or attempt to dematerialize it.

By contrast, my final two texts allude directly to a particular set of crosses that survived the first wave of violent iconoclasm in England. Both plays adhere to the theatrical strategies I have outlined above: they distance their crosses from the threat of idolatry by presenting them in foreign contexts, they attach them to the bodies of individual believers, and they associate them with characters who are effectively powerless and therefore unthreatening. But these two plays, John Webster's *The White Devil* (1612) and Dekker and Ford's *The Spanish Gipsy* (1623), are extraordinary in that their stage properties directly resemble actual crucifixes and invoke recognizable recusant practices, thus allowing the theater companies to explore the positive role these objects played in the lives of English families. These stage crosses reference the small crucifixes, like the one mentioned in the Vaux inventory, which held recusant families together in the face of official pressure to conform. By taking into account the role religious objects played in individual English families and family legacies, the final section of this chapter reveals the theater's interest in treating crucifixes and their owners from a more intimate perspective.

The Domestication of the Cross

In a poem written sometime before his death in 1612 but not published until 1618, Sir John Harrington addresses his wife on the subject of her private devotions. Although it deals with many of the doctrinal issues surrounding the use of material objects in religious worship, the epigram has a warm, almost conversational feel. "My deare," he begins,

> that in your close for devotion,
> To kindle in your brest some godly motion,
> You contemplate, and of your eyes doe fixe
> On some Saints picture, or the Crucifixe;

Tis not amisse; be it of stone or mettle,
It serveth in thy mind good thoughts to settle.[49]

The logic of Harrington's couplets is breezy and practical; if the intention behind the prayer is to settle her thoughts and stir "godly motion" in her heart, the effect cannot be idolatrous. He does warn her against kneeling before the crucifix, which must be used "kindly" rather than superstitiously, but if she treats it like a book, "thereby thy remembrance to acquaint, / With life or death, or vertue of the Saint," she can certainly not be criticized (ll. 19, 9-10). In this he echoes the sentiment expressed in Nicolas Sanders's *A Treatise of the Images of Christ*, which suggests that, "if we see the Image of Christ crucified, we straight lay aside the brass, iron or wood where upon that Image was drawn or made, and we apprehend Christ Himself."[50] As for those who call the crucifix a mere "stocke," a lifeless piece of wood or metal, Harrington concludes that such a person should be chided for abusing her own lord and savior: "Such a one were a stocke, I straight should gather, / That would confesse a stocke to be her father" (ll. 31-2).

Harrington's attitude in this poem is remarkable on a number of different levels. It adopts the argument put forward by writers such as Donne that the sign of the cross could function successfully as a memory aid and extends it even to crucifixes and images of saints. The tone of his address is also noteworthy in the way it demystifies these controversial Catholic objects. He compares the picture of Christ to the picture he keeps of his wife, arguing that in both cases the subject of the image must never be forgotten, and he even accepts the crucifix as a standard part of his household furniture. The poem suggests that the crucifix can be viewed as a positive element of post-Reformation practice when contextualized within the home and anchored in a shared set of family values. Although his open appreciation for the object—and for his wife's devotion to it—is unusual, Harrington's was not the only home that contained a crucifix in post-Reformation England, as documents such as the Vaux inventory indicate. What is unusual about Harrington is that he was not a Catholic writer. Rather, his views indicate the extent to which some moderate Protestants were willing to tolerate material forms of worship as long as they were carefully regulated and confined to the home.

Webster's *The White Devil* provides another answer to the question of how objects associated with traditional religion could be used in sixteenth- and seventeenth-century England, and like Harrington's poem it focuses on the domestic sphere. Set in Catholic Italy, the play contains not one but two crucifixes, and it reproduces a set of anti-Catholic stereotypes that appeared regularly on the early modern stage. Early in the play, Duke Bracciano's wife expresses her devotion to her husband by kissing his portrait, a gesture Protestants would have labeled idol worship. Even more shocking is the performance put on by Bracciano's enemies,

---

[49]   *Epigrams both pleasant and serious, written by that all-worthy knight, Sir Iohn Harrington: and never before printed* (London: [Purslowe], 1618), M6ᵛ-7ʳ.
[50]   Southern, 100.

who disguise themselves as monks and pretend to comfort him during his final moments with a traditional Catholic ritual. But *The White Devil* is not a standard piece of Protestant polemic. Rather, it uses these apparently stereotypical images as a foil for its sympathetic depiction of a small, jeweled crucifix, a Catholic object that functions within the play as the embodiment of family unity. On one level, then, Webster's play deftly skirts the problem of idolatry by distancing Cornelia's crucifix from any kind of religious ceremony and focusing its audience's attention instead on the pathos of a family's disintegration. Through its depiction of Cornelia's struggle to preserve the values she associates with this heirloom, *The White Devil* allows the specific resonance of the family crucifix to come to the forefront. The play does not, however, manage to avoid the associations between crucifixes and idolatry altogether. Instead, the complex interplay between Cornelia's crucifix and a second stage crucifix works to ensure that audience members will not confuse her heirloom with an emblem of idol worship.

Cornelia is one of the few sympathetic characters in *The White Devil*, but she is also the mother of Flamineo, its malcontent anti-hero, and her crucifix becomes the focus of the tragic family drama he provokes in Act 5, scene 2. Flamineo has been arguing with his younger brother, Marcello, and the two have agreed to a duel. Rather than staging their fight, this scene unexpectedly juxtaposes the sword and the crucifix:

> *Marcello.* Was not this crucifix my father's?
> *Cornelia.* Yes.
> *Marcello.* I have heard you say, giving my brother suck,
>   He took the crucifix between his hands *Enter Flamineo,*
>   And broke a limb off.
> *Cornelia.* Yes, but tis mended.
> *Flamineo.* I have brought your weapon back. *Flamineo runs Marcello through.*
> *Cornelia.* Ha, O my horror!
> *Marcello.* You have brought it home indeed.[51]

By bringing "home" his brother's weapon Flamineo emphasizes the connection between the broken crucifix and his broken family. Marcello's death speech, delivered a few lines later, provides an even more explicit link between the desecration of the cross and the desecration of the family unit; he urges his mother to "remember what I told / Of breaking off the crucifix. Farewell, / There are some sins which heaven doth duly punish / In a whole family" (5.2.18-21). The crucifix calls to mind the family tree, which Flamineo has violated by severing one of its branches, and in this scene its theatrical power is associated with its role as a repository of personal memories. Moreover, Cornelia's grief for her son's death might well have evoked Mary sorrowing over Jesus—especially if the actor were

    [51] *The White Devil*, ed. John Russell Brown (Manchester: Manchester University Press, 1996), 5.2.10-14.

to take up the body of the dead Marcello. Yet the play also creates a wholly new kind of iconoclasm in the breaking of the crucifix, for it is not the figure of Christ but the arm of the cross that has been damaged, and the threat of further disruption comes not from outside the family but from within it. Cornelia's heirloom is still a symbol of the Catholic faith, but because of the context in which it is presented it carries an affective charge rather than an overtly religious one, signifying her piety within the realm of the family. I argue here that the precedent for this stage object, which is valued as an heirloom rather than an iconic emblem of Catholicism, lies in the social history of post-Reformation England.

As historians such as Marie Rowlands have shown, English recusancy took many forms and was not always the focus of public controversy. One of the less overtly controversial items associated with recusant life was the "family" crucifix, which functioned as part of an inheritance system and played an important role in the lives of private citizens throughout the sixteenth and early seventeenth centuries. In fact, as we have seen, one of the primary reasons the visitors charged with enforcing religious injunctions had so much difficulty eliminating the use of crosses and crucifixes in England was that in many parishes individuals were hiding them in their homes. In the decades after the Reformation, therefore, objects such as crucifixes and rosary beads continued to function as important anchors of private devotion, but they also served as markers of family unity passed down from generation to generation among those who still adhered to the traditional religion. Cherished by their individual owners, these objects also accumulated a considerable affective value over the years as part of secular inheritance systems. By foregrounding Cornelia's crucifix as a family heirloom, *The White Devil* references the actions of individuals who were determined to preserve Catholic objects as a means of maintaining continuity within their families, and as a result it complicates any simple connection between Catholic objects and idolatry.

Like many recusants, Cornelia has inherited her crucifix from a family member, in this case her husband, and she hopes to pass it on to her children someday. As the events of the play unfold, however, both the status of the crucifix and the stability of Cornelia's family are called into question. Cornelia attaches emotional weight to her husband's crucifix because it was his, and because it connects her to a set of familiar social customs and beliefs. But the fact that the heirloom is broken dramatizes the way in which inherited objects and the traditions associated with them can be jeopardized as they pass from hand to hand, even within the domestic sphere. Thus, although *The White Devil* assigns the crucifix a positive role within the family unit, Cornelia's desire to secure its meaning as a part of an inheritance system is complicated by its fluctuating value within the play. In making the crucifix susceptible to desecration at the hands of her son, Flamineo, the play acknowledges the changing status of religious objects that circulated as family heirlooms, but it also suggests that they maintained an emotional charge even as their worth was being renegotiated.

In order to access the positive potential of the family crucifix, *The White Devil* must overcome typical associations linking religious objects with Catholic superstition. Whereas the Elizabethan homilist announces that the practice of venerating images is in constant danger of being resurrected whenever popish objects are present, this play addresses the survival of Catholic objects by dramatizing the destruction of a small crucifix within the domestic sphere, in which the threat from the inside, from the rotten branch of the family tree, is more real than any possibility that the object will be worshiped on stage. Inviting them to identify with Cornelia, who is struggling to protect her heirloom and the values attached to it, the play prompts audience members to reconsider an object that most Protestants treated as idolatrous by demonstrating how that object could be re-inflected in a new context. Michael O'Connell has argued that early modern playwrights were deeply aware of the antitheatrical critiques linking the theater with Catholic superstition and that this awareness was one of the major forces shaping their work. In this section of the chapter I make a slightly different claim about the way early modern drama responded to antitheatrical rhetoric and the way it staged religious practices. In addition to positing, as O'Connell does, that dramatists developed their craft in opposition to Protestant antitheatricalists, I want to suggest that in some cases the drama encouraged playgoers to step outside the language of iconoclasm altogether.

The White Devil separates Cornelia's crucifix from what Protestants called the ornaments of papist superstition by supplying another crucifix, one that directly invokes familiar anti-Catholic stereotypes. If Cornelia's small, jeweled crucifix is positively inflected as a key element of a family inheritance system, its worth determined by the virtuous woman who continues to believe in its power as a token of family unity, this second crucifix property is a counterfeit liturgical object, falsely appropriated by the men who use it to torture the dying Bracciano. The theme of papist hypocrisy is especially prevalent in this scene, as his murderers— dressed like Capuchin monks—mock the duke with a fake crucifix, the apparent symbol of his salvation, before brutally strangling him. The two properties are also physically distinct, for the property Lodovico and Gasparo taunt Bracciano with is a hand-held object, while Cornelia's crucifix is a piece of jewelry worn about the body. Despite the lack of material resemblance between the two implements, however, the play creates a thematic connection between them that complicates the apparently stereotypical aspects of the revengers' crucifix.

According to the stage direction, Lodovico and Gasparo appear to Bracciano "*in the habit of Capuchins,*" outfitted with "*a Crucifix and hallowed candle*" (5.3.116-18). Murmuring a standard set of Latin phrases, the two murderers perform an imitation of the *commendatio animae*, a Catholic ritual designed to comfort the dying and commit their souls to god.[52] Forms of this ceremony are common to the *ars moriendi*

---

52   Richard Allen Cave reports that in the 1969 Old Vic production, "on Gasparo's command that Brachiano be strangled in private, Lodovico took a grim pleasure in doing so with the aid of the rosary and crucifix that he had but lately used while pretending to administer Holy Unction to the Duke" (*The White Devil and The Duchess of Malfi: Text and Performance* [Basingstoke, Hampshire: Macmillan Education, 1988], 51).

genre, in which the good Christian is lauded for his or her fortitude in the final moments of life. John Fisher's account of the death of Henry VII in 1509, for instance, praises the king's piety by describing his abiding attachment to the symbol of his salvation: "The ymage of the crucyfyxe many a tyme that day full devoutly he dyd beholde with grete reverence, lyftynge up his head as he myght, holdynge up his handes before it, & often embracynge it in his armes & with grete devocion kyssyng it, & betynge ofte his brest."[53] The *commendatio* is also described in several English liturgical guides, including the *Monumenta Ritualia*, which instructs the dying man to "[p]ut alle thi trust in [Christ's] passion and in his deth, and thenke onli theron, and non other thing." The dying man's confessor, meanwhile, is instructed to "have the crosse to fore the."[54] Parodying this tradition, the revengers pretend to offer the crucifix as an image of his salvation, until, left alone with their victim, they begin to curse him, telling Bracciano that he will be damned to hell for his sins, and "forgotten / Before thy funeral service" (5.3.163-4).

We can read this scene as both a mockery of "the good death" and as an indirect attack on Catholicism itself, for by the time the play was first performed the Church of England had dismissed the *commendatio* and other traditional ceremonies as dangerous forms of papist superstition. The hypocritical actions of the revengers, who dress as holy men and pretend to comfort their enemy, echo standard Protestant rhetoric used to critique the false trappings of the priesthood. Priests were accused of being as hollow as stage players, and the mass itself was said to be no more than a set of gestures designed to provoke blind idolatry; Thomas Becon even called the priest's robes "game-players' garments."[55] The falseness of the revengers, who hide their true intentions by donning the clothing and gestures of Capuchin monks, mirrors the falseness that Protestants perceived as being at the heart of the Catholic faith, and the actors playing Lodovico and Gasparo become even more "false" when their characters take on deceptive roles within the fiction of the play. Construed in this way, the crucifix is nothing more than an element of the characters' false show. Emptied of its sacrality, and used satirically as a weapon against Catholicism, its function in the scene seems to directly mirror its function in *The White Devil*.

But although Act 5, scene 3 evokes well-known stereotypes concerning priests and players, the self-conscious use of the crucifix as a property within the fiction emphasizes the potential for abuse rather than prompting the audience to dismiss this aspect of Catholic practice altogether. Because the audience knows

---

[53]   Duffy, 324.

[54]   Ibid., 315. The ceremony of the *commendatio* was apparently still practiced in Henrietta Maria's private chapel, where a group of Capuchins administered last rites to Father Richard Blount in 1638: "The voices of his Brethren mingled with those of the Capuchin Friars in that commendation of a departed soul which for so long a time in England had been uttered only in secret and almost in whispers" (John Morris, *The Troubles of Our Catholic Forefathers Related by Themselves*, vol. 1 [London: Burns and Oats, 1872], 79).

[55]   Becon, 259-60.

that these are not real Capuchins and that their crucifix is a mere device, there is no threat that they will promote idolatry through their actions. The ceremony is rendered ineffective from the moment they don their disguises. Moreover, this scene contains moments of poignancy that capitalize on the sympathetic quality of Cornelia's crucifix, which appears in the previous sequence. The play takes Bracciano's suffering seriously and acknowledges the fact that the crucifix, which should be used to comfort the dying man, has instead become an instrument of torture. By taunting Bracciano with salvation and then confronting him with the consequences of his sin, Lodovico and Gasparo are, like Flamineo, waging an attack upon the traditional objects and customs that preserve social memory. The real duke, whose story was famous enough to make its way into a London playhouse, is here depicted as a man whose life will be summarily erased from the annals of history. Ironically, Webster's theatrical creation, a mere fiction, ultimately succeeds in memorializing Bracciano's life.

If these scenes are similar in their treatment of the issue of remembrance, they are also consciously designed to play off one another, for the spectacular nature of the revengers' false *commendatio* masks the social problem manifested in Act 5, scene 2. The hypocrisy practiced by the fake Capuchins overshadows the more serious implications of Bracciano's murder, namely, the reality that his family can no longer hold itself together through traditional religious practices. In both scenes, Webster uses the crucifix to concretize the threat posed by iconoclastic attacks on memory-laden objects and practices. Although the play ultimately reinforces the controversial nature of the crucifix in post-Reformation England, recalling familiar rhetoric about the evils of papist superstition, both objects promote a more compassionate view of Catholic practice by pointing to the interpenetration of religious rituals and social traditions. This combination is not always fortuitous, however, for the tragedy of *The White Devil* arises when the commingling of sacred and secular concerns—exemplified in Flamineo's campaign to gain influence at court—threatens to corrupt the values manifested in objects such as the crucifix. Thus the play also questions the assumption that objects such as the family crucifix can continue to function in the same way from generation to generation.

Although the Reformation introduced a unique set of problems for Catholic families by forcing them to remove sacred objects from parish churches and perform traditional rituals in secret, Cornelia's belief in the crucifix as the anchor of her family's stability can be traced back through a rich tradition of pre-Reformation practices in England. Gail McMurray Gibson reports, for example, that in the early sixteenth century Sir William Clopton willed to his son "my crosse of gold which I where dayly abowtte my necke." Clopton's bequest was contingent on the son's promise that he and all his heirs would in turn "lenne this same crosse unto women of honeste being with child the tyme of ther laboure and immediately to be surely delivered unto hours ayen."[56] The language of Clopton's will explicitly highlights

---

[56] *The Theater of Devotion: East Anglian Drama and Society in the Late Middle Ages* (Chicago: University of Chicago Press, 1989), 61.

the social value of the gift and suggests that the affective meaning attached to such objects is more likely to endure when they are attached to a stable parish community. In the decades immediately following the Reformation, however, Catholic objects were more likely to be confined to the family, and the historical record provides several seventeenth-century examples of jeweled crucifixes that circulated within individual inheritance systems. In 1614 the Earl of Northhampton bequeathed to the Earl of Suffolk a diamond cross that he, in turn, had inherited from his mother. And in 1623 the head of another prominent recusant household, Viscount Montague, bequeathed his gold reliquary cross "which I usually were about my necke" to his son Francis.[57] It is these aristocratic bequests that resonate most powerfully with Cornelia's "mended" crucifix.

It is also worth remembering, however, that religious objects sometimes made their way into private homes because they had been neglected or were under attack. During the final years of Elizabeth's reign, a churchwarden named Roger Martyn recalled rescuing the crucifix from his church in Long Melford, Suffolk. "[I]n my aisle called 'Jesus aisle,'" he recalls in a diary written sometime around 1600, "[there was] a table with a crucifix on it, with the two thieves hanging, on every side one, which is in my house decayed; and the same I hope my heirs will repair and restore again one day."[58] In order to secure its value and prevent it from falling into the hands of the ecclesiastical visitors, Martyn kept the crucifix in his home and instructed his children to return it to the church when conditions became more favorable. But Martyn's own account acknowledges a problem with the crucifix: namely, it is already "decayed." By making the rood a part of his household, Martyn places his trust in the stability of his family, and in the continuance of intangible beliefs through the preservation of tangible objects. On the other hand, Martyn's journal does not tell us whether the crucifix was ever repaired or returned to the church, and thus it raises more questions than it answers about the life histories of such objects in post-Reformation England. For English recusants such as Martyn, crucifixes were not merely the "sorry relics" of a bygone age.[59] They may have been defaced or dilapidated, but throughout the sixteenth and seventeenth centuries they continued to figure prominently within the inheritance systems of individual families.

Although the rood described in Roger Martyn's diary is an exception to the general rule that parishioners only took small crosses into their homes, the issues raised by this narrative echo those addressed by Webster's play: namely, can a sacred object continue to serve as a conduit of religious traditions in a secular context? And how will its status change as it passes from one generation to the next?

---

[57]   Scarisbrick, *Jewellery in Britain*, 72, 100.

[58]   David Cressy and Lori Anne Ferrell, eds, *Religion and Society in Early Modern England*, 2nd ed. (New York: Routledge, 2005), 11.

[59]   Christopher Haigh, *English Reformations*, 294. In annual inventories, churchwardens regularly defended their parish's possession of altars or crosses by asserting that these objects had long been defaced or "brent."

Although circulation may put the object itself at risk of desecration, *The White Devil* suggests that despite—or perhaps because of—these threats of violence, items such as Cornelia's crucifix continue to carry a powerful affective charge. The focus, then, is not on Flamineo's act of iconoclasm but its aftermath. Iconoclasts often made the breaking of idols into a public spectacle, thereby demystifying them in front of the largest possible number of believers, but rather than replicating this highly theatrical aspect of Protestant policy, the play uses the story of the crucifix as a backdrop to the fratricide. The play does not stage the actual breaking of the limb—such a scene might distract from the spectacle of Marcello's death—and as a result, it draws most directly not on narratives of iconoclasm but on the popular practices surrounding the persistence of Catholic objects.

The loss of a religious object could be devastating to churchwardens and individual parishioners, but in many cases the defacing or breaking of Catholic objects was a necessary condition for their survival. In 1583, a resident of Kelvedon named Thomas Baker was forced to defend himself on a charge of "keeping idols, and images" in his home, although he stoutly asserted that because they had been damaged they were innocuous.[60] For Baker and other recusants, resistance to religious conformity manifested itself in a willingness to hold onto all the physical remnants of the traditional faith, even those that were broken or ruined, and their attachment to these objects was often tolerated as long as they were deemed unusable. In the London injunctions of 1605, Bishop Richard Vaughn asked specifically "[w]hether there be any in your parish who are noted, known, or suspected to conceale or keepe hidden in their houses any masse bookes, portesses, breviaries, or other bookes of popery or superstition, or any chalices, copes, vestments, albes, or other ornaments of superstition, *uncancelled or undefaced*, which is to be coniectured, they doe keepe for a day, as they call it?"[61] One of the first statutes enacted during James's reign, "An Act to prevent and avoid dangers which may grow by Popish recusants," specified that any "crucifix or other relic of price" found in a private home should be defaced and returned to its owner.[62] This statute sets out to preserve the rights of property owners while giving officials legal permission to ensure the desecration of potentially dangerous objects. But such leniency did not change the fact that even small, broken crucifixes made the reformers uneasy. Just as strict Protestants feared the seductive power of visual displays on the public stage, so they feared the influence such objects might exert on individual worshipers. Webster's play picks up on this anxiety, and on the issues surrounding the survival of Catholic objects in private homes, but it tells the story from the point of view of the owners rather than the iconoclasts. What is at

---

[60]   F. G. Emmison, *Elizabethan Life: Morals & the Church Courts* (Chelmsford: Essex County Council, 1973), 96.

[61]   Fincham, *Visitation Articles and Injunctions of the Early Stuart Church*, vol. 1, 37. My italics.

[62]   G. W. Prothero, ed., *Select Statutes and Other Constitutional Documents Illustrative of the Reigns of Elizabeth and James I*, 4th ed. (Oxford: Clarendon Press, 1913), 267-8.

stake in the play, then, is not whether Cornelia's faith will promote acts of idolatry but whether she can preserve the traditional values associated with her crucifix.

Once a community in and of itself, the family and its traditions become subject to the violent tendencies of the court as *The White Devil* approaches its tragic conclusion. In the wake of Marcello's murder, for instance, Cornelia bemoans the fact that the proper function of her winding sheet has been horribly displaced: "This sheet / I have kept this twenty year, and every day / Hallowed it with my prayers. I did not think / He should have wore it" (5.4.70-73). Cornelia believes that her virtue is rooted in her sons, and their quarrel ultimately destroys her, but that destruction is located very concretely in objects such as the winding sheet and the crucifix, the physical connections between family stability and traditional faith. Rather than adopting his mother's crucifix, Flamineo has broken it, and rather than burying her in her hallowed winding sheet he has caused Marcello to be buried in it. More so than the winding sheet, the crucifix clearly references Catholic practices, but both objects demonstrate the problem of maintaining the affective meaning of an object from generation to generation, even within a single family. In examining Cornelia's role as the purveyor of family heirlooms, it is important to pay attention to the name Webster chose to give her. Cornelia was the mother of the Gracchi, two of the most renowned landowners in Republican Rome, and she gained notoriety for her unflinching devotion to her sons. When one of her wealthy houseguests encouraged her to display her collection of jewelry, Cornelia is said to have pointed to her sons and replied, "[t]here, madam, the richest jewels in my house."[63] Along the same lines, Webster's character views her children and her crucifix as two portions of the same inheritance, the best gifts her husband has left her.

Even as it links Cornelia to the stoic Roman matron, however, *The White Devil* draws upon the social realities of post-Reformation religion in England in order to challenge the assumption that the meaning of objects such as Cornelia's crucifix can be fixed. By contrasting the virtue of Cornelia's crucifix, a family heirloom, with the fake Capuchins' malevolent appropriation of a crucifix in Act 5, scene 3, the play suggests that the value of a given object is determined in part by the way the theater appropriates these objects for its own purposes. Their counterfeit performance thus reflects the perceived similarity between Catholicism and theater, and the play uses this association to vilify the revengers, while Cornelia's character promotes a more positive view of the crucifix as an integral part of an inheritance system. *The White Devil* does acknowledge, however, that objects such as Cornelia's heirloom often survive only because they have been somehow altered or adapted to suit their new surroundings. Through the use of both stage properties the play emphasizes the fact that corruption within the family can threaten both sacred objects and the faith systems associated with them once they have been removed from a purely religious context.

---

[63]   Charles R. Forker, *Skull Beneath the Skin: The Achievement of John Webster* (Carbondale: Southern Illinois University Press, 1986), 48.

The White Devil's use of two crucifix properties is certainly exceptional; because of their highly contested status in post-Reformation England such objects were seldom brought on stage. But Webster's is not the only Jacobean play to present a crucifix as a key element of a family inheritance system. In Dekker and Ford's *The Spanish Gipsy* (1623) a crucifix property allows Clara, a young woman who has been raped, to recognize and claim her right to marry the young nobleman who ravished her. Rather than staging the breakdown of the family unit, this tragicomedy presents its crucifix as an object whose value is only temporarily called into question as it circulates from hand to hand. And while the themes of *The Spanish Gipsy* parallel those of *The White Devil*, the tragicomic ending of Dekker and Ford's play—in which the young man's father correctly identifies the crucifix as his son's and oversees his marriage to the heroine—requires that the crucifix remain intact as an indicator of aristocratic virtue and family unity. In *The Spanish Gipsy*, the recovery of the crucifix successfully preserves the family honor of both the rapist and his victim while simultaneously forging a new alliance between their two noble houses.

Although *The White Devil* exposes the corruption of Cornelia's family by juxtaposing the story of the crucifix with Flamineo's act of fratricide, this play uses its crucifix to smooth over the events of the play's opening scenes, in which a hot-headed nobleman named Roderigo decides to rape a girl he has never seen before, an attractive "thing" he notices on the public road late at night. His companion, Lewys, reluctantly agrees to help him kidnap the girl, but since neither of them is looking at her face, Lewys fails to recognize her as his own betrothed. For his part, Roderigo is hardly interested in her facial features. In fact, Clara's personality does not emerge at all until after the rape, which happens off stage. But she is eloquent in condemning the deed afterward, calling her attacker a "[d]isease of natures sloth; / Birth of some monstrous sinne, or scourge of virtue."[64]

Roderigo attempts to shut her up by locking her in his father's garden, but she continues to protest, marveling at the beauty of her surroundings while contrasting them to Roderigo's sinful actions:

> Oh Heaven! the stars appeare 'too, ha! A chamber,
> A goodly one, dwells Rape in such a paradice!
> Help me my quickned senses, 'tis a garden
> To which this window guides the covetous prospect,
> A large one and a faire one, in the midst
> A curious Alabaster Fountaine stands,
> Fram'd like—like what? no matter, swift remembrance,
> Rich furniture within too! and what's this?
> A precious Crucifix? I have enough. ...
> (1.3.42-50)

---

[64] *The Spanish Gipsy by Thomas Middleton and William Rowley: A critical edition*, ed. Kate Parker Smith (Northwestern University, 1944), 1.3.22-3.

Clara's discovery of the crucifix is carefully framed by her description of the garden, and later she makes the connection between Roderigo's family and the crucifix when she finds herself in a room overlooking the same courtyard. In this speech, she is already assessing the possibility of marrying her attacker as she evaluates the marks of his social status, inscribing them in her memory so she can identify him later, not by his person but by his surroundings. Roderigo has not told her his name, but evidently he comes from a noble family and is thus a suitable prospect for marriage. Such a reversal may seem forced to modern readers, but within the sexual economy depicted in plays such as *The Spanish Gipsy*, a woman who has been raped must choose either death or marriage: being the heroine of a tragicomedy rather than a tragedy, Clara chooses the latter. Unlike *The White Devil*, which consistently questions the stability of objects, this play presents pieces of property such as the crucifix and the garden as no less recognizable than faces, perhaps even more so because they are associated with the permanence of the aristocratic family unit. The only "thing" that is irrevocably broken here, the thing the play itself never fully addresses, is Clara's maidenhead.

After Roderigo releases her, Clara returns to her parents, but soon she falls ill under the strain of her secret. Luckily, her travels lead her to Roderigo's ancestral home, where she is confined to a room on his father's estate. Unable to rise from her bed, she asks her father to describe the view outside her window. "Easie suite," he replies, "*Clara* it over-viewes a spacious Garden, / Amidst which stands an Alabaster Fountaine, / A goodly one" (3.3.6-8). On the strength of this description, which fits her memory of the place where she was imprisoned by Roderigo, she asks to speak with the owner of the house, and during this interview she produces her most important piece of evidence. "My Lord," she asks, "d'ee know this Crucifix?" The sight of the object, which he recognizes immediately, prompts Roderigo's father, Fernando, to reveal the connection between the crucifix and his own lineage:

> You drive me to amazement, 'twas my Sonnes,
> A Legacy bequeathed him from his Mother
> Upon her Death-bed, deare to him as Life;
> On Earth there cannot be another treasure
> Hee values at like rate as hee does this.
> (3.3.40-45)

Fernando's identification of the crucifix serves as a kind of confirmation of the rape, but within the context of an imminent resolution in which Clara's wrongs will be righted through marriage, Fernando's initial ignorance of his son's misdeed also foreshadows the effacement of the crime itself. In a crude way, the crucifix seems to be a kind of compensation for Clara's suffering, and it is the crucifix that eventually becomes the focus of the play's comic resolution.

The Spanish Gipsy's presentation of a family crucifix differs significantly from that of Webster's *The White Devil*, largely because the text rejects a tragic outcome in favor of a comic one. Roderigo's mother is designated as the keeper of the family legacy and the original owner of the crucifix, but because she is already dead the drama never stages the moment in which she feels the loss of her children or their legacies, and all the requisite marriages restore a semblance of social order in the end. Like the handkerchief in *Othello*, which I address in the final section of the book, the crucifix in this play travels from the mother to the son and from him to his future wife. Clara, however, manages to avoid the threat of sexual promiscuity that eventually destroys Desdemona because she is merely the means by which the crucifix is reestablished as a marker of family continuity. The social order celebrated in the final act of the play is predicated on erasing the rape, and any anxiety about Clara's sexual status, by ritualistically confusing her identity. Fernando tells Roderigo that he must be married but allows him to choose his own bride, and when his son chooses Clara from among the audience of women at a court performance, Fernando exacts a kind of confession from him about the rape by declaring that his bride has already been deflowered. Finally, Clara turns Roderigo's shame into "comforts" when she reveals herself and announces, "[b]y this Crucifix / You may remember me" (5.1.46-7). The scene ends with a typical fatherly promise that all will be revealed in due time: "No more; hereafter / Wee shall have time to talke at large of all" (5.1.51-2).

Although Clara's union with her rapist is unsettling in and of itself, Dekker and Ford's play uses the crucifix, and the marriage, to salvage Roderigo's role in the family lineage. Through his father's description of his attachment to the crucifix, and through its association with his virtuous mother, Roderigo is successfully recuperated as a suitable husband, the opposite of the iconoclastic Flamineo. Such a reading, however, is the most tidy interpretation possible, for the original contract between Clara and Lewys has been broken, and the rape itself has been dismissed. When Roderigo asks, "art thou / That Lady wrong'd?" Clara replies, "I was, but now am / Righted in noble satisfaction" (5.1.47-9). Fernando's speech cuts off Roderigo's apology, and Clara is effectively disassociated from the girl who was ravished in Act 1. The play ultimately affirms the power of the crucifix to cement family ties, but it does so at the expense of her integrity. Both plays re-contextualize the crucifix within the private realm of the family while distancing the object from its ritual context and from the physical landscape of post-Reformation England. Unlike *The White Devil*, however, *The Spanish Gipsy* creates an artificial happy ending that leaves its audience emotionally distanced from Roderigo's family—even from Clara herself. *The Spanish Gipsy* does not raise the specter of iconoclasm, nor does it introduce the possibility that the crucifix might lose its value as it passes from generation to generation.

In contrast to this forced resolution, elements of revenge tragedy consistently darken the relationship between family inheritance and religious objects in *The White Devil*. The audience witnesses a mother mourning her son's death at the hands of his own brother, forced to admit that her crucifix is not truly mended and that she will have no one to whom she can pass it on. As a piece of property once belonging to Flamineo's father and now owned by his mother, the crucifix ought to be an appropriate emblem for the way lineage can overcome mortality, but the first time it is introduced Marcello immediately alerts the audience to the fact that it is broken, indicating that neither the cross nor the family has survived the consequences of Flamineo's ambition. By foregrounding the continual threat posed to Cornelia and her crucifix by Flamineo's attacks, Webster's play creates a heightened level of empathy for the heirloom and its owner that is entirely absent from *The Spanish Gipsy*. These acts of desecration, which draw the audience's attention to Webster's suffering mother, also highlight the dangers associated with taking the crucifix out of a religious context and subjecting it to a violently unsettled secular environment. By foregrounding the violation of familiar objects and rituals, the play uses Cornelia's fictional tragedy to evoke the localized aftereffects of the Reformation.

In his 1622 eulogy for a former Catholic named Mary Gunter, the Protestant minister Thomas Taylor offhandedly mentions the disintegration of her recusant family before going on to describe her successful conversion to the true faith. From Taylor's point of view, Gunter's acceptance of Protestantism after the death of her papist parents made her "an happie instrument of Gods glory in earth." He inadvertently betrays the pathos of her situation, however, when he relates the details of the young woman's spiritual awakening. After the death of her mother and father, Gunter was placed in the custody of another Catholic, an old woman who raised her according to the traditional faith. But when her guardian died the girl came under the protection of the Countess of Leicester, and this pious lady recognized immediately that her charge was "a most zeelous Papist." Even worse, Mary had plans to "convey her selfe beyond the Seas, and become a Nunne" as soon as possible.[65] To quell such ambitions, and to separate her from her Catholic friends, the countess began to keep close watch over her, preventing her from praying alone in a popish manner or from seeking out the company of anyone outside the household. Finally, she "tooke from her all her Popish Bookes, and Beads, Images, and all such trumpery." Although Gunter struggled to maintain her faith, keeping "her heart for Popery," she eventually adopted all the precepts and practices dictated by the countess.[66] As Taylor's narrative indirectly acknowledges, the growth of Mary Gunter as a virtuous Protestant is predicated on the violence done to the young girl of fourteen who dreamed of being a nun. By taking away all her "trumpery," the countess cut her off not only from her supporters, but also from her memories of her parents and the recusant woman who raised her; the act of removing them effectively severed any remaining ties between the girl and her natural family. Taylor avoids discussing the fate of the girl's possessions, but the theater, which relied heavily on material objects itself, was not so quick to dismiss an issue that played out both in public and private spheres. In 1604, James I assured his wary subjects, some of whom suspected he would support a return to

---

[65]   Thomas Taylor, *The Pilgrims profession, or a sermon preached at the funeral of Mris Mary Gunter* (London: Dawson, 1622), G3^r-v.

[66]   Ibid., G5^v, G7^v.

Catholicism in England, that "the materiall Crosses, which in the time of Popery were made for men to fall down before them … are demolished as you desire."[67] For all his protestations, James had developed a relatively tolerant attitude toward recusants, which facilitated the production of these images and the circulation of crucifixes such as Cornelia's. But it was not until 1625, when his son Charles and his Catholic wife, Henrietta Maria, took the throne, that "materiall Crosses" in the traditional sense of the term began to be displayed more openly.

Upon arriving in London, Henrietta Maria established her own private chapel where she and her maidservants heard mass; she even had her own Capuchin monks to minister to her spiritual needs.[68] As patron of the Queen's Men, she also oversaw the revival of *The White Devil* at the Cockpit in 1630-31. The two performances of Webster's play thus bracket the period in which religious objects began to appear with increasing frequency on the public stage. The first thirty years of the seventeenth century also mark the rise of the anti-Calvinist movement, headed by figures such as Lancelot Andrewes and William Laud, who advocated returning some elements of traditional worship to the churches and cathedrals of England. The second performance of the play coincided with an extraordinary historical moment, when Henrietta was actively promoting tolerance for English Catholics and Laud's attempt to re-beautify English churches was gaining momentum. In 1634, at the height of the anti-Calvinist movement, the author of the visitation articles for Lincoln demanded, "[a]re all crucifixes and any scandalous pictures of the persons of the Trinity abolished in your churches?"[69] Patrick Collinson documents the dramatic rise of Arminianism or anti-Calvinism by citing examples such as "the large painted crucifix" that hung in the parlor of the vicar of Sturry and, more surprisingly, "the large crucifix behind the altar" that adorned the chapel of St. John's College Cambridge in the mid-1630s.[70] Although Webster himself could not have foreseen this shift in royal policy, his play may well have been revived because of its sympathetic portrayal of traditional religion. For the most part, seventeenth-century plays tended to reflect the growing intensity surrounding contested objects such as crucifixes by avoiding them altogether. But some, most notably *The White Devil*, successfully dramatized the power that continued to

---

[67]   William Barlow, *The summe and substance of the conference … at Hampton Court. January 14. 1603* (London: John Windet [and T. Creede], 1604), 74.

[68]   Morris, vol. 1, 78.

[69]   Fincham, *Visitation Articles and Injunctions of the Early Stuart Church*, vol. 2, 104. The author of the Lincoln articles had cause for concern, as did the parishioners of All Hallows Barking in London, where, they complained in a 1637 petition, "there is a new font erected, over which certain carved images and a cross are placed … and certain images placed over the raile which stands about the table, all which, as we conceive, tends much to the dishonour of God" (Aston, 462). For more on the so-called Laudian reforms and the reaction against them, see Chapter 2.

[70]   Collinson, 120.

adhere to the physical remnants of the pre-Reformation church while raising a larger set of questions about their status as sacred objects.

In my readings of these play scripts, I have worked to uncover the connections between post-Reformation practices, which included the persistent attachment to material crosses, and the strategies employed by the public theater companies. By tying the crucifix to questions about the survival of the family, questions that were vital for Protestants and Catholics alike, plays such as *The White Devil* reveal the complicated aftermath of the Reformation and shift their audience's sympathies toward, rather than away from, the crucifix itself. And although I began with plays that stage the cross, the less controversial materialization of the crucifix, in these plays, too, the association between the cross and the body of the believer is crucial to the theater's positive materialization of religious practice. Inspired by the reformers' own ambivalence toward the symbolic anchor of the Christian faith, the theater presented a wide variety of stage crosses, with a wide variety of affective values associated with them, to suit the particular demands of each production. As the Elizabethan homilist was too well aware, it was nearly impossible to control the reception and the use of such objects in the context of popular religious practice—or, for that matter, in the space of the popular theater, where the playing companies were rapidly finding new ways to address the political events that were impacting English playgoers on a personal, material level.

Chapter 4

The Performance of Piety: Book Properties and the Paradox of Dematerialized Devotion[1]

The aspect of English Protestantism most familiar to modern scholars is its preference for books over idols, its reliance on the word of God rather than the authority of the priest. Historians of the Reformation have recently sought to complicate these simple oppositions, but the central place of the book in Protestant doctrine and propaganda is undisputed. This chapter focuses on the use of religious books as stage properties rather than as devotional aids, but the two functions were not altogether dissimilar, and in the case of the theater it is especially useful to consider evidence that questions the absolute dichotomy between books and images in post-Reformation practice. In the preceding sections, I have examined the persistence of material forms of devotion in England in order to better understand the appearance of these objects and ceremonies on the public stage. In the case of the sacred book, the phenomenon of its enduring materiality was especially antithetical to the stated project of the Reformation, and the theater companies' practice of using books as stage properties often drew attention to this contradiction. For if faith was an internal phenomenon, how could it be measured through acts of piety, namely prayer and meditation, that involved objects such as the codex?

From Luther to Calvin to Tyndale, the reformers argued that salvation resulted not from the priest's intervention in the miracle of the eucharist but from the individual believer's understanding of the word of God, which was to be enshrined in his or her heart. They often disagreed about how scripture was to be interpreted, but all Protestant polemicists called for a ministry based on the reading of the Bible in the vernacular and for an end to the Latin mass; the faithful were no longer to pay attention to the sound of the words but to their arrangement on a page. Accordingly, the images that once hung over the altar were replaced by tablets embossed with the ten commandments, and those who could read were encouraged to bring their own copies of the scriptures or the psalms to church so they could follow along during the minister's sermon. The process of replacing popish idols with godly books was not an easy one, but by the time Elizabeth came to the throne in 1558 English Bibles and prayer manuals had become a staple

[1] Parts of this chapter are reprinted with permission from *English Literary Renaissance* 39, no. 1 (February, 2009): 371-95. Reproduced with permission of Wiley-Blackwell.

of Protestant life, and by the time of James's coronation in 1603 these objects were familiar to most English worshipers. Patrick Collinson describes the radical shift in English culture during this period in terms of an opposition between images and books. "In 1500," he observes, "for a lay person of humble status to be found in possession of a book (almost any book) was to be suspected of heresy. It seems that by 1600 to be found in possession of a picture (almost any picture) was to be a suspected papist."[2] Yet in many sacred books, including the 1560 Geneva Bible, explanatory pictures were printed alongside the words. Later generations of English Calvinists would eliminate such illustrations, but even the strictest reformers could not dispute the centrality of images and material objects to Protestant life. By stressing the importance of making books available to all the faithful, Protestants paradoxically confirmed the fact that one could not have the word of God without a vessel to convey it in. These vessels, moreover, could be quite beautiful. Alexandra Walsham observes that the elaborately embroidered bindings that once protected Catholic primers were often reattached to Protestant texts without any particular fanfare. "Such bindings," she writes, "seem to have weathered the storm of the Reformation very successfully, becoming exquisite emblems of continuity absorbing, embracing, and mediating change."[3]

The common features shared by Catholic and Protestant prayer manuals, both of which were frequently transformed into sumptuous accessories, provides a particularly striking example of the physicality of reformed devotion, a problem that was accentuated by the relatively conservative nature of the Elizabethan settlement. Because Elizabeth refused to outlaw gestures such as kneeling outright, the proper manner of praying continued to be hotly debated throughout her reign, and well into James's.[4] But even the otherwise decorous use of inexpensive black-letter quartos brought with it an underlying problem: before the believer could

---

[2]   Collinson, 118.

[3]   Alexandra Walsham, "Jewels for Gentlewomen: Religious Books as Artefacts in Late Medieval and Early Modern England," in *The Church and the Book*, ed. R. N. Swanson (Woodbridge: Boydell and Brewer, 2004), 123-42, 131. For more on the reprinting of Catholic books see McClain, 49-53.

[4]   As Ramie Targoff notes, the boundary that has been drawn between Protestant prayer (spontaneous and private) from Catholic prayer (prescripted and public) is complicated both by the central role of the Book of Common Prayer in post-Reformation worship and by the fact that traditional Catholicism included a strong focus on private devotion using prayer manuals such as books of hours (*Common Prayer: The Language of Public Devotion in Early Modern England* [Chicago: University of Chicago Press, 2001], 5). This issue has been explored in depth by Lori Anne Ferrell in *Government by Polemic: James I, the King's Preachers, and the Rhetorics of Conformity, 1603-1625* (Stanford: Stanford University Press, 1998), 148ff. Judith Maltby argues that some Protestants considered the "set forms" established by the Book of Common Prayer to be "a shallow exercise," a latter-day equivalent of the popery Tyndale protested against one hundred years earlier (*Prayer Book and People in Elizabethan and Early Stuart England* [Cambridge: Cambridge University Press, 1998], 30). The potential controversy over the prayer book's status may make more

internalize the word, she had to get her hands on a copy of it, and the material presence of those objects was dangerously analogous to the place of objects such as the crucifix in pre-Reformation devotion. While it is true that books were not necessary for the exchange of prayers between the preacher and the congregation, and many churchgoers had key passages from the scriptures memorized, Protestant ministers strongly encouraged individual congregants to have their own books and to carry on the work of the sermon in their own homes. The faithful were thus constantly confronted with the physical presence of books themselves, as well as with the contradiction they posed. In this chapter, I argue that the drama's reliance on material properties made it uniquely suited to draw out and comment upon that inescapable physicality. Protestants associated the reading of holy books with a form of piety uncorrupted by the superficial trappings of the Catholic church, and the theater actively appropriated that affective technology by putting acts of prayer on stage, but it also highlighted the similarity between such godly activities and professional actors' use of books as properties.

Protestant polemicists routinely asserted that the Reformation would eventually restore the church to its original or "primitive" state, free from the grossly material objects that had corrupted the truth faith. But an anonymous play depicting the early days of the Christian church suggests that such fantasies still relied on the presence of material things, especially books. *The Two Noble Ladies* (1622), a tragicomedy first performed at the Red Bull, follows the adventures of the pagan conjurer Cyprian, who uses his magical powers to protect himself and his friends from being touched by the violent struggle between Egypt and Antioch. As with Prospero, Cyprian's power is said to reside in his books, and at one point the poor scholar Barebones attempts to hide behind them, hoping they will provide a literal shield against marauding soldiers. Cyprian also uses his necromancy to more serious ends, including prophesying the future of the play's hero, Lysander. In a Faustian act of conjuring, Cyprian summons "a Spirit" to reveal Lysander's birthright to him, but the scene is suddenly interrupted by an angel, who enters "*shaped like a patriarch*" and bearing "*a red crossier staffe*" in his hand.[5] This stage direction is particularly unusual, for the crosier was associated with the papacy or, at the very least, with the Catholic hierarchy of bishops, as in the dumb show at the beginning of Dekker's *Whore of Babylon* (1606). Here and elsewhere the play works to rescue the classic implements of Christianity from their association with Catholic superstition by contrasting them to the tools of the necromancer, and the appearance of the angel is taken as a definitively positive sign, providing the first indication that a conversion is about to take place. "[S]uch a light Ile bring shall make thee see," the angel promises, "thou to that houre liv'd'st in obscurities,"

---

sense when we recall the difference between the private prayer manual and the prayer book as liturgical guide.

[5] *The Two Noble Ladies*, ed. Rebecca Garrett Rhoads (London: Printed for the Malone Society by J. Johnson at the Oxford University Press, 1930), ll. 1101-3.

thus invoking the recognizably Protestant trope of the Bible as the light of the world (ll. 1121-2).

The conversion scene itself combines two sacred texts, a Bible and a prayer book, in a striking display of the physical power of the true faith. Cyprian has fallen in love with a Christian woman named Justina, whose virtue has so far successfully repelled all his charms. Near the end of the play he manages to cast her into a heavy sleep, and she appears to be powerless. The stage direction reads: "*Justina is discovered in a chaire asleep, in her hands a prayer book, divells about her*" (ll. 1752-3). The magician has underestimated her vigilance, however; she suddenly awakens from the spell and "*looks in her booke*," an action that immediately prompts the spirits to fly from her. "Her faith," the demons marvel, "beats downe our incantations" (l. 1802). That faith is located directly in the prayer book, and a few lines later Justina teaches Cyprian to use her book against the demons who threaten to tear him apart when he agrees to give up his magic spells in favor of hers. "Call on that pow'rfull name / those pray'rs so oft repeat," she urges him, eventually convincing him that the "charmes" contained in her book are more effective—and can be called upon in much the same way—as the ones in his own (ll. 1845-7).

The language of this scene reads as distinctly Protestant in that Justina urges Cyprian to discover the power contained in the words on the page, including the name of Christ himself, yet the way in which those words are turned into talismans, analogous to the conjurer's black arts, suggests the surprisingly magical potential of the Christians' holy book. As in Fletcher, Field, and Massinger's *The Knight of Malta* (1618), a play that deploys crosses as shields against foreign enemies, the Bible in *The Two Noble Ladies* takes on inexplicable powers that seem to remain untainted by the threat of superstition. The spectacle of Cyprian's conversion does not end here, however. Once he has renounced his necromancy, the "*patriarch-like*" angel reappears "*with his crosier staffe in one hand, and a book in the other*," driving out the devils for good (ll. 1856-8). The angel proceeds to give Cyprian another book, which he urges him to study well, and converts his lust for Justina into "love of heav'n" by touching his breast with the cross (l. 1870). Cyprian dutifully promises to spend the rest of his life studying the angel's book, presumably a copy of the scriptures. Rather than being dragged under the stage by the devils as Faustus is, he throws his necromantic books down after them in a gesture reminiscent of Prospero's promise to drown his entire library.

Set in the early days of the Christian church, *The Two Noble Ladies* relegates the trauma of religious division to the realm of ancient history. But what is perhaps most unusual about this play is that it literalizes the connection between Protestantism and the primitive church by radically recontextualizing a set of values that the reformers had staked out for themselves, specifically, the valorization of a woman's chastity as embodied in her dedication to her prayer book. The prayer book was a distinctly contemporary object, and by placing it within the context of early Christianity and lending it talismanic powers, the play seems to be taking the Protestants' dedication to the word of God to its furthest possible extreme.

The Two Noble Ladies does not express any particular concern about the potentially blasphemous use of the book as a magical demon repellant, in part because the setting is so far removed from early modern England. The play does suggest, however, that the state-sanctioned religion was inextricably linked to a matrix of popular practices that included both traditional Catholic worship and activities typically associated with magic or witchcraft.

Although it raises a familiar set of questions about the nature of Protestants' attachment to material objects such as prayer books and bibles, *The Two Noble Ladies* is nearly unique among early modern play texts in that it seems to call for a copy of the scriptures to be brought on stage. The Bible appears in only three other surviving play scripts; the vast majority of religious book properties mentioned are ordinary prayer books used as tokens of personal devotion. In fact, religious books appear in a wide variety of both Elizabethan and Jacobean plays, but none of them are listed in Philip Henslowe's inventory of stage properties, probably because they did not need to be specially fabricated; the visual appearance of the book was important only insofar as it allowed the actor, and on another level the character, to perform the act of reading.[6] Although these books, unlike other religious objects, were not presented as especially controversial, they were used to explore a central issue in Christian practice: the expression of inner piety through outward gestures such as prayer. And while *The Two Noble Ladies* is unusual in the way it uses both prayer books and Bibles as magical talismans, several other scripts tackle the materiality of prayer in subtler ways, using recognizably contemporary settings. What was at stake in the theater companies' use of books was the physicality of religious practice, both Catholic and Protestant, and the drama highlighted that physicality by creating an analogy between the actor's use of the book as property and the worshiper's use of the book as an aid to spiritual meditation.

The label "prayer book" might refer to a variety of texts, both Protestant and Catholic, for although devotional works designed for the individual believer were a crucial element of traditional piety, they continued to be printed and sold widely in post-Reformation England. The term "prayer book" could also refer to the Book of Common Prayer, first circulated in 1549 as a reformed version of the Catholic mass book and printed in English so that parishioners could study it at home and follow along during the service. Judith Maltby has uncovered evidence from household inventories and printers' records to suggest that although they could not afford their own Bibles, many English families owned copies of the Book of Common Prayer. Given that the print run allowed for the Prayer Book was double

---

[6] By my count, prayer books are called for in at least eighteen of the surviving plays first produced before 1642. Prayer books were so prevalent on the stage that in Webster's *The White Devil* (1612) Lodovico jokes about their absence, complaining that he and his co-conspirators should have poisoned one and used it as a murder weapon against Bracciano. Two years later, Webster answered his own challenge by having the Cardinal force his mistress Julia to swear an oath on a poisoned book—presumably a prayer book or Bible—in *The Duchess of Malfi* (1614).

the usual permitted maximum, over half a million copies were probably put into circulation before the civil war. Furthermore, the type size was sometimes quite small, suggesting that such books were intended for personal use in church or home, rather than for liturgical use.[7] Despite the important role the Prayer Book proper played in Protestant society, there is no indication that any of the prayer books used on stage were meant to represent the Book of Common Prayer specifically. It is more likely that the properties used in the public theater resonated with private prayer manuals, such as Edward Dering's *Godlye private praiers for housholders to meditate upon, and to say in their families* (1578), Anne Wheathill's *A handfull of holesome (though homelie) hearbs* (1584), Johann Habermann's *The enimie of securitie, or, A daily exercise of godlie meditations* (1591), and Arthur Dent's *A Plaine Man's Pathway to Heaven* (1601). These kinds of manuals were immensely popular and provided a convenient framework for daily devotion, but they were also similar in theme to Catholic texts with identical functions. In other words, both the Book of Common Prayer and the private prayer manual cut across the lines the reformers attempted to draw between idolatrous Catholic practice and appropriate Protestant worship. The reformers had removed books from altars, and even altars as well, but the very materiality of the Bible and the prayer book, which resembled that of Catholic books, continued to haunt Protestant theology and Protestant practice.

In a majority of early modern dramas, prayer book properties are used to represent devotional acts without explicitly challenging the nature of those practices. The altar called for in *The Knight of Malta* has a book on it, perhaps a missal, but that book is never referred to in the dialogue and might have existed merely as part of the recognizable furniture of a Catholic altar. Prayer books also differ from the objects discussed in earlier chapters—where I focus on plays first staged in the first three decades of the seventeenth century—in that they appear in several scripts performed as early as 1591. These earlier plays include a flurry of English histories, many of which directly address the gendered nature of prayer. The reformers prided themselves on putting the word of God into the hands of all the members of the church, including women, but the archetype of the godly woman reader was complicated by the fact that a rich tradition of women's literacy was eliminated when the English nunneries were dissolved. Moreover, many Protestant polemicists were deeply anxious about the possibility that women's moral and physical frailty would lead to the abuse of religious objects such as prayer books. This was an unsettling thought, for the increasingly important role women played in the nuclear Protestant household meant that their treatment of books, including prayer manuals, had serious ideological implications for the project of constructing the Protestant state. As a model for her children and a companion to her husband, the virtuous wife was central to the maintenance of the godly household. Because of her perceived fragility, however, she was also seen

---

[7]   Maltby, 24-5.

as a threat to the project of godly reading that served as one of the cornerstones of post-Reformation practice.

Because of their association with sexual chastity, the stakes of women's reading practices in post-Reformation England could not have been higher, but the theater was also interested in the question of what happened when sacred books came into the hands of foreign infidels, or, conversely, what happened when Christians were confronted with religious systems and objects that were alien to them. In a handful of plays the Qur'an itself appears as an alternative to Christian books, and I will address the most complex of these, Marlowe's *Tamburlaine* (1587-8), in the final section of this chapter. I begin, however, by addressing two texts, *Hamlet* (1601) and *Richard III* (1592), which explicitly take up the controversies within Christianity about the performance and interpretation of godly prayer by employing sophisticated metatheatrical strategies to illuminate the paradox of using material prayer books to anchor immaterial devotion.

Devotion's Visage

Although we know relatively little about the actual book properties used in the early modern theater, we do have evidence that such properties played an important role in Shakespearean performances during subsequent centuries as actors continued to experiment with the implications of bringing sacred books on stage. One of the treasures in the Folger Library's collection of manufactured stage properties is a prayer book bound in velvet once owned by Charles Kean and used in his production of *Hamlet*. The manuscript has eighty-eight real pages that can be turned, but those pages are covered with watercolors rather than illuminations and decorative calligraphy rather than devotional instructions. Consciously or unconsciously, the creator of this book has managed to hone in on the objective behind the theatrical gesture of reading. Instead of using a real book, which might tempt the actor to follow the words in front of him, the prop master has created a fake book with lines that lead the eye across the page without becoming distractingly legible. The book was also a crucial part of the actor's appearance. Kean was famous for his attempts to add historical accuracy to his theatrical interpretations, and this "Handsome Book for Hamlet" was designed to look like an illuminated manuscript from the medieval period. Records of the performance do not indicate whether other characters also used the property, but if Kean himself carried it on stage in Act 2, scene 2, it would have lent an iconoclastic undertone to the prince's exchange with Polonius. Hamlet describes his reading material as nothing more than "[w]ords, words, words," perhaps implying that the lines on the page are without substance (2.2.192). This critique echoes the accusations Protestants made against Catholic devotional manuals, but it also resonates with the fact that the book Kean was holding was literally illegible.

The fact that Kean's *Hamlet* property is a fake book underscores the problem articulated by the play script itself, which suggests that acts of piety are disturbingly easy to falsify. The object's purple velvet and crude watercolors evoke the aesthetics of the Catholic prayer manual just as gestures and words were used on the stage to represent devotion; the very design of the object mirrors the notion that books, even sacred ones, are often evaluated by their appearance. Setting aside, for a moment, the fact that it was made to look distinctly medieval, thus allowing Kean to skip over the early modern period altogether, the existence of this property also points to one of the differences in theatrical practice between the seventeenth and the nineteenth centuries. In 1600, it would have been easy for the Chamberlain's Men to purchase or borrow a real book. Books were becoming cheaper as a result of new printing technologies, and devotional works were among the most common texts to be mass-produced. By contrast, Kean would have had to pay a hefty sum for a four- or five-hundred-year-old book in 1850. What remains constant, however, is the fact that the book, like all stage properties, oscillates between being relatively worthless and absolutely necessary. On stage, a book brings with it a host of cultural meanings and accrues additional ones as a result of being incorporated into dramatic fictions. Off stage, the property is easily replaceable and consequently valueless. What makes the book property unique is its ability to present a particularly vivid analogy between theatrical practice, which relies upon material objects and visual displays, and religious practice, which, even in Protestant England, depended upon the material presence of sacred things.

The Folger catalogue identifies Charles Kean's book as the one he used when playing the Danish prince, but this intriguing stage property also resonates with issues that come to the foreground in Act 3, scene 1 of *Hamlet*, in which Polonius instructs Ophelia to pretend to read her prayer book so that she has an excuse to confront the prince in the courtyard. Like the performance of "The Mousetrap," this deception is designed to provoke a revelation of truth, but as Polonius himself admits there is a shameful precedent for such falsehoods:

> *Polonius.* Ophelia, walk you here.
> ... Read on this book,
> That show of such an exercise may color
> Your loneliness. We are oft to blame in this—
> 'Tis too much prov'd—that with devotion's visage,
> And pious action, we do sugar o'er
> The devil himself.
> (3.1.43-8)

On one level, Polonius seems eager to articulate what his daughter is *not* doing. By following her father's instructions, she risks a comparison between her show of devotion and the false acts of prayer that frequently took place off stage, and Polonius quickly tries to distance her from this possibility by asserting his awareness of the precedent. On another level, by referring to "pious action" and "devotion's visage" Polonius's speech points beyond the particular problem of Ophelia's fake reading to the play's exploration of the performative nature of religious practice, and to the anxieties that surrounded those performances, especially when the character in question was a woman.

Several variants between the folio and second quarto help draw out the gendered implications of Polonius's words, which obliquely refer to the falseness of women as well as the hypocrisy of those who pray insincerely. Many apparently religious people, Polonius remarks in the folio version of the play, use material gestures to "surge o'er" their hidden faults, but for the folio's "surge," Q2 reads "sugar," a word that complements the associations between Ophelia's attractive outside and the unpleasant task she has been ordered to fulfill. The folio also reads "lowliness," for Q2's "loneliness," a choice that makes little sense unless we read the word as a description of her deceitful actions. It is not Ophelia's deception that needs to be smoothed over, however, but her father's; like Guildenstern, she has not "craft enough to color" her intentions (2.2.280). The fact that Ophelia is first instructed by her father and then rebuked by Hamlet calls attention, as many of the plays discussed in this chapter do, to the charged nature of female piety. Although women were praised for their devotion, negative stereotypes linking members of the female sex to falseness and changeability often caused their pious acts to be questioned. Hamlet pointedly observes, for instance, that "the power of beauty will sooner transform honesty from what it is to a bawd than the force of honesty can translate beauty into his likeness" (3.1.110-13). But despite these lewd suggestions about the separation between honesty and chastity, Ophelia is neither a good actor nor a whore. Indeed, her inability to hide the fact that she is acting highlights the facility with which other characters, including Hamlet, mislead one another.

Polonius's references to "action" and "visage" seem to encourage audience members to read Ophelia's actions within the context of anti-Catholic attacks, such as William Tyndale's critique of "a false kind of praying, wherein the tongue and lips labour … but the heart talketh not … nor hath any confidence in the promises of God." Would-be believers, Tyndale remarks, ground their faith "in the multitude of words, and in the pain and tediousness of the length of the prayer," rather than in its substance. Nor were such fears altogether unfounded for, as Alexandra Walsham argues, "conformity could be an excellent cloak behind which to engage in subversive, anti-Protestant activity."[8] In his commentary on the book of Matthew, Tyndale invokes this problem using the language an antitheatricalist might apply to the false shows put on by stage players. Tyndale is not, however, particularly concerned with the theater. Instead, he compares the fake penitent to a "conjuror" who, like Cyprian in *The Two Noble Ladies*, grounds his faith in "circles, characters, and the superstitious words of his conjuration," eliding popery

---

[8] "'Yielding to the Extremity of Time': Conformity, Orthodoxy, and the Post-Reformation Catholic Community," in *Conformity and Orthodoxy in the English Church, 1560-1660*, eds. Peter Lake and Michael Questier (Woodbridge: Boydell Press, 2000), 211-36, 213.

with necromancy and presenting Catholic prayer as a form of idolatry.[9] Although in practice Protestants could not forego all physical forms of worship and focus exclusively on the heart, spirit, and mind, the language used by the reformers often attempts to align Protestantism with inner faith and Catholicism with outer shows. Highlighting this contradiction, *Hamlet* demonstrates the difficulties that arise from associating material objects such as books with genuine devotion, a concept that, according to Protestant doctrine, was based on the understanding and acceptance of the immaterial word of God.

In Act 3, scene 1, Polonius's meditation on the opposition between genuine prayer and mere performance is underscored by Claudius's response, delivered as an aside to the audience:

> *King.* O, 'tis too true!
> How smart a lash that speech doth give my conscience!
> The harlot's cheek, beautied with plast'ring art,
> Is not more ugly to the thing that helps it
> Than is my deed to my most painted word.
> O heavy burthen!
> (3.1.48-53)

Struck by Polonius's remarks on false prayer, Claudius immediately recognizes the parallel between his actions and the conduct of those who conceal "the devil himself" in their hearts. Claudius calls his own words, which he has used to cover up the act of fratricide, "painted," and thus shallow, superficial. His allusion to the "harlot's cheek" and Polonius's use of the term "color" underscore one of the play's pervasive metaphors, the idea that cosmetics cover over blemishes but also damage the skin underneath. The phrase "painted word" may also refer to manuscript illuminations, drawing a contrast between these adornments, which were associated with Catholic books of hours, and the simplicity of the black ink used in printed books. Prompted by Ophelia's feigned act of devotion, Claudius is forced to acknowledge the disjunct in his own life between the lips and the heart, organs which, to use Cranmer's words, were meant to "go together in prayer."[10]

Two scenes later, alone at prayer after the performance of "The Mousetrap," Claudius laments the insufficiency of his painted or superficial speech in more detail. As he struggles to repent his act of fratricide, he admits that "[m]y words fly up, my thoughts remain below: / Words without thoughts, never to heaven go" (3.3.96-7). Even more than Ophelia's performance, which has no pretensions to actual piety, this scene presents a direct indictment of unsuccessful prayer, the kind that has no "sweetness," to use Tyndale's terminology. There is, however, some pathos in this moment of attempted penance. Having willfully murdered his

---

[9]   *Expositions and Notes on Sundry Portions of the Holy Scriptures, Together with The Practice of Prelates* (Cambridge: Cambridge University Press, 1849), 9.

[10]   *The Works of Thomas Cranmer* vol. 2, 173.

brother, Claudius cannot think of any reasonable text that could excuse his sins; he has failed to internalize the word of God and is thus left speechless at the moment of his greatest spiritual need. What is most ironic about the scene, however, is that Hamlet takes Claudius's outward gestures at face value. Assuming that the king is repenting in earnest, he resists the temptation to kill him, believing that if he does he will send his soul to heaven.

From Hamlet's standpoint, it is impossible to distinguish Ophelia's form of deception from Claudius's, since both the would-be penitent and the actor pretending to pray use an object and gestures to communicate their intentions. In addition to referencing the logic of reformers such as Tyndale, the play's various stagings of prayer also suggest that, given the right property, anyone can fake the act of devotional reading. And although the play does not charge Ophelia with the crime of falsifying her religious belief, her performance with the prayer book reinforces the unsettling analogy between theatrical practice and religious practice by demonstrating the ease with which even a bad actor can imitate true piety. It is important to remember that in this scene Ophelia is construed as an actress rather than a failed penitent. The problem here is not that she is pretending to be pious, but rather that it is impossible to tell genuine devotion from false devotion, a slippage which is accentuated by the audience's awareness of the fact that members of Shakespeare's company were themselves mimicking the gesture of reading. The troubling similarity between Ophelia's act of prayer and Claudius's emphasizes the theater's ability to illuminate the analogies between stage properties and the physical books used to support acts of devotion. Hinting at the ironies surrounding the unreformed materiality of prayer manuals, the theater referenced a pressing set of issues surrounding the supposed moral frailty of the ordinary people who were handling them.

In addition to pointing out some of the contradictions inherent in Protestant notions of a dematerialized faith, the play also seems to destabilize the metaphors that linked women with false shows by drawing a crucial distinction between Ophelia's acting and Claudius's fake piety. Watching Ophelia duly performing her role, Claudius is reminded that he is the one playing the harlot by covering his sins with "painted" words. It is he, not Ophelia, whose thoughts are severed from his prayers, rendering them fruitless. In this sense, *Hamlet* also alludes to the values and stereotypes associated with the figure of the woman reader in post-Reformation England. The focus on the sincerity of female virtue was an enduring one, as Patricia Crawford demonstrates, citing a 1682 funeral sermon in which the deceased was praised not only for a perfect attendance record at communion, but also for her earnestness; her diligence, the preacher suggests, "was not 'an affected Out-side' but an example of very real piety."[11] For this and other qualities, the virtuous Protestant woman was celebrated as an anchor of the household, even though she posed a potential threat to domestic peace because of her supposedly frail physicality. The image of the woman reader was crucial to

---

[11]   *Women and Religion in England, 1500-1720* (London: Routledge, 1993), 78.

Protestant propaganda, yet stereotypes about "painted" or undependable women provide another example of the way certain misogynist claims failed to hold up in practice.

If Ophelia's use of her prayer book addresses the way Protestant claims about an immaterial faith tend to break down under pressure, the performance of prayer in *Richard III* (1592) openly links its protagonist's Machiavellian tendencies with the errors of traditional religion, presenting an apparently straightforward endorsement of anti-Catholic stereotypes. Just before arranging for the death of his nephews, Richard stages a public appearance with his prayer book, hoping to convince the citizens of London that, despite all the evidence to the contrary, he is a deeply pious man. This scene presents both a classic example of election propaganda and a quintessentially performative use of the prayer book as a "mere property." At the beginning of the scene, Catesby sadly informs the mayor and citizens of London that the Duke of Gloucester cannot appear to speak with them because he is busy "with two right reverend fathers, / Divinely bent to meditation," and cannot be torn away "from his holy exercise" (3.7.61-2, 64). Just then, however, Richard appears in person "*aloft, between two* BISHOPS" (94 sd.). Presenting himself with two spiritual "companions"—either bishops turned reluctant actors or actors hired by Richard to dress up like bishops—he sets out to give the citizens the perfect image of aristocratic devotion. His visual appearance is then interpreted for the on-stage spectators:

> *Buckingham.* Ah ha, my lord, this prince is not an Edward!
> He is not lulling on a lewd love-bed,
> But on his knees at meditation;
> Not dallying with a brace of courtezans,
> But meditating with two deep divines;
> Not sleeping, to engross his idle body,
> But praying, to enrich his watchful soul.
> (3.7.71-7)

Buckingham's speech epitomizes the duplicity Protestants associated with Catholicism's false shows. Ironically, although many of the citizens are aware that Richard is no god-fearing man, his gestures seem to convince the mayor that he is. His body's devotion is directly equated with his pious soul.

A few lines later, speaking as much to the audience at the Globe as to the fictional audience of citizens, Buckingham provides a further gloss on Richard's appearance:

> *Mayor.* See where his Grace stands, 'tween two clergymen!
> *Buckingham.* Two props of virtue for a Christian prince,
> To stay him from the fall of vanity;

> And see, a book of prayer in his hand—
> True ornaments to know a holy man.
> (3.7.95-9)

In contrast to Polonius, who decries the practice of using religious gestures to hide the devil underneath, Richard, Buckingham, and their followers hope that by prompting the citizens to draw a connection between outward ornaments such as the prayer book and his personal devotion, Richard will convince them to endorse his bid for the crown.[12] Buckingham helps the mayor to read the tableaux as a pious one, but in fact it is wholly a display, featuring the book and the friars as accessories. This is perhaps the theater's most explicit statement of the way books were used both on stage and off to falsify the act of prayer.

Shakespeare's audience would have been well aware that both book and bishops are hollow tokens of Richard's piety, and here is where the reading of this scene as a straightforward example of anti-Catholic satire begins to fall apart. Because the dialogue is so explicit about the prayer book's status as a mere property, it opens up a space for the performer playing Richard to share with the audience a moment in which the spectators, the actor, and the character are all simultaneously aware of the similarity between the object within the drama and the property used in the theatrical production. By celebrating the talents of both the player and the would-be king, this scene "invites the audience to suspend their moral judgment and evaluate [Richard's] actions simply as theatrical performances."[13] And if it is possible to separate the protagonist's personal charisma from the wickedness of his deeds, scenes such as this also allow us to conclude that the theater as a medium is neither moral nor immoral, Catholic nor anti-Catholic—it is simply a form of entertainment that relies on actors' ingenuity. In an all-female production of the play at the reconstructed Globe in 2003, the actor playing Richard held the book upside down for a moment, then, grinning at the audience, quickly turned it right side up. J. P. Kemble, for his part, made a show of flinging it from him as soon as the citizens left the stage, as did David Garrick before him.[14] And in the World War II-era film adaptation starring Ian McKellen, Buckingham hands Richard a popular novel with the dust jacket removed to serve as his prayer book. Through Richard's misuse of the prayer book property, which is also a prop for the narrative he and his supporters are working to construct, the play calls attention to the theater's own investment in the business of creating fictions and forgeries.

---

[12] As John Jowett points out in his edition of the play, the two lines from Buckingham's speech that specifically refer to the prayer book are missing from the quarto. He speculates that perhaps they constituted "an anachronistic reference to *Common Prayer* that affronted the established church" (*The Tragedy of King Richard III* [Oxford: Oxford University Press, 2000], 272).

[13] Jean Howard and Phyllis Rackin, *Engendering a Nation: a feminist account of Shakespeare's English histories* (London and New York: Routledge, 1997), 111.

[14] Jowett, 272.

Richard's staged appearance with the prayer book represents the most extreme example of the use of a prayer book as a negatively-inflected theatrical device, but an equally intriguing aspect of this scene is that the performance is not entirely Richard's idea. Richard does tell Buckingham in Act 3, scene 5 that they will find him "well accompanied / With reverend fathers, and well-learned bishops" when they seek him out, but the business with the prayer book seems to be Buckingham's invention (99-100). Before the citizens and the mayor appear, Buckingham urges Richard to "get a prayer-book in your hand, / And stand between two churchmen, good my lord— / For on that ground I'll build a holy descant." He goes on to emphasize that Richard must not appear too eager: "And be not easily won to our requests: / Play the maid's part, still answer nay, and take it" (3.7.47-51). Richard's part has literally been scripted for him. The book's status as a property is further underscored by the fact that the scene contains not one actor, but several, who conspire to create this vision of pious royalty. Richard's performance, a more overt version of the trick by which Polonius becomes his daughter's prompter, is carefully choreographed by Catesby and Buckingham, and supported by the two "bishops" who accompany him.

Shakespeare's Richard is a highly self-conscious manipulator who shares with his audience a pleasurable sense of appreciation for his own abilities as an actor. By contrast to *Hamlet*, in which Ophelia is forced to commit an act of deception that is entirely unsuited to her temperament, in this play the audience sees a man whose skill in prevarication may be equaled only by that of the actor who portrays him. Confronted with the spectacle of Ophelia reluctantly posing with her book, playgoers are encouraged to take Polonius's Protestant rhetoric as a legitimate critique, while acknowledging the disturbing fact that it is ultimately impossible to tell false prayer from playacting. In this way, *Hamlet* undermines standard Protestant attacks against women and Catholics by providing the exception to the rule, in which a woman is forced to play along with the hypocrisy of the men who surround her. *Richard III*, on the other hand, is less concerned with Protestantism's highly fraught relationship with materiality and more interested in debunking the stereotypes that indiscriminately grouped actors, women, and Catholics together as "bad" readers.

Through their highly self-conscious dramatization of the book as property, these plays seek to defend the theater against charges of superficiality by pointing out that objects were just as central to religious practice as they were to theatrical practice. But the most radical implication of the scenes discussed above is that even godly Protestants who despised idolatry and artifice had to employ outward signs in order to indicate to anyone who might be watching that an act of prayer was taking place. Just as an actor used a prayer book property to represent a state of devotion, so an otherwise modest Protestant was expected to demonstrate that she was engaging in a holy exercise by maintaining a physical proximity to her copy of Dering's *Godlye private praiers* or its equivalent. And by incorporating a physical object into a visual representation of the act of worship, even the most devout churchgoer laid herself open to charges of falsifying her faith through outward shows.

The fact that Hamlet and Richard both do so much self-conscious posing helps to undermine the rhetoric that associated women with false superficiality, and even as these plays reference the language that linked women to bad actors and to false Catholics, they suggest that the problem lies not in women's weakness but in the unreformed materiality of the prayer book as a prop for lay devotion. Both plays, however, focus on gender only as an adjunct to their exploration of the inherently theatrical nature of piety, giving little subversive space to female characters. This absence belies the fact that women readers occupied a position of prominence in contemporary Protestant propaganda. As John M. King has argued, contemporary woodcut illustrations frequently celebrated women "as embodiments of pious intellectuality and divine wisdom," and images of reading, especially on the part of female parishioners, were one of the most familiar elements of Protestant iconography.[15] If it was easier to hold up an ideal image of godly womanhood than to trust real women with their prayer books, early modern playwrights were also powerfully aware that the most potent image of the godly woman reader was not an anonymous churchgoer, but Elizabeth I herself.

Defender of the Faith

The Shakespearean scenes described above are unusual in their very pointed treatment of prayer book properties. By contrast, most early modern dramas appropriate prayer books as properties without drawing undue attention to their materiality. Even in plays depicting the life of Queen Elizabeth, prayer books and Bibles function as relatively stable emblems of her devotion to the word of God and her desire to see it made accessible to all her subjects. It is worth noting, however, that the prayer book was used to represent the familiar, everyday nature of Elizabeth's piety, while the Bible takes on a supernatural quality. In each of the two polemical plays produced just after Elizabeth's death, *The Whore of Babylon* (1606) and *If You Know Not Me You Know Nobody*, part 1 (1604), the Bible figures prominently as the magical attribute of her power and virtue. Thus, although the plays do not emphasize the materiality of prayer in the way that *Richard III* and *Hamlet* do, the contrast between the Bible and the prayer book, and the carefully coded language used to describe the queen's devotions, pick up on some of the issues introduced by Ophelia's "pious action" and tie into a larger discourse about women's devotional practices in post-Reformation England.

Produced three years after the queen's death and in the shadow of the Gunpowder Plot, Dekker's *The Whore of Babylon* opens with a strong declaration of Elizabeth's providential right to the throne—a dumb show in which Truth and Time appear to the Faerie Queene and present her with a book. The script does not explicitly refer to the book as a Bible, but its identity is confirmed when, in a gesture reminiscent of

---

[15] "The Godly Woman in Elizabethan Iconography," *Renaissance Quarterly* 38 (1985): 41-84, 41.

the 1558 coronation pageant, the queen kisses and displays the property to "those about her." Her supporters in turn vow to defend her and it at all costs before driving out "*those Cardinals, Friers &c. (that came in before) with Images, Croziar staues &c*" ("Dumb Shew" sd.). The dumb show thus confirms what the audience already knows about Elizabeth's triumph over popery, but the play does briefly represent the perspective of the queen's Catholic enemies. The title character, identified as the Empress of Rome, complains early in the play that Elizabeth's book of "holy Spels" has charmed the ears of English Catholics and made them deaf to their former faith (1.1.69). Here the Empress is represented, like Cyprian in *The Two Noble Ladies*, as a juggler who cannot understand the book's power except in terms of magical tricks. And yet this clash of viewpoints raises the question of whether a clear distinction can be drawn between Catholic books and Protestant ones.

Heywood's *If You Know Not Me You Know Nobody* makes a similar point about the supernatural quality of the Bible when Queen Elizabeth's jailor Beningfield picks up a book in her room and is immediately overcome with horror upon discovering what it is: "Marry a God, whats here an English bible? / *Sanctum Maria* pardon this prophanation of my hart, / Water *Barwick*, water, Ile meddle with't no more."[16] Like *The Whore of Babylon*, this play assigns the English Bible a power that is incomprehensible, and therefore terrifying, to Catholic characters whom the playwright uses to affirm the potency of this physical symbol of the Protestant faith. In addition to performing a sort of prophetic role within the fiction, the Bible would have been particularly noticeable on stage. Unlike Ophelia's prayer book, which could easily be represented by any small volume, the Bible could not be realistically represented by anything but the Bible; it was potentially blasphemous to bring any religious subject matter on the stage, but far worse to falsify the holy scriptures. I would like to speculate, then, that for their performance of this play the company bought or borrowed an actual copy of the scriptures.

The visual impact the Bible might have had on stage and the degree to which it manifested Elizabeth's status as defender of the Protestant faith against the threat of popery is evident in several popular images of the queen. At St. Clements Eastcheap, for example, a monument to Elizabeth was created "in the figure of a book," and it described the queen as "Britain's Blessing, England's Splendour, Religion's Nurse, the Faith's Defender." At St. Mary le Bow she appeared with angels, who held a Bible over her head inscribed with the words "*Verbum Dei.*" The title page of Heywood's *England's Elizabeth* (1631) shows her standing next to a table with a Bible on it, meditating on the meaning of Psalm 66. A more formal example of this type of imagery can be found in the memorial portrait executed by Crispin van de Passe (Figure 4.1).

---

[16]   *If you know not me, you know no bodie: or, The troubles of Queene Elizabeth* (London: Purfoot, 1605), ll. 1039-41.

Figure 4.1   Van de Passe, "Portrait of Queen Elizabeth," 1603-1604. By permission of the Folger Shakespeare Library

Here Elizabeth stands majestically holding the scepter and orb, but on a table next to her are two equally important objects: a sword and a book labeled "Verbum Dei." Although in this portrait the book is closed, acting as a more or less static attribute of Elizabeth's virtue, *the female figure of Religion* in the public pageant *Brittania's honor* (1628) appears in a white robe with a book open in her hand. It is crucial that the object held by the pageant figure is described as being open, both because it suggests the practice of reading and because it refers to the Protestant project of giving the word of God back to the laity. In a much earlier play by martyrologist John Foxe, "thrones descend 'as if from heaven' and ... the power of the Word is dramatized by a reading from the open Bibles on the thrones."[17]

The gesture of opening the Bible, signifying its accessibility to all the queen's subjects, is a crucial element of the depiction of Elizabeth in *If You Know Not Me You Know Nobody*, a play that focuses on the persecution of the young Elizabeth during the reign of her sister, Mary. This play ends where Dekker's begins, with a reference to the coronation pageant and to Elizabeth's kissing of the Bible in front of her subjects, and her final speech clearly emphasizes the significance the play attaches to the act of giving the Bible back to the people:

> *Elizabeth.* We thanke you all: but first this booke I kisse,
> Thou art the way to honor; thou to blisse,
> An English Bible, thanks my good Lord Maior,
> You of our bodie and our soule haue care,
> This is the Jewell that we still love best,
> This was our solace when we were distrest,
> This booke that hath so long conceald it selfe,
> So long shut up, so long hid; now Lords see,
> We here unclaspe, for ever it is free:
> . . . .
> Who builds on this, dwel's in a happy state,
> This is the fountaine cleere imaculate,
> That happy yssue that shall us succeed,
> And in our populous Kingdome this booke read:
> For them as for our owne selves we humbly pray,
> They may live long and blest; so lead the way.
> (ll. 1578-98)

Here Elizabeth functions as a model of the devout Protestant, and in kissing the Bible she emphasizes her dedication to God's word as opposed to the ecclesiastical authority of Mary's church. Furthermore, the public unclasping and opening of this book ensure not only the salvation of the queen's soul but her people's, as she imagines the entire kingdom eagerly reading the long-lost English scriptures. Heywood's script, inspired by actual accounts of the coronation, cleverly conflates

[17] Dawson and Yachnin, 144.

the Bible given to Elizabeth with the multiple copies of the text that were to be read by her subjects. This elision, like the one between "fake" properties and "real" scriptures, allows the play to point outward beyond the fiction to the status of the Bible in post-Reformation practice.

This scene may have reminded some playgoers that Elizabeth's triumph over her enemies was analogous to the long-awaited resurfacing of the English Bible itself. When copies of William Tyndale's translation were first circulated in England in April of 1526, the authorities promptly had them burned at Paul's Cross, and it was not until 1539 that state sanctioned copies of the so-called Great Bible were made available for purchase by parishes wealthy enough to own one.[18] The title page of this latter volume depicted Elizabeth's father Henry distributing the word of God to Cranmer and Cromwell, who would then distribute it to the people. But by 1543 Cranmer had begun to push for a more authentic translation "corrected by the Vulgate," and an act was passed to prohibit "the use of Tyndale or any other annotated Bible in English."[19] Ten years after her ascension, in 1569, Elizabeth herself finally appeared on the cover of a newly sanctioned edition of *The Bishops' Bible*. Theologians might still have disagreed about which version of the English Bible was best, but by the time of Elizabeth's reign the scriptures had officially become a fixture in English parish life. Thus the princess's triumph over her tormentors in *If You Know Not Me* could be equated, in the long history of the Reformation told from the Protestant point of view, with the victory of the English Bible over its detractors.

Plays such as Heywood's celebrate Elizabeth's legacy by recounting in dramatic form the mythology that had developed around her affection for the English Bible. But by bringing the coronation procession on stage, the play also reminds its audience that Elizabeth's public image, which was based on Protestant ideals about the immateriality of faith, was very much rooted in physical gestures and in the Bible itself as a material object. The play explicitly draws upon the account of Elizabeth's first public appearance as ruler in *The Quenes Majesties Passage*, where her gestures are described as almost liturgical: "[b]ut she as soone as she had received the booke, kyssed it, and with both her handes held up the same, and so laid it upon her brest, with great thankes to the citie therefore."[20] Another observer, Richard Mulcaster, marveled at "how reverently did she with both her hands take it, kiss it, and lay it upon her breast," before promising "the reading thereof most

---

[18]   P. R. Ackroyd, Christopher Evans, S. L. Greenslade, and G. W. H. Lampe, eds, *The Cambridge History of the Bible* vol. 3 (Cambridge: Cambridge University Press, 1963), 142.

[19]   Ibid., 152-3.

[20]   *The passage of our most drad Soueraigne Lady Quene Elyzabeth through the citie of London to westminster the daye before her coronacion Anno 1558* (London: Tottill, 1558), C2ᵛ.

diligently."[21] These outward gestures were crucial components of Elizabeth's attempt to cement her public image, and her physical demonstration of her love for the Bible echoes, on a larger scale, the argument implicit in *Hamlet*. Just as objects and gestures are necessary for one worshiper to communicate with another, it was Elizabeth's project as queen to create engaging spectacles that would make her subjects believe she would defend them and their faith at all costs.

The physical presence of the Bible is also crucial to an earlier scene from Heywood's play in which the book figures prominently as a symbol of both divine providence and Elizabeth's personal salvation. Confined to the Tower, Elizabeth is about to be attacked by her enemies when a pair of angels arrives to rescue her:

> *A dumb show. Enter Winchester, Constable, Barwick, and Fryars: at the other dore 2. Angels: the Fryar steps to her, offering to kill her: the Angels drive them back. Exeunt. The Angel opens the Bible, and puts it in her hand as she sleepes, Exeunt Angels, she wakes.* (ll. 1049-53)

This dumb show, like the one at the beginning of *The Whore of Babylon*, makes manifest the Bible's symbolic power, but it also represents the book as a literal shield against Elizabeth's detractors. Moreover, it serves as a tool for divination when she wakes and reads the lines underneath her finger out loud: "*Who so putteth his trust in the Lord, / Shall not be confounded*" (ll. 1064-5). The scene of Elizabeth's rescue is different in two crucial ways from the one in *The Two Noble Ladies*, although the staging in the later play may have been inspired by this one. First, a Bible, and not a prayer book, is associated with driving away demons—or in this case, Catholic friars. Second, Elizabeth is assisted by angels and sleeps through the entire event, whereas Justina actively uses her prayer book to repel her would-be attackers. In contrast to the scene in which Elizabeth makes a show of kissing the Bible and displaying it to her subjects, this scene celebrates her role as an exemplary woman reader rather than as defender of the faith.

It is possible that Heywood created a more passive role for the princess in this scene because he did not want the play to suggest that the young Elizabeth was in the habit of summoning angels to do her bidding. The play is also consciously constructing a providential account of her girlhood, reading the queen's political savvy as an adult back onto her experiences as an adolescent and confirming that she was destined through providence to become the defender of the true faith. Heywood may even have been inspired by popular Protestant polemics, for Richard Fletcher had already articulated a similar account of Elizabeth's early years in 1587. When he preached before the queen in February of that year, Fletcher reminded her of how God's angel had smote her enemies "in the hinder part[es]," rousing her and loosening her chains as he had done when freeing

---

[21]   Leah Marcus, Janel Mueller, and Mary Beth Rose, eds, *Elizabeth I: Complete Works* (Chicago: University of Chicago Press, 2000), 55.

St. Peter from prison, before finally leading her to her succession.[22] Curiously, Fletcher's narrative, which stands conveniently between John Foxe's account of Elizabeth's providential life history in the *Acts and Monuments* and Heywood's, does not include the Bible. All three narratives emphasize the providential nature of Elizabeth's triumph, but only *If You Know Not Me* accentuates the role the English scriptures played in the development of her public image by giving them a kind of dramatic agency in her deliverance.

Although it reveals the contradiction between Elizabeth's iconographic public image and the Protestant notion that the word of God was itself immaterial, *If You Know Not Me You Know Nobody* supplies a resolution to this problem through an act of reading which, unlike Justina's in *The Two Noble Ladies*, is construed as properly dematerialized. Confined to the Tower and interrogated about her faith, the young Elizabeth calls for her "book" and tells her maid to "leade me where you please / From sight of day; or in a dungeon; I shall see to pray" (ll. 607-8). In this scene the act of reading is almost metaphysical—the princess asserts that she has internalized the words in her personal prayer book by committing them to memory—and it is this transcendent attitude that allows her to escape any charge of counterfeit reading. Ironically, this claim precedes the Constable's idle threat that he will "lay her in a dungeon where her eyes, / Should not have light to read her prayer booke." He hopes, by putting her through a series of tortures, to make her curse "her faythles prayer," but she is already destined to confound his expectations (ll. 718-19, 723). Another way to read the centrality of both the Bible and the prayer book in this play is to suggest that these two objects represent another iteration of the theory of the king's two bodies. Her dedication to the Bible indicates Elizabeth's status as future head of the Protestant church and identifies her with the male reformers who struggled to get an English translation of the scriptures into print, while her prayer book represents the more circumscribed set of reading practices that were acceptable for young aristocratic ladies. As we will see, other female characters in English history plays are presented as devout readers, but only Elizabeth is presented both as a Bible reader and a prayer book user.

The only concrete clue we have about the physical characteristics of the various book properties in this script is that at least one of them would have to have been large enough to play a prominent role in the dumb show. Both types of books were appropriate signs of Elizabeth's personal faith, but a folio copy of the Bible would have been too heavy for the actor to carry around on stage for any duration of time, while the more portable prayer book could have been used to display the princess's fondness for devotional reading in several different scenes. The close proximity between the reader's body and the prayer book also facilitated the kind of regular reading that for Heywood's Elizabeth eventually resulted in her internalization of the words themselves. Although they could be covered with velvet or gilding, printed books were relatively inexpensive, and thus came to be associated with

[22]   Peter McCullough, "Out of Egypt," in *Dissing Elizabeth*, ed. Julia Walker (Durham: Duke University Press, 1998), 118-49, 129.

a more widespread and diverse set of reading practices. In practical terms, this meant that prayer books could be more readily appropriated as properties, but an actor holding a "prayer book" might just as easily be carrying a printed sermon, a treatise against the use of cosmetics, or a play script. On the one hand, then, the fact that prayer books were relatively cheap meant that playing companies could easily borrow or buy one for a performance. On the other hand, the prayer book, when put on stage, was indistinguishable from any other small volume. The reformed faith was rooted in the project, promoted by writers such as Tyndale, of solidifying a particular set of values—what I have been calling an "affective technology"— even though in everyday life those values were constituted by a disparate group of practices and beliefs. The theater used its own visual techniques to demonstrate the contradiction inherent in the ideal of a dematerialized faith, not as an attack on Protestantism *per se* but as an exercise in exploring the ideological intricacies of the material practices that were so often associated with actors and papists.

If, as I have been arguing, Heywood's play was performed with an actual Bible on stage, an object whose presence would have given particular weight to the fictional events being depicted, we might ask to what extent Elizabeth is identified in this play with the boy actor who takes on her role. When the newly-crowned queen put the Bible to her chest and promised to commit its contents to memory, she was indicating, as Heywood's character does when she says that she can read her prayer book without any light, that the book is part of her. This process of internalization defuses the threat that either book might be a mere thing, capable of being misused or misidentified, but it also alludes to the analogy between theatrical and theological practice, for by committing the book to heart Elizabeth was doing precisely what an actor did in memorizing his role. The actor playing Elizabeth uses the book as a powerful theatrical property while simultaneously asserting that if you know how to pray you do not need the book at all. *If You Know Not Me You Know Nobody* simultaneously works to represent the positive aspects of Elizabeth's public image and to acknowledge the innate theatricality of her dedication to the word of God.

Common Prayer

If the plays that depict Elizabeth's attachment to her books present the most extreme example of the central role women played in Protestant iconography, other dramatic texts present a broad spectrum of female characters who use prayer books—all of whom, to varying degrees, make reference to the pervasive image of the godly woman reader. In what follows I provide further evidence for my contention that the theater was actively commenting upon the central role played by women, ordinary English citizens as well as queens and princesses, in Protestant propaganda. In 1543 an act of parliament restricted the privilege of reading the scriptures in public to "licensed persons" and forbade all women and lower-class persons from reading the Bible at all.[23] According to Susan Wabuda, "[n]oblewomen or gentlewomen might read the Scriptures to themselves, but only in the greatest privacy, out of the range of hearing of any other person." Although this act was withdrawn later, in Edward's reign, the English Bible was suppressed once again during the reign of Elizabeth's sister Mary. John Foxe reports that a woman who was caught smuggling religious books into London was reprimanded by the Bishop of London and told that, "[i]t is more fit for thee to meddle with thy distaff, than to meddle with the scriptures."[24] Such anecdotes tell us as much about the Protestant view of Catholic tyranny as they do about the actual lives of early modern women, but they nonetheless underscore the centrality of the female reader, especially the ordinary female reader, to Protestant ideology.

Just as widely circulating images of Elizabeth emphasized the importance of the Bible to her personal iconography, a series of woodcuts from Protestant texts helps us understand the role women and their prayer books played in telling the history of the Reformation. The title page of Foxe's *Actes and Monuments* (1563), for example, famously juxtaposes scenes of pre and post-Reformation devotion in order to show his readers how far they have come. His engraver's representation of godly religion shows a Protestant minister preaching to a group of men and women; in the front row, one woman holds a book open in her lap to indicate that she is reading the Word as it is being preached. In the engraver's depiction of Catholicism, on the other hand, women are fingering their rosary beads, distracted by the popish procession taking place in the background. Rosary beads were among the first objects banned by the early reformers, and here these "trifles" are directly contrasted to the acts of devotional reading taking place on the other side of the image.

In general, the theater exploited the pervasiveness of this imagery rather than challenging it, as *Hamlet* does through the character of Ophelia, and several plays self-consciously cater to audience members' desire to see characters acting out the cultural fantasy of the godly woman. Just before Anne Saunders, the wayward wife of *A Warning for Fair Women* (1599), is led away to the gallows, she repents her husband's murder and, as part of her penance, gives her prayer book to her children. Instructing them to benefit from its lessons and from her mistakes, she exclaims, "[o]h children learne, learne by your mothers fall / To follow vertue, and beware of sinne, / Whose baites are sweete and pleasing to the eie, / But being tainted, more infect than poison."[25] The book she gives them is no generic prayer manual, however; it is specifically identified as the *Godlie Meditations* of

---

[23]   Ackroyd et al., vol. 3, 153.

[24]   Susan Wabuda, "The woman with the rock: the controversy on women and Bible reading," in *Belief and Practice in Reformation England*, eds Caroline Lintzenberger and Susan Wabuda (Aldershot and Brookfield, VT: Ashgate, 1998), 40-59, 42, 58.

[25]   *A Warning for Fair Women. A Critical Edition*, ed. Charles Dale Cannon (The Hague: Mouton, 1975), ll. 2686-9.

John Bradford, originally published in 1562.[26] By dramatizing this recognizably contemporary moment of penance, in which a former adulteress performs her proper function as a moral example to her children and identifies herself with the writings of a Protestant martyr, the play reinscribes the values that were threatened by Anne's initial transgression.

A more extensive portrait of the repentant adulteress with her prayer book appears in Heywood's *Edward IV*, part 2 (1599), first produced the same year as *A Warning for Fair Women*. While part 1 of the play details Edward's seduction of Jane Shore, part 2 focuses almost exclusively on her humility. After her lover the king dies, Jane stages her penance publicly, but she also performs a private display with her prayer book in her jail cell, a performance to which the audience is given voyeuristic access. Jean Howard has described Jane as a "desexualized" being who poses no threat to the male hierarchies depicted in the play. Howard also argues that through her suffering and humility she "becomes the city's fantasy of its own virtue."[27] This fantasy, constructed in part through Jane's devotion to her prayer book, places audience members in a viewing position analogous to the individual male characters who watch and pity her throughout the play.

The prayer book that figures prominently in *Edward IV* is not Jane's personal prayer book but one given to her by her jailor, Brackenbury. Because she once pleaded successfully for his kinsman's life, he declares his intention to provide her with spiritual as well as physical nourishment, and the stage direction conflates these two gifts: "*Enter Brakenburie with a prayer booke, and some releefe in a cloath.*"[28] Brackenbury begins by addressing the audience on the subject of Jane's suffering, describing her as "basely wronged" and "vildly used," and he specifically directs the spectator's gaze to her body. "See where she sits," he urges them, focusing attention on the spectacle of Jane's suffering (K6^v-K7^r). Addressing Jane herself, Brackenbury then explains the theological importance of the prayer book he is about to give her:

> First take that to releeve thy bodie with,
> And next, receive this booke, wherein is foode,
> Manna of heaven to refresh thy soule:
> These holy meditations mistris Shoare,
> Will yeeld much comfort in this miserie,

---

[26]   Viviana Comensoli, "'*Household Business*'": *Domestic Plays of Early Modern England* (Toronto: University of Toronto Press, 1996), 97.

[27]   "Other Englands," in *Other Voices, Other Views*, eds Helen Ostovich, Mary Silcox, and Graham Roebuck (Newark; London: University of Delaware; Associated University Press, 1999), 135-53, 148.

[28]   *The first and second partes of King Edward the Fourth Containing his mery pastime with the tanner of Tamworth, as also his love to faire Mistrisse Shoare* (London: Kingston, 1600), K6^v.

Whereon contemplate still, and never linne,
That God may be unmindfull of thy sinne.
(K7ʳ)

The book is described as food for the soul and proof of God's mercy, even for the sinner. Jane herself picks up the theme of holy book as sustenance, addressing the object as "sweete prayer booke, foode of my life, / The soveraigne balme for my sicke conscience" (K7ʳ). This self-conscious explication of the prayer book and its connection to spiritual well-being further emphasizes what Brackenbury has already told us about Jane, namely, that she has been mistreated and now has become a sincere penitent. Having established the lens through which the audience is to read Jane's character, Brackenbury leaves her alone on stage, giving the audience exclusive access to her solitude, at which point Jane begins "*weeping & praying*" (K7ʳ).

Though she and Anne Saunders are intended to serve as negative examples to women who might be similarly tempted to sin, the language Jane and Brackenbury use to describe the prayer book speaks to the role it was meant to play in the household routine of every English woman. Most parishioners took communion only rarely, but the comfort provided by the prayer book was available on a regular basis, and it could be used to prepare the churchgoer for receiving the sacrament in the proper frame of mind. The meditations contained in prayer books were, like bread, something that must be consumed daily in order to sustain life, and not just by aristocratic ladies but by middle-class women as well. Brackenbury's speech and Jane's reply constitute a kind of catechism on this subject of the prayer book as nourishment, and as such the scene acknowledges the importance of absorbing the words and ideas contained in the book itself. By comparing her prayer book to something she can internalize, Jane, like the young Elizabeth, avoids treating the book as a mere property, but by turning the demonstration of her piety into a theatrical spectacle the drama once again demonstrates that even this act of properly dematerialized reading is itself a performance.

Like *2 Edward IV*, Dekker and Webster's *Sir Thomas Wyatt* (1602), uses prayer book properties to highlight the visual aspects of female piety, but this later play provides a more dynamic exploration of reformed devotion. Set against the backdrop of Mary's Catholic court, the play retells the story of Lady Jane Grey and her husband, both of whom are portrayed as pawns in their fathers' strategy to get Jane crowned queen of England. When Mary first enters, complaining of having been passed over for the throne in favor of her brother Edward, she enters "*with a Prayer Booke in her hand, like a Nun,*" having apparently embraced a life of poverty (1.3.0 sd.). Unlike Edward, who lives in "pompe and state," Mary has rejected all worldly pleasures for a humble abbey and "a rich prayer Booke," which she addresses affectionately in a speech that echoes Brackenbury's:

> The Golden Mines of wealthy India,
> Is all as drosse compared to thy sweetnesse.
> Thou art the joy, and comfort of the poore,
> The everlasting blisse in thee we finde.
> This little volume inclosed in this hand,
> Is richer then the Empire of this land.
> (1.3.4, 8-14)

Mary concludes—correctly, from a Protestant as well as a Catholic point of view—that the prayer book is "the joy, and comfort of the poore," and the path to "everlasting blisse." Contrasting heavenly joys to earthly ones, she appears to have absorbed the lessons contained in the prayer book, lessons that would have been appropriate in either a pre- or a post-Reformation context. Her words may even have reminded the audience that Catholic prayer books, many of which were still being produced in places such as St. Omer and smuggled into England, were essentially similar in function to books of Protestant prayer. But when her advisers enter a few lines later and alert her that she may soon achieve the throne, she abandons her nunnery and eagerly follows their suggestion that she show herself publicly like a queen in order to stir up support for her cause. The rapidity with which she leaves the prayer book and the cloister behind renders ironic her stated fondness for its riches and its "sweetnesse." Like *If You Know Not Me You Know Nobody*, this play can be read as dramatizing two different sides of the Protestant dynamic that elevated Elizabeth's piety via her attachment to the Bible and accused Mary of hypocrisy because of her preference for glittering idols.

In *Sir Thomas Wyatt*, Lady Jane Grey, famous during her lifetime for her homiletic writings, experiences a sense of relief in escaping the material world that provides a striking contrast to Mary's eagerness for the crown and serves as a kind of stand-in for Elizabeth.[29] Indeed, according to the stage direction, both Jane and her husband Guilford make their final appearances reading. Sentenced to die for conspiring to put Jane on the throne, the lovers turn to prayer books shortly before their deaths, just as Anne Saunders does. Unlike Anne, however, these two characters have nothing particularly sinful to atone for, and their meditations are focused less on penance than on the standard tropes of the *memento mori*:

> *Guilford.* What were you reading?
> *Jane.*   On a prayer booke.
> *Guilford.* Trust me so was I, wee hade neede to pray,
>   For see, the Ministers of death drawe neere.
> *Jane.*   To a prepared minde death is a pleasure,
>   I long in soule, till I have spent my breath.
>   (5.2.46-51)

---

[29]   King, "The Godly Woman in Elizabethan Iconography," 74.

This brief exchange focuses on the spiritual message contained in the prayer book, and its conversational quality further normalizes their preparation for death. Jane in particular is given the chance to express her willingness to die in the final scene, relying on her book for comfort. In this she follows the example set by women such as Grace Mildmay, who says of her daily meditations, "when I present them to [God], in the sincere devotion of my mind, my soul receiveth unspeakable consolation."[30] On the other hand, Jane's performance, which makes her—like Jane Shore in *Edward IV, part 2*—the object of the audience members' admiration and pity, is also designed to remind them of their own interest in the material spectacle of her penance, just as it reminds them of the inescapable physicality of Jane's use of the prayer book. According to contemporary accounts, the real Jane Grey did indeed go to her death with "a black velvet book hanging before her," and Alexandra Walsham notes that such accessories had a dual signification: they were both decorative luxury items and supposed proof of the intimacy between the owner and her text, the devotional ideal exemplified in Elizabeth's assertion in *If You Know Not Me You Know Nobody* that she can read her prayer book in the dark.[31]

Sir Thomas Wyatt heightens the contradiction between Jane's womanhood and her high-minded devotion by contrasting her desire to escape her body with her husband's desire to hold onto it. Guilford chides the executioner for daring to do violence to "a face so faire" and insists on lamenting her loss in physical terms (5.2.113). Even when confronted with her severed head, he praises it for retaining its beauty, noting "a ruddie lippe, / A cleere reflecting eye, / Cheekes purer then the Maiden oreant pearle" (164-6). His uxoriousness in the face of this bloody spectacle might prompt the audience to think twice about their own attachment to Jane's beauty, for they, like Guilford, have been made to attend to her physical actions and gestures, including any stage business with the prayer book property, throughout the course of the play. Through its use of such properties *Sir Thomas Wyatt* contrasts Jane's enduring devotion with Mary's fleeting interest in her prayer book in an attempt to distinguish between Protestant and Catholic practice. On a visual level, however, this distinction is threatened not only by the cross-dressed boy actor's distracting beauty but also by the material resemblance between the two books. The similarity between the various prayer book properties—Mary's "little volume" may have reappeared in Jane's hand, or in Guilford's—points out the difficulty in distinguishing Jane's sincerity from Mary's temporary devotion to her book. This play, like the others discussed in this section, can also be fruitfully read alongside the scene of Ophelia's fake reading, for what they each expose is a basic instability in the way a male-dominated Protestant rhetoric articulated the role of the woman reader. Because of her sensual beauty and her perceived corruptibility, a woman by her very nature endangered the project of godly reading. Yet as a model for her children and a companion to her husband,

30 Linda Pollock, *With Faith and Physic: The Life of a Tudor Gentlewoman, Lady Grace Mildmay* (London: Collins and Brown, 1993), 84.
31 "Jewels for Gentlewomen," 129.

she was absolutely central to the composition of the godly household. Each of these texts explores this duality embedded in the ideal of the virtuous woman, but among surviving play scripts, only *Sir Thomas Wyatt* demonstrates the potential disruption of that chain of ideological signification by highlighting the vulnerability of the prayer book as well as the supposed fragility of the female body.

The scenes of prayer book reading discussed above have been implicitly labeled as either "public," like Richard's and Jane Grey's, or "private" acts made public to the audience at the theater, like Jane Shore's. As Lena Cowen Orlin has shown, however, the separation between these two terms was not a clean one; contrary to our twenty-first-century understanding of the nuclear family, the early modern household was not an arena of undisturbed privacy. The model of the godly household was always under scrutiny, relying upon the presence of a competent wife as well as a careful husband precisely because the success of this microcosm reflected the success of the Protestant project. Flying in the face of this ideal, and in the face of the example set by characters such as Anne Saunders, the anti-heroine of *Arden of Faversham* (1591) rejects both her earthly husband and her divine paramour. A flagrant adulteress, Alice Arden uses her prayer book not to display her sense of sorrow for the wrongs she has done her husband, as Anne Saunders and Jane Grey do, but to impress her lover with her lack of reverence for this emblem of domestic loyalty. In order to contextualize Alice's transgression and her misuse of the prayer book, it is worth exploring in more detail the ideal of domesticity she so violently resists.

In post-Reformation England, "the archetypal good woman was a godly matron, obeying her husband, caring for her children and servants, and spending her spare time in private devotion."[32] This set of values, which centered around acts of reading, is manifested in nondramatic works such as *A Pattern for Women* (1619), an instructional text that describes the daily life of one Lucy Thornton, a devout and learned lady whose religious habits dominated her entire household: "In her private familie, prayers morning and evening, reading of the Scriptures, and singing of Psalmes, were never wanting in manie yeeres." The anonymous "bachelor of divinitie," who authored a short biographical pamphlet in her honor, celebrates Lucy for her ability to "readily recite fit texts of Scripture for any purpose, and finde them out." Unlike the "dul Hebrue," who had the text but not the understanding, she "was capable of great mysteries" in her use of holy books, and these mysteries were not superstitious ones, but useful lessons for herself and the members of her household.[33] In a more personal account, a Somerset clothier describes his dead wife as "full of virtues … godly of mind, a diligent hearer of the

---

[32]   Lena Cowen Orlin, *Private Matters and Public Culture in Post-Reformation England* (Ithaca: Cornell University Press, 1994), 39.

[33]   John Mayer, *A patterne for women: setting forth the most Christian life, & most comfortable death of Mrs. Lucy late wife to the worshipfull Roger Thornton* (London: Griffin, 1619), A8ʳ-B1ᵛ.

word preached, devout in her secret prayers."[34] This sense of nostalgic admiration for a woman humble enough to keep her devotions to herself is echoed in *The Revenger's Tragedy* (1606). "I mark'd not this before," Lord Antonio says of his wife after her death, "[a] prayer book the pillow to her cheek, / This was her rich confection."[35] Through a husband's discovery, the play creates the portrait of a woman whose prayers are free from any taint of false theatricality precisely because no one ever sees them. The scene thus attempts to instantiate the fantasy of a purely dematerialized faith, but it does so using the example of a woman whose sexuality has been contained once and for all, suggesting to the audience that perhaps the fantasy is less easily "proved" than Lord Antonio suggests. Underscoring the irony of making this otherwise private woman into a spectacle, this piece of dialogue describes a nameless character whose early death—along with the absent presence of the virtuous Gloriana's skull, which her lover Vindice dresses up as a prostitute—makes way for a distinctly misogynist view of the outward showiness of female sexuality.

Although many early modern women were lauded for their chaste dedication to prayer and/or learning, the presence of books in the private home had the potential to take on more erotic overtones, as in Richard Crashaw's ode "praefixed to a little Prayer book given to a young Gentlewoman." This poem, which admittedly reflects the poet's own preference for the material objects associated with traditional religion, lingers over the physical nature of the book, its proximity to the reader's body, and the many pleasures associated with divine love. The speaker of Crashaw's "Prayer" calls the book "a nest of new-born sweets" who desire to be cradled in "kind hands. ... And confidently look / To find the rest / Of a rich binding in your brest." And though he urges the owner of the book to keep those hands "pure" and her eyes "chast and true," he refers not to a withdrawal from sensuality but to her constant devotion to a single lover. Inverting an entire set of gendered metaphors, the poem gives the young gentlewoman the right "[t]o rifle and deflour / The rich and roseall spring of those rare sweets / Which with a swelling bosome there she meets / Boundles and infinite / Bottomless treasures / Of pure inebriating pleasures." The speaker also warns that anyone wishing to study this craft "[m]ust be a sure house-keeper," and not allow her lover to find her absent, mentally or physically, when he comes to call.[36] In this sense Crashaw's poem picks up on the values espoused elsewhere in *A Pattern for Women*. Whether construed as a probing lover or a well-trained reader, the female prayer book owner must treat the book with care lest she violate the sanctity of her home.

Despite such warnings, the threat of violation was ever present, and it is vividly dramatized in *Arden of Faversham*, in which Alice's deviant attitude toward her

---

[34]   Collinson, 73.

[35]   Cyril Tourneur, *The Revenger's Tragedy*, ed. Lawrence J. Ross (Lincoln: University of Nebraska Press, 1966), 1.4.12-14.

[36]   *Steps to the temple sacred poems with other delights of the muses* (T. W.: London, 1646), E2[r-v].

role as homemaker begins with her preference for Mosby over her husband. While Arden is away on business, Alice makes Mosby head of her household, asserting that it is her husband who unjustly "usurps" her lover's place: "Sweet Mosby is the man that hath my heart; / And he usurps it, having nought but this, / That I am tied to him by marriage. / Love is a god, and marriage is but words; / And therefore Mosby's title is the best."[37] Marriage, Alice argues, is nominal, while love is sacred, and therefore Mosby, not Arden, has the best claim to her affections. By displacing existing legal structures in favor of the doctrine of romance, Alice injures not only her husband but also the social structures that make him her superior. Mosby, according to Alice, is master of her heart and thus may be master of the house. But the full extent of Alice's apostasy is not revealed until she threatens to destroy a crucial emblem of domestic virtue.

Like husband and wife, Alice and Mosby are constantly quarrelling, and after a particularly brutal exchange she begs for his forgiveness, using her prayer book as a marker of her sincerity:

> I will do penance for offending thee,
> And burn this prayerbook, where I here use
> The holy word that had converted me.
> See, Mosby, I will tear away the leaves,
> And all the leaves, and in this golden cover
> Shall thy sweet phrases and thy letters dwell;
> And thereon will I chiefly meditate
> And hold no other sect but such devotion.
> (8.115-22)

Compounding sin with sin, Alice has replaced her husband with her lover and the god who blessed her marriage with the god of love; worse still, she threatens to tear out her prayer book pages and replace them with Mosby's letters. Ironically, the acts Alice promises to do in the name of penance are closer to Protestant iconoclasm than to traditional gestures of repentance. First she offers to burn the book, which she admits has "converted" her. Like any good iconoclast, however, she knows that the defaced object is a more powerful reminder than one that has been destroyed altogether, and so she offers to "tear away" the leaves themselves. Finally, she proposes to put Mosby's love notes in her prayer book, making them, rather than the word of God, the object of her spiritual meditations. Although her proposed deeds echo sanctioned forms of Protestant iconoclasm, Alice's threat is the ultimate manifestation of the godly home turned upside down. Rather than serving as proof of her piety, the prayer book becomes the focus of her rejection of the godly ideals epitomized in images such as Foxe's. And unlike Ophelia's "pious actions," which are analogous to the false gestures of the actor, Alice's

---

[37] *The Tragedy of Master Arden of Faversham,* ed. Martin L. Wine (London: Methuen, 1973), 11.98-102.

words refer to actual crimes that she is more than willing to commit and that represent a real danger to the patriarchal family unit. The play thus demonstrates the potential disruption of the associations between women and domestic virtue by highlighting the vulnerability of the prayer book as well as the supposed weakness of the female body. In contrast to the men and women who erect what Ramie Targoff calls "a pretense of conformity that successfully masked their unreachable inwardness," *Arden of Faversham* focuses on a woman who is eager to bring her unholy thoughts to light.[38]

The play seems to emphasize the fact that Alice's actions have broad ideological implications by refusing to have her carry them out, though the language of books and leaves continues to haunt the text. "If," says Arden, "love of me or care of womanhood … fear of God or common speech of men" would make her repent, "[n]o question then but she would turn the leaf / And sorrow for her dissolution" (4.2-3, 7-8). But since Alice has no love for her husband, no fear of God or concern about her reputation—which, as Arden indicates, is grounded in the immaterial concept of "womanhood"—she would rather destroy the leaf than turn it. She expresses regret only after being sentenced to hang, and even then the play denies the audience any satisfactory display of repentance. When she declares her intention to "meditate upon my Saviour Christ / Whose blood must save me for the blood I shed," she seems to overestimate Christ's willingness to fulfill his part of the bargain, and she is immediately interrupted by Mosby, who calls her a strumpet and exclaims that "[f]ie upon women!" is the only doctrine he adheres to (18.10-11, 34).

The shock value of Alice Arden's attack on her prayer book is considerable, but the play manages to preserve the possibility that the social order can be reestablished. Following the historical events on which it was based, *Arden of Faversham* never allows Alice to carry out her threat and later emphasizes the severity of her punishment for the murder of her husband. In this sense the play answers Orlin's definition of the purpose of domestic tragedy: "to identify disorder and to imagine that in this way it is mastered, to participate in communal restoration of the preferred order of domestic things."[39] Because the domestic tragedy is ultimately concerned with social stability, the destruction of the prayer book is one crime it is not willing to stage. Although *Arden of Faversham* deprives spectators of the chance to see Alice repent as Anne Saunders does, refusing to recuperate her as an exemplary godly woman, it nonetheless reminds its audience how important their acts of piety were to the dominant value systems in post-Reformation England.

In contrast to other dramatic depictions of female devotion, this play alerts its audience to the potential for the misuse of religious texts that accompanies their broad distribution. On the other hand it makes clear that Alice is not the only one at fault here. When he chooses to tolerate the affair between Alice and Mosby, Arden

---

[38]   Targoff, 2.

[39]   Orlin, 8.

abdicates his proper role in the household and, quite literally, leaves the door open for Alice's betrayal. By accentuating his cowardice, as well as the inappropriate amount of control she has over him and all the other men in the play, *Arden of Faversham* exposes existing fears about the state of a religion that valorizes the widespread use of prayer books, making them available to unscrupulous women such as Alice Arden. If the piety of Jane Shore and Lady Jane Grey is meant to represent the purity of the new Protestant nation state, Alice poses a threat to that ideal that is purposefully confined to a village on the outskirts of London.

This chapter began with the assertion that the playing companies justified their own reliance on properties and costumes by pointing out Protestantism's dependence on physical objects such as books. *Arden of Faversham* goes one step further in eliding the difference between the book property and the thing it is designed to represent. When Alice abandons her book, she also abandons the object that stands in for her book, which exits the fiction and re-enters the tiring house. It becomes temporarily useless, worth no more than the paper it is printed on. Yet the virtue of the property, especially this type of property, lay precisely in its anonymity, which made it reusable. It could easily reappear in a scene of secular reading or as another woman's prayer book—even as a Catholic character's primer. Thus the fluctuation in the prayer book property's status, from an emblem of domestic loyalty to a symbol of Alice's transgression to an anonymous sheaf of papers, also speaks to Walsham's research on the transformation of Catholic prayer books into Protestant ones. Neither the outlawed book of hours nor the discarded stage property was entirely valueless, for each might be transformed in the next moment, endowed with a new set of meanings and reestablished as something different but not entirely unrecognizable. The Catholic prayer book that the king carries with him into the woods in *3 Henry VI* (1591) might, for instance, have reappeared in Gloucester's hands a year later. Similarly, the copy of Bradford's meditations that Anne Saunders gives to her children in *A Warning for Fair Women* might have been reintroduced as the book that Polonius presses on the hapless Ophelia. Small codexes were inexpensive enough that it would be foolish to try to make a definitive statement about the possibility that a single prayer book would be reused over and over again by the same company. Nonetheless, the theoretical point remains a compelling one. Through the actions of its iconoclastic protagonist, *Arden of Faversham* suggests that, like stage properties, prayer books cannot maintain a fixed value. The very materiality of the prayer book resists the symbolic functions assigned to it by the reformers, undermining its role as a clear alternative to the false theatricality embodied in the gestures of the priest. In everyday practice, however, the adaptability of private prayer manuals was an asset to their owners, just as it was an asset to the playing companies.

Because so much is at stake in *Arden of Faversham*'s representation of English domesticity, Alice's mistreatment of her prayer book is perhaps the most dramatic example of the way in which religious books can be misused, and it focuses less on the elision of playacting and pious gestures than it does on the vulnerability of the prayer book itself, a vulnerability that jeopardizes the affective technologies associated with it. In fact the implications of Alice's speech may be more radical and more interesting than a mere challenge to patriarchal values. If she were to burn it on stage, we could group her with iconoclasts whose acts of destruction ironically confirm the power of the things they hate. Instead, she discards her prayer book as if it were a stage property that no longer has any value. Whether using it to perform the role of devout wife or convince Mosby of the fierceness of her love, Alice, like the members of the company performing *Arden of Faversham*, views the prayer book as immanently replaceable. In this sense, the play anticipates Richard's theatrical use of his prayer book, but neither *Arden* nor *Richard III* goes so far as to destroy a sacred book on stage, leaving unanswered the question of how audiences might respond to such an act of desecration.

The Scourge of God

In contrast to *Arden of Faversham*, which merely threatens to destroy a sacred text on stage, Marlowe's *Tamburlaine*, part 2 (1588) makes good on this threat by enacting the burning of a holy book, in this case the Qur'an. In a period characterized by growing awareness of the Turks' military superiority, English Protestants often sought to downplay the value of the Muslim religion. Polemical works dismissed the Qur'an as mere superstition and Islam as a religion with "no doctrinal depth," riddled with the same idolatrous tendencies as Catholicism.[40] The author of *The Policy of the Turkish Empire* (1597), for instance, compares a certain group of Muslim holy men to "the Friars mendicants in the Papacie" and the imam to a high priest. He notes the preponderance of saints and relic worship in Islam, and describes their prayers as no more than "a wonderfull shew of devotion."[41] These types of analogies allowed Protestant writers to dismiss the Muslim religion as a game, even if they could not entirely ignore the power of the Turkish empire. But although anti-Islamic Protestants often used the same terms to dismiss both Muslims and Catholics, it was also true that for all Christians the Qur'an represented an unfathomable set of beliefs; that is, both reformers and their Catholic counterparts identified the Turks' holy book as the antithesis of the Bible. If anything, *Tamburlaine* comes closest to this view, but in the end the play takes a more measured approach to this unfamiliar icon of Islamic culture, revealing the underlying similarity between type and anti-type. The Qur'an in this play serves both as an example of the kind of sacred text that could be burned on stage without exciting controversy and, ironically, as proof of how much theatrical and symbolic meaning the theater was able to attach to an otherwise ordinary property.

---

[40]   Nabil Matar, *Islam in Britain, 1558-1685* (Cambridge: Cambridge University Press, 1998), 149.

[41]   Giles Fletcher, *The policy of the Turkish empire. The first booke* (London: Windet, 1597), V1ᵛ, H4ᵛ.

James Kearney has suggested that the absence of book properties in Shakespeare's *The Tempest* (1611) points toward Protestant anxiety about the physical nature of the book, for although Prospero's magical texts give him power over Caliban and the other characters, they are also potential indicators of a materialism "that must be repudiated or abjured if the European Prospero is to take his proper place in the emergent order of a 'reformed' imperialism," and that must therefore be destroyed.[42] In this play, then, the promise of book desecration can be read as an affirmation of Protestant beliefs and values, although Shakespeare wisely avoids making that act of destruction into its own spectacle, a mistake whereby many iconoclasts ironically confirmed the power of the objects they were attacking. The protagonist of Marlowe's *Tamburlaine*, by contrast, is counting on the fact that the Qur'an is a mere thing, one with no religious power attached to it. The conqueror who is identified both in the play and on its title page as "the scourge of God" burns a copy of the Qur'an in a final attempt to assert his superiority by humiliating his Turkish enemies. When he calls for it to burned, he mocks Mahomet as a worldly enemy rather than a holy prophet.

Tamburlaine's goal is to demystify the book by demonstrating its physical vulnerability, and immediately after giving the order for the Qur'an to be flung into the fire he mockingly calls upon the prophet himself to show his might:

> Now Mahomet, if thou have any power,
> Come down thy self and work a miracle,
> Thou art not worthy to be worshipped
> That suffers flames of fire to burn the writ
> Wherein the sum of thy religion rests.
> Why send'st thou not a furious whirlwind down,
> To blow thy Alcaron up to thy throne,
> Where men report thou sitt'st by God himself,
> Or vengeance on the head of Tamburlaine,
> That shakes his sword against thy majesty
> And spurns the Abstracts of thy foolish laws?
> Well, soldiers, Mahomet remains in hell—
> He cannot hear the voice of Tamburlaine.
> Seek out another godhead to adore,
> The God that sits in heaven, if any god,
> For he is God alone, and none but he.[43]

Tamburlaine openly acknowledges the religious and social beliefs tied to this sacred book, just as Alice Arden tells the audience that her prayer book once converted her. He labels the Qur'an "the sum of thy religion" and calls to mind its role as a

---

[42]   *Matters of the Book* (Philadelphia, 2001), 224.

[43]   *Tamburlaine Parts One and Two*, ed. Anthony B. Dawson (London and New York: A&C Black and Norton, 1997), 5.1.185-200.

collection of legal precepts. A few lines earlier, he even refers to Mahomet as one "[w]hom I have thought a God" (175). As he desecrates the book, Tamburlaine reminds his audience of its supposed powers in order to juxtapose the Turks' belief in the sacredness of the Qur'an with the destruction of the fragile material thing.

Tamburlaine's speech is in many ways a model of Protestant iconomachy, but his stated purpose in destroying the Qur'an is complicated by the play's sympathetic portrayal of its Muslim characters. In contrast to the conniving Christians and to Tamburlaine himself, the Turks are presented as the only ones who do not betray their religious principles. This crucial difference is introduced in Act 1, scene 2 when the leaders of Natolia and Hungary agree to a military truce, each swearing by his own god to keep their treaty. The Christians recant, however, and justify their betrayal by referring to the Turks as those "in whom no faith nor true religion rest" (2.1.34). Because the Turkish oaths are based on empty, profane belief, Baldwine reasons, they are of little consequence. This scene expresses the Christian characters' disdain for what they see as a superstitious and irrational religion, a sentiment that was quickly becoming one of the mainstays of English nationalism. Similarly, in *Guy Earl of Warwick* (1593), the Sultan swears by the Qur'an to make the Christians who have scorned the prophet stoop to kiss his feet. On the other hand, the Christians' perjury in *Tamburlaine* immediately establishes the Turkish characters as victims rather than aggressors, and when the Christians are defeated their leader Sigismund accepts the loss as retribution for his broken oath. This reversal, in which the Turks are morally justified in seeking revenge, is the first of a series of events that sets the stage for a more complex reaction to Tamburlaine's act of iconoclasm against the Qur'an. Displacing the opposition between the Bible and the Turks' holy book, the play instead attempts to establish an opposition between religion and its absence. When, in part one, Bajazeth swears on the "holy Alcoran" that he will make Tamburlaine stoop to his will, Tamburlaine replies by swearing on his sword and on his own fame (3.3.76). Part two of Marlowe's play extends this analogy, making Tamburlaine's iconoclasm an act of atheistic impiety rather than Christian vengeance.

Giles Fletcher's translation of *The Policy of the Turkish Empire* provides one of the earliest and most vituperative accounts of Islam, and although it was published after the first performances of *Tamburlaine* we can see how this type of language played upon contemporary Protestant polemics. Among other epithets, *The Policy of the Turkish Empire* refers to the teachings of the Qur'an as "divelish doctrines and illusions" foisted upon "people full of simplicity and ignorance." It labels Islam, like Roman Catholicism, "monstrous," as well as "divelish" and "superstitious"; the author of the *Policy* likewise associates Mohammed with "faigned myracles" and empty acts of devotion.[44] This account even alludes to the belief that Turks considered it an act of piety to give false evidence against a Christian. References to false oaths were apparently a common part of anti-Islamic rhetoric, for in *Soliman and Perseda* (1592), two witnesses are paid to accuse a loyal Christian of

---

[44]   Fletcher, B1ʳ, B2ʳ, B2ᵛ-B3ʳ, C1ʳ.

treason and subsequently swear on a copy of the Qur'an that they are telling the truth. Unlike *Soliman and Perseda*, which adheres to the stereotypical depiction of Turks as those people who have no respect for sacred books, *Tamburlaine* figures the Qur'an not as an idol associated with oath swearing but as a sacred object destroyed by a tyrant's wrath. In this sense the play also displaces the association between superstitious books and oath swearing, a practice that was one of the earliest condemned by English reformers.[45] Eventually, the practice of swearing on holy books would come to be connected not only with idolatrous Catholics but also with "barbarous non-Europeans."[46] Those who refused or were unable to comprehend the word of God were considered most likely to falsely privilege the material book.

By the 1620s and 30s, references to the Qur'an in public theater plays were becoming both more casual and more overtly negative. In Philip Massinger's *The Renegado* (1624), the Qur'an becomes the focus of an attack on the supposedly magical or superstitious aspects of the Muslim religion. "Dare you," the protagonist Vitelli rages, "bring / Your juggling prophet in comparison with / The most inscrutable, and infinite essence / That made this all and comprehends his work?"[47] Here Vitelli, like the author of *The Policy of the Turkish Empire*, claims to expose Mohammad as a juggler who blinded the naive peoples of the Arab world with his talk of angels and miracles. In Thomas Randolph's *The Muses looking glass* (1630), Acolast concludes a lengthy description of his libertine pursuits by declaring his intention to "reade the Alcoran, / And what delights that promises in future I'le practise in the present," and a character in William D'Avenant's *The cruel brother* (1627) condemns a group of conspirators with a single, opaque sentence: "All this is Alcaron."[48] An in-depth study of such allusions might bear out Nabil Matar's thesis that the Qur'an was a more dangerous entity in the imaginations of mid-seventeenth century Londoners than it was fifty or eighty years earlier, but as *Tamburlaine* itself demonstrates, this sacred text was already being contrasted to the Bible—and not always unsympathetically—in the 1580s and 90s. What is unique about this historical moment, or at least about Marlowe's play, is the relative freedom he is able to exercise in complicating the negative associations surrounding the Turks' holy book.

Ian Gaskell, who sees a direct connection between Tamburlaine's insult to the prophet and his sudden illness and defeat in the next scene, has read these two events as constituting a carefully negotiated rejection of the idea of divine intervention. The audience cannot, and should not, accept the idea that Tamburlaine's death is the result of Mahomet's revenge, but because they are forced to dismiss that

---

[45]   *Actes and Monuments*, 487.

[46]   Kearney, 223.

[47]   *The Renegado*, in *Three Turk Plays from Early Modern England*, ed. Daniel J. Vitkus (New York: Columbia University Press, 2000), 4.3.114-17.

[48]   *The muses looking-glasse* (London: n.p., 1643), B6ᵛ; *The cruell brother A tragedy* (London: M[athewes], 1630), D3ʳ.

premise they are left, in Gaskell's words, to "concentrate on the ethical significance of Tamburlaine's demise."[49] In theatrical terms, however, Tamburlaine's act of iconoclasm deserves its own reading, distinct from the circumstances of his death. Designed to shock its audience, the desecration of the Qur'an is construed as an act of blind tyranny. After establishing the Turks as a kind of ethical standard in this otherwise corrupt world, the play encourages its audience to sustain the analogy between the Bible and the Qur'an by framing Tamburlaine's actions within a broader perspective in which the Turks are seen as faithful believers rather than false idolaters; as Jonathan Burton argues, the second part of *Tamburlaine* makes it "impossible to see Christianity as an exemplary negation of Islam."[50] By allowing the Turks to occupy the moral high ground in the play, Marlowe underscores the idea that Tamburlaine is a tyrant—albeit a charismatic one—who must be destroyed, and implicitly aligns the audience's sympathies with his victims. Just before calling for the burning of the Qur'an, Tamburlaine orders the murder of every man, woman, and child in Babylon. This massacre, along with the killing of his own son, serves as a prelude to the book burning and prompts spectators to draw connections between these three examples of excessive violence rather than dismissing the destruction of the Qur'an as somehow justifiable.

Tamburlaine's supremely confident performance of iconoclasm has led Gaskell and others to conclude that, "[f]or a Christian audience in an age of religious intolerance this exhibition presumably merited considerable applause."[51] I would argue, however, that although Tamburlaine himself is assured of the book's worthlessness, his attack upon it prompts its audience to confront, from a safe geographical distance, the profound impact of such an act of desecration. In other words, while the acting companies would never go so far as to burn a Bible on stage, Tamburlaine's role as the tyrannical unbeliever prompts the audience to imagine how they might feel if their own sacred texts were treated in a similar fashion. Playgoers might have been familiar, for instance, with the story of the infamous recusant Robert Goldesborowe, who in 1589 openly defaced a copy of the scriptures as a protest against the most recent English translation. Alexandra Walsham also cites the case of the Yorkshire vicar accused of attacking a Bible with a knife in the 1550s and the systematic burnings of English Bibles during the Northern Rising in 1569, while Steven Mullaney recounts a case of Bible burning committed by a Parliamentary soldier, who in 1649 performed a "last rite for Christian ritual" by burning a copy of the scriptures in a parish churchyard.[52] Recusants, too, suffered the destruction of their cherished books; in 1617 a large

[49]   "*2 Tamburlaine*," *English Studies in Canada* 11, no. 2 (June 1985): 178-92, 186, 188.

[50]   "Anglo-Ottoman Relations and the Image of the Turk in *Tamburlaine*," *Journal of Medieval and Early Modern Studies* 30, no. 1 (Winter 2000): 125-56, 150.

[51]   Gaskell, 184.

[52]   "Unclasping the book? Post-reformation English Catholicism and the vernacular Bible," *Journal of British Studies* 42, no. 2 (April 2003): 141-66, 141; Mullaney, 85.

number of devotional texts discovered at the home of a Catholic printer were burned in a public bonfire at Saint Paul's.[53] Protestants eschewed the materiality of religious objects and often displaced these vices onto Muslims as well as Catholics, but the spectacle of the Qur'an being burned on stage encouraged spectators to consider the disturbing possibility that in another time and place they might be watching the destruction of their own book, thus forcing them to acknowledge some degree of attachment to the vessel of the word.

I have been suggesting that *Arden of Faversham* and, to a greater extent, *Tamburlaine* present examples of the phenomenon whereby the theater exposed Protestantism's residual interest in the materiality of religious books by offering to do violence to them. Although Alice never carries out her threat to destroy the prayer book, *Arden of Faversham* resembles Marlowe's play in that it makes the object's vulnerability the emotional focus of the scene. For its part, *Tamburlaine* encourages playgoers to admit that they would not want to see their own book treated in such a way, even though they might have labeled it a "mere property" in the context of the theatrical fiction. Neither play explicitly sets out to highlight the similarity between Catholic and Protestant practices. Rather, these two dramatic fictions draw their audience's attention to what is at stake in the book's physical existence by highlighting its susceptibility to violence. Alice and Tamburlaine, the two iconoclasts, can also be said to occupy the same position as outsiders who reject the roles assigned to them. Alice refuses to play the part of the godly housekeeper while Tamburlaine, who might have been figured as a Christian convert, refuses to rely on his god to help him defeat his enemies, turning instead to an act of violence that threatens the sanctity of all holy books.

Arden of Faversham and *Tamburlaine* also share something in common with the two texts discussed at the beginning of this chapter. I have suggested that in Shakespeare's plays, theatrical practice mirrors the doctrinal crux at the heart of Protestant practice by revealing the contradiction involved in designating books and reading as indicators of an immaterial quality called piety. But in fact all four of these plays bring the audience back to their own attachment to religious books by posing the question of whether there is a difference between theatrical properties and books used in the daily performance of devotion. *Hamlet* makes this move despite the geographical and chronological distance between its characters and Elizabethan playgoers, while in *Richard III* a moment of Catholic hypocrisy set in the days before the Reformation ironically points to the very contemporary problem of distinguishing genuine faith from its insubstantial shadow. *Arden of Faversham* draws upon the powerful cultural image of the woman as godly reader in order to

---

[53]   McClain, 53. Reading the play in light of other contemporary accounts of radical book burning, Roger Moore argues that Tamburlaine's iconoclasm actually deemphasizes the book's materiality. "The Spirit and the Letter: Marlowe's *Tamburlaine* and Elizabethan Religious Radicalism," *Studies in Philology* 99:2 (Spring 2002): 123-51, 124. His approach fails to address the emotional reality of the theatrical spectacle, but it does provide an intriguing way of recuperating Tamburlaine's radical individualism.

intensify the seriousness of Alice's betrayal, while at the same time allowing for the possibility that the book is a mere accessory and therefore inconsequential. Despite the large gap between characters and playgoers, *Tamburlaine* draws an implicit analogy between Muslim books and Christian books, and requires the most spectacular, and most affecting, theatrical device: the image of a sacred text being cast into a roaring bonfire. If these plays use Christian books to prompt audiences to consider the overlap between theatrical practice and religious practice, and thus normalize the theater's reliance on material properties, *Tamburlaine* takes the analogy one step further. By contrasting Tamburlaine's mistreatment of the Muslim scriptures with its otherwise sympathetic portrait of the Turks and their religion, Marlowe's play presents the spectacle of the book's desecration as disturbing rather than triumphant.

This strikingly irreverent theatrical spectacle, along with all the other derogatory comments he makes about Mahomet, has led many scholars to connect Tamburlaine's actions with the supposed views of Marlowe himself. Although Marlowe and Tamburlaine both became famous for their atheism after the playwright's death, there is no clear evidence to suggest that Marlowe's personal belief, or lack thereof, was the driving force behind the play. Peter Hall, who staged the Qur'an desecration with great zeal at the National Theatre, is surely right to argue that at "the core of the play" is a man "attempting to prove that there is no God," a leader who seeks to gain political power by demystifying the legend of the prophet and terrorizing his followers. But it does not necessarily follow that, as Hall claims, *Tamburlaine* "is the first atheist play, and in a way the first existential play."[54] The character's beliefs do not automatically correspond to Marlowe's, nor to the perspective articulated by the play as a whole, particularly when we take the sympathetic depiction of the Turks and their religious beliefs into account.

Like *Tamburlaine*, *Doctor Faustus* (1592) addresses religious practice with a complex combination of orthodoxy and skepticism. In the opening scene of the later play, the title character appears in his study perusing a pile of books—works by Aristotle, Galen, and Justinian, as well as the Vulgate Bible—all of which he eventually discards in favor of "heavenly" necromancy. Although God's angel urges him to cast aside his magic texts and "[r]ead, read the Scriptures," Faustus is ultimately dissatisfied with what he perceives as the harsh lessons of Romans 6:23.[55] Of course, Faustus famously leaves out the second part of the verse, which reassures the reader that although "the wages of sin is death … the gift of God is eternal life through Jesus Christ our Lord."[56] Faustus, like Tamburlaine, is eventually brought down by his lack of faith, but the fact that he remains unsaved allows the doubt behind his initial questions to linger over the play: what makes

---

[54]   John Goodwin, ed., *Peter Hall's Diaries* (New York: Limelight Editions, 1985), 256.

[55]   *Doctor Faustus: the 1604-version*, ed. Michael Keefer (Peterborough, Ont: Broadview Press, 1991), 1.1.74.

[56]   Keefer, 7.

the Bible superior to books of black magic and what guarantees do the Christian scriptures provide? Presenting a critique of mainstream theology rather than a wholesale rejection of religion *per se*, Marlowe subtly reminds playgoers that one character's holy book could be another character's meaningless conjuration, for unlike Cyprian, Faustus is incapable of being saved by holy books and the intervention of angels. *Tamburlaine* thus points to the irresolvable project of proving that one religion, Protestantism, is superior to the blind superstition of Islam and Catholicism.

In both *Doctor Faustus* and *Tamburlaine*, Marlowe articulates a perspective that is more radical than simple atheism: namely, that there is little distinction to be made between the more spectacular aspects of mainstream Christianity, including martyrology and iconoclasm, and the superstitious beliefs typically associated with Islam and Catholicism. Keefer, for instance, suggests that by infiltrating recusant communities on behalf of England's Protestant government Marlowe discovered that the two warring religions were surprisingly interchangeable. Keefer also argues that during this period atheism was as much about power as about belief; the government's ministers were eager to suppress atheism only so far as it produced "any public demystification of religious authority," and they accomplished this suppression through their own forms of public violence, either by burning heretical books or imprisoning their authors.[57] In this sense *Tamburlaine* is very much about atheism, and David Farr's 2005 production of the play at the Barbican underscored this reading by having Tamburlaine destroy a whole group of volumes representing the world's major religions. By staging the burning of the Qur'an, the play is not merely valorizing the excesses of its protagonist. This spectacle pointedly undermines the uniqueness of individual holy books and emphasizes their materiality, rather than advocating the wholesale rejection of religious beliefs and practices.

So what did early modern audience members actually see when they watched Tamburlaine's henchmen destroying the Qur'an? There are very few instances of an object being burned on stage, and one of them is the firing of the town in Act 3 of *Tamburlaine*, part 2. For this scene and the scene of the book burning, the company may have used a brazier set out on the stage or, as Peter Hall did at the National Theatre in 1976, a fiery pit below a trap door. Anthony Dawson's note on the passage in his edition of the play reads as follows: "Again, here, as with the burning of the bodies in II.iv, a trap might have been used. But a simpler expedient would have been a brazier of some sort in which a fire could be quickly kindled. The books, flung into the fire on Tamburlaine's orders, would then continue to burn onstage during his challenge to Mahomet and the subsequent onset of his distemper—producing a telling ironic effect."[58] As we know from the accident that caused the destruction of the Globe in 1613, the theaters themselves were extremely susceptible to incineration. One could argue, then, that the threat posed

---

[57]   Ibid., xxvi-xxvii.

[58]   Dawson, *Tamburlaine*, 162.

by the presence of a flame on stage would have intensified the sense of danger aroused by the Qur'an's desecration—the perception that, however exciting, this act is also flagrantly irresponsible. As for the property itself, it is possible that the Admiral's Men might have been able to get their hands on commentaries of the Qur'an, but translations of the book itself were not readily available in England until the mid-seventeenth century. The book property might have been large and exotic looking, but unlike the company who performed *If You Know Not Me You Know Nobody*, the Admiral's Men were unlikely to be able secure a copy of the actual item. During a performance of *Tamburlaine* the audience at the Rose could never be entirely certain what it was that was being destroyed, or whether it was being destroyed at all.[59] The property used by the Admiral's Men could just as easily be a Bible, and though it undoubtedly was not, the scene introduces the imaginative possibility that there could be a Christian text in Tamburlaine's fire.

The uncertainty about what kind of book the actor playing Tamburlaine was burning returns us once again to the irony of using a real book as a stage property. When the theatrical fiction dealt with texts such as the Bible that possessed nationalistic significance, it made a considerable difference whether there was really a Bible on stage or whether the actors could substitute any small book for the prayer manual called for in the script. In Marlowe's play, as in Shakespeare's, the players could have used more or less any book as a property, but the potential difference between the object represented in the fiction and the object brought out on stage would have substantially altered the meaning of the scene. In *Tamburlaine*, a Christian book might have been substituted for the Turkish one, while *Hamlet* raises the question of whether a secular book could be substituted for a sacred one. In each case, and especially in *Tamburlaine*, the use of books as properties demonstrates the impossibility, even for Protestant polemicists, of maintaining a faith that was entirely pure, entirely dematerialized.

For the most part, the public theater did not challenge mainstream Protestant practice through its appropriation of sacred texts, but it did defend its own use of books and other religious objects as properties by revealing some of the crucial ways in which material objects and gestures were still an important aspect of post-Reformation worship. If Marlowe's audience was prompted to view the Qur'an sympathetically because it was the object of Tamburlaine's blind aggression, they might also have been drawn to it precisely because it was a book, a recognizable emblem of their own reformed belief. Despite the reformers' assertions to the contrary, the practice of Christian religion in England did have something in common with the religion of the Turks, for both were deeply tied to the materiality of holy texts. The surprising likeness between theatrical properties and religious ones, often revealed in the drama through the similarities between different types

---

[59] On the other hand, audience members might draw connections between this play and other contemporary productions. In the early 1630s, *Tamburlaine* became a staple at the Red Bull, a venue known for spectacular effects such as those that characterize the final act of *Two Noble Ladies* (Gurr, *Playgoing in Shakespeare's London*, 189).

of religious books, points to the investment in material things that Protestants, whether they admitted to it or not, shared with Catholics, and with the commercial theater.

Unconsidered Trifles:
Stage Properties as Theatrical Relics

In each of the preceding chapters, I have addressed plays that were performed during a particular historical moment and under specific cultural conditions. The religious stage properties employed in these plays have often been overlooked, even while careful attention has been paid to theological or political references within the dialogue. By returning our attention to individual objects and groups of objects, I have worked to demonstrate that the visual apparatus of the theater was just as important as verbal allusion in allowing the playing companies to engage with the complexities of post-Reformation religious practice. I would like now to take a step back in order to consider some of the implications of this methodological focus on stage properties, for, as Andrew Sofer has shown, the centrality of properties on the British stage did not end with the closing of the theaters in 1642. But whereas Sofer's *The Stage Life of Props* offers phenomenological readings of several play scripts from the fifteenth to the twentieth century, in this section I consider the circulation of stage objects in two slightly different, but firmly historicized contexts. First, I explore the shifting status of the handkerchief in Shakespeare's *Othello* (1604) in light of the emerging discourse of the "trifle" in early modern England. Second, I turn to the long history of Shakespearean performance, and to the conventions through which "mere" properties became relics thanks to their association with famous British and American actors. Both these approaches allow for a more theoretically-oriented consideration of the relationship between the stage property's value off stage and the meanings it takes on within dramatic fictions. Finally, I end with a brief discussion of a twentieth-century novel that satirizes the practice of enshrining old properties as sacred objects while underscoring the powerful memorializing impulse behind such acts. By considering the role stage properties have played in our modern obsession with Shakespeare, I hope to account for the various meanings assigned to these relics, objects that link us not to some original moment of transcendent genius but to a dynamic theatrical tradition.

The Circulation of Stage Objects

Thomas Rymer, author of "A Short View of Tragedy" (1692) and the first to point out the striking prominence of the handkerchief in *Othello*, remains one of the play's most provocative critics. "Why was not this call'd the *Tragedy of the Handkerchief?*" he famously exclaimed, deriding the play for its obsession with a trifle. Rymer's indignation is based upon his view that Shakespeare let the handkerchief run away with him, giving the property its own personified agency. To attribute value to such an object, he argued, was "barbarous" and "against all Justice and Reason." "Had it been *Desdemona*'s Garter," Rymer continues, "the Sagacious *Moor* might have smelt a Rat: but the Handkerchief is so remote a trifle no Booby on this side *Mauritania* cou'd make any consequence from it."[1] According to the play's title page, Othello is "the Moore of *Venice*," but for Rymer his tragic mistake is understandable only if he comes from the other side of Mauritania—the side, that is, farthest from "us." In other words, if Othello had been born on the far side of Mauritania his geographical distance from England would make his barbaric obsession with a "trifle" understandable, for by the late seventeenth century it had become the very mark of "savage" people that they failed to distinguish people from things.

As William Pietz has argued, barbarism was radically redefined during this period when it was interpreted through an emergent discourse of the fetish. "The fetish," Pietz writes, "as an idea and a problem, and as a novel object not proper to any prior discrete society, originated in the cross-cultural spaces of the coast of West Africa during the sixteenth and seventeenth centuries. It was Portuguese merchants who first conceptualized the *fetisso* as the mark of Africans' supposed irrational propensity to personify material objects."[2] And though Pietz's research operates largely outside the confessional divide, the concept of the "fetish" was itself an offshoot of the mercantile language of the "trifle," a term used by Protestants to dismiss various forms of material worship as meaningless. In what follows I argue that *Othello* explores the processes through which objects gain and lose meaning and consequently reveals the pervasive social values embedded in "mere trifles." It does so by employing a property, the handkerchief, that is characterized by its shifting value, which changes throughout the play but also within the playhouse as it passes from the tiring room to the stage and back again. Thus, in addition to illuminating the complicated status of objects in cross-cultural spaces, *Othello* points to the long history of stage properties themselves.

The discourse of the trifle, like the discourse of the fetish, demonstrates the overlap between the ideology of new world exploration and that of the Reformation: in both cases, Europeans sought to fix the value of an object whose status was in question by using labels such as "trifle," as well as "trinket" and "toy."[3] In a

---

[1] "A short view of tragedy," in Brian Vickers, ed., *Shakespeare: The Critical Heritage* (London; Boston: Routledge; Kegan Paul, 1974), 51-4, 51.

[2] "The problem of the fetish, I," *Res* 9 (1985): 5-17, 5; "The problem of the fetish, II," *Res* 13 (1987): 23-45, 23.

[3] For more on the discourse of the trifle, see James Kearney, "Trinket, Idol, Fetish: Some Notes on Iconoclasm and the Language of Materiality in Reformation England," *Shakespeare Studies* 28 (2000): 257-61. Kearney's reading, like mine, is indebted to the work of William Pietz and Peter Stallybrass. It is also possible, of course, to focus on the

1608 account of his first encounter with the natives of Virginia, Francis Perkins remarks that they "came aboard naked bringing us potatoes, bananas, pineapples … and other things which they gave us in exchange for iron hatchets, saws, knives, rosaries, little bells, and other similar trifles which they esteem very highly and are of great worth to those who take them along on similar voyages."[4] Perkins is describing a set of exchanges in which he considers himself the clear beneficiary, but his list is more puzzling than it first appears. Hatchets, saws, and knives, after all, served essential practical functions, but what were the uses of "little bells" and "rosaries"? Perkins's account of these objects points to the fact that the mercantile trifle was always intertwined with a discourse of religious value. In Udall's 1548 translation of Erasmus's paraphrases, the Pharisees are described as those who "teache and observe supersticiously … folysh trifles" (*OED* "trifle," 1.a). In fact, it was in the 1530s and 1540s that the dismissive language of trifles, along with the terms "trinket" and "toy," was first appropriated by Protestants in their attacks on Catholic idolatry. "Toy" took on the meaning of "a thing of no value" during the radical upheavals of the 1530s, while at the same time "trinket" was first used to mean "a small ornament" (1533), "a small article" (1536), or "religious rites, ceremonies, beliefs etc. which the speaker thinks vain or trivial" (1538) Like "trifle" and "toy," this was a term used to denote objects that, for Protestants, had no intrinsic worth (*OED* "toy," II.5, "trinket" 2, 1.a, 3). On the other hand, the reformers were simultaneously anxious about the profusion of such objects, both at home and abroad.

In John Foxe's 1570 encyclopedia of Protestantism, a woodcut depicting the Edwardian attacks on traditional religion is accompanied by the caption, "Ship over your trinkets and be packing you papists."[5] Foxe's depiction of the banishment of Catholic objects provides one possible explanation for the presence of rosaries and little bells among the "trifles" the English traded to the natives of Virginia. But despite the optimism of this image, which suggests that popish trinkets could

---

sacredness of the handkerchief, and Andrew Sofer has pointed out the resonances between this "mere" stage property and the various sacred cloths associated with Christ's passion (65-72).

[4] Philip Barbour, ed., *The Jamestown Voyages Under the First Charter 1606-1609* (London: Published for the Hakluyt Society by Cambridge University Press, 1969), 159. This dismissive attitude toward the items traded with native peoples appears as early as 1549 in Sir Thomas Smith's *Discourse of the Commonweal*, but the particular language of trifles and trinkets emerged several decades later. See also John Gee's *New Shreds of an Old Snare:* "Why doe we laugh at the barbarous *Indians* for imparting to us their richest commodities in exchange for glasse, beads, peny whistles, copper rings, &c? But the *Popes Benediction*, or any the least touch of Sainting Miracle-monging fiction is able to infuse the highest worth into the basest baggagely New-nothing to hang upon the sleeve of admiring adoring ghostly Children of the *Jesuites*" (London: [Printed (by J. Dawson) for Robert Mylbourne], H2^{r-v}).

[5] *The First[-Second] Volume of the Ecclesiasticall History* (Imprinted at London: By John Day, 1570), 1483.

be permanently exiled, the reformers were never able to find and confiscate all the material remnants of English Catholicism. As late as 1571, Grindal's injunctions for the province of York, a stronghold of the old faith, stipulated that "the churchwardens and minister shall see that … all vestments, albs, tunicles, stoles, fanon, pyxes, paxes, hand-bells, sacring-bells, censers, christmatories, crosses, candlesticks, holy-water stocks, or fat images, and all other relics and monuments of superstition and idolatry, be utterly defaced, broken and destroyed."[6] In 1607 the York visitors were still asking whether there were any "praying for the dead at crosses or places where crosses have beene, in the way to the church, or any other superstitious use of crosses with towells, palmes, met-wands, or other memories of idolatry at burialls." In the diocese of Lincoln, in 1634 and again in 1635, the officials anxiously inquired, "[a]re all crucifixes and scandalous pictures of any of the persons of the Trinity abolished in your churches?"[7] Even in London, some churchwardens disobeyed the royal edicts against traditional church furnishings and, during the years leading up to the Civil War, began to publicly reinstate the objects that had been officially outlawed during the first waves of Protestant iconoclasm. These dramatic examples of the continuing use of traditional objects were preceded, however, by a more common set of practices: throughout the late sixteenth and early seventeenth centuries, individual parishes routinely disregarded the visitation articles, either because they did not want to expend additional time and money destroying the items they had recently replaced during Mary's reign, or because their parishioners were genuinely sympathetic to the ornaments of the old faith.

One of the primary reasons the ecclesiastical visitors had so much difficulty eliminating traditional objects was that in many parishes residents were storing them in their homes. As I argue in Chapter 3, iconoclasm actually facilitated the circulation of Catholic church furnishings, since they were frequently sold to or stolen by private citizens to prevent their desecration. Thus, in the London injunctions of 1605, Bishop Richard Vaughn demanded to know "whether there be any in your parish who are noted, known, or suspected to conceale or keepe hidden in their houses any … ornaments of superstition, uncancelled or undefaced, which is to be conjectured, they doe keepe for a day, as they call it?"[8] While some parishioners preserved Catholic objects, others sold them to international traders such as Perkins. Banished to foreign shores, these "ornaments of superstition" would later be rediscovered as further examples of the fetishism of barbarians. Thus, both at home and abroad, religious objects were subject to opposing modes of valuation: in England, the term "trifle" designated the conflict between Catholics and Protestants, while in foreign countries populated by non-Christians the word was used to express the distinction between English traders and native peoples.

---

[6]   Cardwell, vol. 1, 336.

[7]   Fincham, *Visitation Articles and Injunctions of the Early Stuart Church*, vol. 1, 59; vol. 2, 104.

[8]   Ibid., vol. 1, 37.

William Perkins's treatise on the uses and abuses of idols, *A Warning against the Idolatrie of the last times* (1601), does not, for the most part, deal with religions other than Catholicism. Its primary aim is to anatomize the disease of idolatry and attack the recusants who have not yet cured themselves of it. In the dedication to the work, however, he stoutly maintains that "[i]f the things which have been done in England, had bin done in Barbarie, or Turkie, or America, it may be they would have repented in sakecloath and ashes, and have turned more earnestly unto God than we have done."[9] His reference to "Barbarie, or Turkie, or America" is surprising, but the analogy between Catholics and pagans is quite calculated, and highly evocative. Like the handkerchief in *Othello*, Perkins's text raises questions about how early modern cultures perceived each other's religious and social values—or more precisely, it reveals the efforts of English Protestants to understand the established value systems they encountered in places such as "Barbarie, or Turkie, or America" by comparing them to Catholic idolatry.

It is worth noting that Perkins is not an adventurer, nor is he writing in the style of one. His text is concerned with establishing a common set of Protestant values, but because he has no direct contact with the inhabitants of "Barbarie, or Turkie, or America," he is able to promote the fantasy that they will be more amenable to the "true faith" than the subjects of his treatise. Ultimately, he is concerned with the more familiar excesses of English recusants, and in order to chastise them as dramatically as possible he describes their religious practices as being more barbarous than the barbarians. According to Perkins, even heathens would be ashamed of worshiping wooden crosses, bits of bone, and rotten cloth, and he imagines them doing penance for the sin of idolatry by converting to the Protestant faith. Conversely, the fact that Catholics, as Christians, should be closer to the truth of God's divinity than heathens makes their faults even more egregious. This comparison emphasizes the fact that the contrast between Protestants and foreign idolaters is a mere shadow of the conflict between Catholics and Protestants at home. The unflattering comparison Perkins draws between Catholics and barbarians, in which the barbarians actually emerge as the less dangerous of the two parties, suggests one answer to the question of why *Othello*, a play in which all the characters are Christian, is so interested in the language of trifles and trinkets. It also provides a useful footnote to the work of William Pietz, who has shown that English and Dutch Protestants frequently dismissed foreign and Catholic idolatry under the same rubric.

Even more troubling for some strict Protestants than either the supposed fetishism of Africans and Native Americans or the private idolatry of parishioners in England was the public flaunting of idols on the London stage. Although aristocratic fashions from the previous season might appear in Shakespeare's history plays, conveying an authentic, if anachronistic, picture of the English nobility, confiscated vestments worn by an actor playing a bishop breathed new life into what iconoclasts labeled "the ornaments of superstition." Writing during

---

[9] *A Warning against the Idolatrie of the last times* ([Cambridge]: Legat, 1601), 2ʳ.

the first flush of Edwardian iconomachy, Thomas Becon had mocked the robes of Catholic priests as "game-players' garments," but later reformers were appalled when Becon's metaphor was literalized in the professional theaters. The well-documented circulation of vestments from the church to the stage reminds us that the Reformation made a variety of Catholic objects available, both physically and imaginatively, to public theater practitioners.[10]

Robert N. Watson has recently drawn a similar set of connections between Iago's use of the word "trifle" and the reformers' attacks on Catholic objects by citing the work of Samuel Harsnet, among others. "Who doth not bewaile the sely doating Indian Nation that falls downe and performes divine adoration to a rag of red cloth?" Harsnet asked in 1603. As Watson notes, *A Declaration of Egregious Popish Impostures* repeats the Protestant tendency to treat all forms of misguided believers, from the followers of Baal to itinerant English priests to American heathens, as idolaters—"Would God," he laments, "your bewitched dotage were not as palpable, and more lamentable than theirs."[11] I am not convinced, however, by his argument that *Othello* can be read as unilaterally promoting a Protestant point of view. By allowing the handkerchief to circulate from character to character throughout the course of the action, the play makes room for interactions and conflicts between a number of distinct value systems. Taking into account the theater's own investment in material objects, the displacement, circulation, and re-evaluation of Catholic "trifles" provides a framework for exploring the ways it used stage properties to pose broader questions about the social and economic value of objects. The handkerchief in *Othello* is both situated within the discourse of the fetish and the trifle, and holds those discourses up to critical scrutiny. Thus the handkerchief, which has proved to be such a knotty problem for modern Shakespearean scholars, is in fact more useful as a problem then as a key to the heart of *Othello*'s mystery, precisely because it illuminates those moments of cross-cultural confrontation characterized by religious difference and economic imbalance.

If, as Rymer jeered, the handkerchief has the status of a person, it is because it can act as "an external organ of the body," thus materializing "a subversion of the ideal of the autonomously determined self."[12] At the same time, the relentless transference of the handkerchief from character to character reveals the inextricable relations between the evaluation and devaluation of people and things. As the handkerchief gains and loses value within the fiction of the play, it demonstrates the difficulty of attaching any meaning—cultural, economic, or religious—to an object that is constantly in circulation. Indeed, *Othello* dramatizes what Igor Kopytoff calls the cultural biography of a thing: "the story of [its] various singularizations, classifications and reclassifications in an uncertain world of categories whose importance shifts with every minor change in context."[13]

---

[10]   Becon, 259-60.

[11]   *A Declaration of Egregious Popish Impostures* (London: Roberts, 1603), A2ᵛ-3ʳ.

[12]   Pietz, "The problem of the fetish, II," 23.

[13]   Kopytoff, 90.

Kopytoff, whose work accounts for and accepts the elision between subject and object, provides a kind of alternative to Rymer's language of trifles and trinkets. But what would it mean, from this perspective, to make the cultural biography of a thing the subject of a play? At least one important consequence of reading *Othello* in this light is that we can see more clearly the shifts in the handkerchief's value as well as the degree to which those shifts depend on the value systems the characters bring to bear on the object.

In *Plays Confuted in Five Actions* (1582), Stephen Gosson argues that the theater is simultaneously trivial and idolatrous, and he anticipates Rymer in pointing out that there can be nothing edifying about dramatic fictions whose plots are resolved by posies, rings, and handkerchiefs. All these objects were commonly used as love tokens, but cockle shells were worn by pilgrims, particularly those traveling to Compostela in Spain. Gosson thus identifies the knights of theatrical romance with pilgrims returning home covered with Catholic "trinkets."[14] He contends that such persons place too much stock in objects, and their failure to recognize the "real" value of trifles in turn allows Gosson to critique the misguided attitude both the theater and the Catholic church have adopted toward such things.

Precisely because its characters adopt a range of attitudes toward the handkerchief, *Othello* is useful for thinking about the contested value of objects that circulate outside their original context. Among those attitudes is Iago's crude skepticism, which maps closely onto Gosson's contempt for the idolatrous properties strewn about the public stage. Iago sees objects like the handkerchief as "[t]rifles light as air," but, echoing the antitheatricalists, he also believes that the gullible will find in them "confirmations strong / As proof of holy writ" (3.3.322-4). Other early modern play scripts similarly use the language of trifles to keep the object in its humble place or designate a fundamental disagreement over its value. When Falstaff swears in *1 Henry IV* (1597) that a ring stolen from him by thieves is a priceless inheritance from his grandfather, Hal mockingly responds that Falstaff's stolen ring was "a trifle, some eight-penny matter" (3.3.104). The multiple valuations of Bassanio's ring in *The Merchant of Venice* (1596) have even deeper causes and consequences. In exchange for Portia's services as the lawyer Balthasar, Bassanio urges him/her to "[t]ake some remembrance of us as a tribute, / Not as fee" (4.1.422-3). Portia consents, agreeing to accept Antonio's gloves and Bassanio's ring—the same ring she gave him to wear as a pledge of his fidelity. But rather than protesting its significance as a token of love, Bassanio tries to undermine its value. "This ring good sir, alas it is a trifle," he protests, "I will not shame my self to give you this" (430-31). Despite his efforts to define the ring as an object of no consequence, Bassanio's position is ultimately complicated by the fact that he has already distinguished between a "remembrance" given in gratitude and a "fee" that can be assessed in purely financial terms.

In *Othello*, as in *The Merchant of Venice*, the concept of the "trifle" emerges through the conflicting value systems in which objects circulate. At first, Iago

---

[14] Gosson, C6^r.

reminds Othello that handkerchiefs, like any other commodity, are common objects of circulation:

> *Iago.*   … But if I give my wife a handkerchief—
> *Othello.* What then?
> *Iago.*   Why then 'tis hers (my Lord) and being hers,
>   She may, I think, bestow't on any man.
>   (4.1.10-13)

In other words, if it is merely "a handkerchief," why should there be any problem about its circulation? Iago's strategy here is to reevaluate all that Othello holds dear (the handkerchief, Desdemona, Cassio) as common trifles. "Have you not sometimes seen a handkerchief … in your wive's hand?" he asks (3.3.436-7). In this exchange Iago cleverly specifies *any* handkerchief, already suggesting all the common things that may pass through Desdemona's hands. If the handkerchief is common, Desdemona's status as "your wife"—a person no longer in circulation because she is Othello's property—is also called into question. As proof, Iago casually remarks that "such a handkerchief (I am sure it was your wive's) did I to-day / See Cassio wipe his Beard with" (437-9). Here the dialogue specifies "a handkerchief," one that can just as easily be used to wipe Cassio's beard as Othello's brow. When Iago returns again to the question of the handkerchief, it is to suggest that any kind of circulation undoes all relations of "mine" and "thine." If the handkerchief that Cassio used to wipe his beard is identical to the handkerchief that Othello gave to Desdemona, "or any [that] was hers, / It speaks against her" (440-41). Iago now argues that Desdemona must not only hold on to gifts from Othello, but also should not circulate anything else, even if it is "hers." This suggestion simultaneously prevents Iago from having to prove anything about the particular handkerchief in Cassio's hand and implies that there is no such thing as a unique handkerchief.

   Throughout the play, Iago constantly manipulates contradictory systems of valuation. On the one hand, the handkerchief is a trifle that reveals the trifling of Cassio with Desdemona. On the other, he suggests, the handkerchief is the physical materialization of Desdemona's honor:

> Her honor is an essence that's not seen;
> They have it very oft, that have it not.
> But for the handkerchief—
> (4.1.16-19)

In this speech Iago returns to the view that the handkerchief is indeed unique—as unique and fragile as Desdemona's honor. And he reiterates this position after he and Othello have overheard the conversation between Cassio and Bianca: "And did you see the handkerchief?" (4.1.174). Shifting between "a" handkerchief and "the" handkerchief, Iago implies that the object is simultaneously priceless and valueless.

In response to the threat of the handkerchief's circulation as a mere commodity, Othello narrates the story of the handkerchief's magical origins:

> That handkerchief
> Did an Egyptian to my Mother give;
> She was a charmer, and could almost read
> The thoughts of people. She told her, while she kept it,
> 'Twould make her amiable, and subdue my Father
> Entirely to her love
>
> . . . .
> There's magic in the web of it.
> A sybil, that had numb'red in the world
> The sun to course two hundred compasses,
> In her prophetic furie sew'd the work;
> The worms were hallowed that did breed the silk,
> And it was dy'd in mummy which the skillful
> Conserv'd of maidens' hearts.
> (3.4.55-75)

Recall Thomas Rymer's objection to the play: "the Handkerchief is so remote a trifle no Booby on this side *Mauritania* cou'd make any consequence from it." Although Rymer wants to distinguish between the "Justice and Reason" of the civilized and the gullibility of the barbarian, he in fact points to a problem at the heart of the play, for in this speech, Othello, the Christian convert and Venetian general, is required to stand in for what can only be called a highly exoticized fantasy of how an object might resist commodification. In other words, it is easy to reject Rymer, but to what extent is Shakespeare's representation of the trifle simply the other side of Rymer's dualistic splitting of subject from object? In what ways does the language of the trifle construct as its imaginary opposite fantasies of sacred silkworms, two-hundred-year-old sibyls sewing in prophetic fury, dyes made of maidens' hearts, Egyptian charmers, and handkerchiefs that can overturn the patriarchal order, subduing men to women?

Nor is the problem entirely an external one. For if Iago gives contradictory accounts of the handkerchief, so too does Othello. After Desdemona's death, Othello returns to the absent object as proof that Desdemona "did gratify" Cassio's love (5.2.213). In giving away Othello's remembrance, he claims, she gave away "an antique token / My father gave my mother" (5.2.216-17). In this speech the handkerchief is not a magical charm but a "token" whose value is derived from the memorial function attributed to it. At the same time, Othello overturns a narrative in which the handkerchief is entirely the product of women's actual bodies, of women's labor, and of women's circulation—the sibyl to Othello's mother, Othello's mother to Othello's father. In this second account, the handkerchief was the gift of a husband to his wife, foreshadowing his own gift of the handkerchief to Desdemona.

Othello's contradictory narratives point to one of the weaknesses in scholarly readings that attribute the manipulation of value entirely to the demonized figure of Iago, because each character who comes into contact with the handkerchief offers a conflicting account of its worth. In the final scene, Emilia wonders why her husband should treat "such a trifle" with "solemn earnestness" (5.2.227-8). Yet it is Emilia who describes the power of the handkerchief to materialize an absent presence:

> This was her first remembrance from the Moor
>
> . . . . : . . . .
>
> she so loves the token
> (For he conjur'd her she should ever keep it)
> That she reserves it evermore about her,
> To kiss and talk to.
> (3.3.291-6)

Although the play never shows Desdemona talking to the handkerchief, the implication is that for her the handkerchief is not an "it" but a "he," an animate substitute for Othello himself. Even here, however, the power of the object to act as a living presence is framed within the language of the "token," one of the most slippery concepts in the play. Like the trifle, the token problematically elides the economic and the spiritual. If a token can be "an act serving to demonstrate divine power or authority" or "something ... to be kept as a memorial; a keepsake or present given especially at parting," it can also mean "something serving as proof of a fact or statement; an evidence" or "a stamped piece of metal, often having the general appearance of a coin, issued as a medium of exchange by a private person or company" (*OED* "token," 4, 9.a, 3.a, 11.a.). The token is clearly designated as a thing of no value in Massinger's *A new way to pay old debts* (1625), when Tapwell taunts Wellborn by telling him that his credit is "not worth a token."[15] The token may be exchanged for something valuable, but the thing itself is incommensurate with what it has bought.

In a more famous exchange, Cressida gives Troilus's sleeve to Diomedes as a "token" or promise of her love (5.2.60). In this case, as in *Othello*, the identification of the love token as a remembrance is sullied by the suggestion that it has already passed through more than one pair of hands.[16] In fact, by the end of the sixteenth century, there was an increasing tendency to use the word "token" to refer to a

---

[15]   *A new way to pay old debts* (London: E[lizabeth] P[urslowe], 1633), B2ʳ.

[16]   This exchange is prompted by Diomedes, who demands the token as "surety" of her pledge. An earlier conversation between Pandarus and Cressida provides an important backdrop to this one: "*Pandarus.* Ay, a token from Troilus. / *Cressida.* By the same token, you are a bawd" (1.2.280-81).

thing with merely provisional value. In *The Spanish Tragedy* (1587), Hieronimo invokes the memory of his dead son by calling the bloody handkerchief "a token twixt thy soul and me, / That of thy death revenged I should be" (3.13.88-9). Even here, however, the handkerchief is also a love token that changes hands more or less indiscriminately, as Bel Imperia first gives it to Don Andrea and then to Horatio. Similarly, the handkerchief in *Othello*, which is five times referred to as a "token," travels from Othello to Desdemona, from Desdemona to Othello, from Othello to Emilia, from Emilia to Iago, from Iago to Cassio, and from Cassio to Bianca. It functions at one moment as an ordinary medicinal aid, at another as an object worth more than a "purse / Full of crusadoes" (3.4.25-6), and at yet another as a thing of "wonder" (3.4.101).

The different registers of the "token" are most complexly enacted in an exchange between Cassio and Bianca in Act 3, scene 4. Guessing that she is not the first person to be given the handkerchief, Bianca complains that "[t]his is some token from a newer friend," to which Cassio responds that the handkerchief is no "remembrance" from a lover but merely a piece of attractive linen (3.4.181, 186). Cassio has no interest in the handkerchief's history or in its sentimental value—he simply wants to see it duplicated before someone demands it back—but in asking for the handkerchief to be reproduced, he evacuates Desdemona's "first remembrance" of the sacred singularity that Othello tries so hard to establish. In the process, Cassio reduces Othello to the almost comic exclamation: "By heaven, that should be my handkerchief!" (4.1.157). In this moment, Othello definitively claims the handkerchief as his, associating its loss with his wife's betrayal, and as the two men watch the physical movement of the handkerchief from Cassio to Bianca, Iago interprets the movement typologically as the physical movement of Desdemona to Cassio. If *Othello* stages Rymer's perspective in Iago's dismissal of the handkerchief as a trifle, it also introduces competing and contradictory views on the object. Othello's description of the object's genesis is haunted by the language of witchcraft, and in reproducing the handkerchief Bianca would not only erase the object's uniqueness but also make problematic the attachment of a magical genesis to a particular thing.

In *Othello*, the threat of having the handkerchief copied ensures that it can never be returned to its original status as Desdemona's first gift from the Moor, for it turns any relation between remembrance and object into the play of competing fictions. More broadly speaking, the oscillation of the handkerchief between trifle and personified remembrance enacts synchronically the diachronic conflicts in which Catholic relics were rewritten as ornaments of idolatry. These same objects that Protestants disdained as trinkets repeatedly reappeared as valuable relics not only within private households but also on the London stages. This is not to say that the theaters were in reality the preservers of Catholic idolatry that strict Protestants accused them of being. Rather, dramatists and playing companies were typically opportunistic in their use of the Catholic trinkets they acquired or represented on stage, and the appropriation of these charged objects raised crucial questions about their fluctuating status. As I have suggested throughout the book, these appropriations call for an approach that takes into account all the intricacies of post-Reformation worship—including the persistence of various material forms of devotion.

Ironically, the dramatic fictions in which religious objects were re-inscribed often owe as much to the histrionics of Protestant demystification as to traditional Catholic rituals, for as Huston Diehl has shown, a certain theatricality characterized the reformers' public attacks on Catholic objects. Among their favorite targets were the large wooden crucifixes that were said to work miracles, the most famous of which was the so-called Boxley rood at the Cistercian Abbey in Kent, which was "cunningly" able to "to nod with his head, to scowl with his eyes, to wag his beard, to curve his body, to reject and to receive the prayers of pilgrims." In 1538, to the great satisfaction of its critics, the Rood of Grace was revealed as a mere puppet in front of the Bishop of Rochester and a large crowd of curious citizens. Geoffrey Chamber told Cromwell that he himself discovered "certain engines and old wire" that caused the eyes and lips to move.[17] In a letter to Bullinger written that same year, Nicholas Partridge drew a clear connection between the false theatricality of the idol, a lifeless hulk manipulated by unscrupulous priests, and the seductiveness of the crucifix itself. According to Partridge, "the trickery of the wicked knaves was so publicly exposed in the image of the crucifix, that everyone was indignant against the monks and imposters of that kind, and execrated both the idols and those who worshiped them."[18] Partridge's account, like many iconoclastic critiques, depends upon the belief that by exposing the rood's theatrical mechanics, the power of the idolatrous illusion will be destroyed.

Just as iconoclasts were invested in debunking Catholic idols, the theater's most virulent critics argued that the companies used "engines and wires" to revive papist idolatry. Yet those critics paradoxically rejected any possibility of revealing theatrical performance as "only" performance through an exposure of its fictions. There could be, they argued, no gap between popery and the representation of popery. Whether part of a critical or celebratory staging of Catholicism, a cross, for instance, could never be just a stage property; despite being a "fake," it still materialized the seductive power of false religion. In his *Histrio-mastix* (1633), William Prynne concluded that plays were incapable of being reformed: "let Stage-Players perish, *yea, for ever perish, which thus revive the cursed memory of Pagan Idols, and their infernall wickednesses*, whose remembrances should for ever be forgotten lest we perish by them."[19] For Prynne, the public theater was no different

---

[17]   Philips, 73.

[18]   Another later example of the practice of exposing Catholic idols is the case of a marble statue of Christ at the Cathedral in Dublin, which marvelously bled through its crown of thorns. When the image was examined, its attackers found a blood-filled sponge inside the head, and they eventually charged a former monk with perpetrating the fraud. According to Phillips, the monk had been trying to bring about the return of images to the church through this miracle (ibid., 117).

[19]   Prynne, 94.

from the guild-sponsored biblical drama or the pagan plays of heathen Rome. Any performance of a play was an incitement to idolatry, a spectacle that might cause the audience to mistake the signifier for the thing it was designed to represent.

The rhetorical trajectory linking the theater to Catholic idolatry is well known to scholars of the early modern period, but we have also unconsciously inherited some of the reformers' distaste for the objects that occupied the commercial stage. Consequently, our readings of dramatic scripts tend to ignore stage properties and the range of meanings they carried with them. As Jonathan Gil Harris points out, even the recent turn to an object-oriented historicism is tinged with a lack of regard for antiquarian collectors who contribute to our understanding of the diachronic dimension of stage objects, past and present, by providing us with a more nuanced picture of the dynamic relationship between the theater and modern capitalist economies.[20] Stage properties continue to be seen as trifles, but this was not the only label they acquired when they entered the marketplace. For what Gosson or Prynne could never have predicted was that in later centuries stage properties might be valued precisely as stage properties—not for what they signified within the dramatic fiction but for their ability to commemorate a performer or a production. Because of the resonance these properties took on as a result of their proximity to famous nineteenth-century actors, many of them were carefully preserved in private collections and museums as "relics" of the theatrical past.

Following Kopytoff's concept of the cultural biography of things, the stage property may be said to have four very different social lives, each of which corresponds to a particular type of value. In its first life, the property is a commodity, a financial investment made by a theatrical company. In the second, it undergoes a kind of transformation as part of a theatrical performance. In *Othello*, for instance, an ordinary handkerchief is first represented as a love token, then as a kind of magical charm once it is lost, then as a piece of needlework to be copied in Bianca's hands, and finally as an "antique token" in Othello's narrative of Desdemona's infidelity. In its third life, the object returns to obscurity, to be reused in a later play, pawned or sold, and, when worn out, recycled or discarded. Finally, collectors give the property a fourth life as the physical trace of a theatrical event. Both the theater and the private collector thus participate in a narrative of singularization that is "real" insofar as the consumers continue to accept the narratives that describe the object's value.

The church, the library, and the stage can all be seen as locations that lend the theatrical relic a set of meanings commensurate with their respective value systems. At the same time, by thinking about the ways in which an object circulates

---

[20]   As Harris notes in his article on Shakespeare's hair: "for all that the antiquarians of the eighteenth and nineteenth centuries placed a naïve faith in objects as the unmediated residue of the past, they were nonetheless attentive to a dimension of materiality that object criticism has all too frequently overlooked; the diachronic trajectories of things through time and space" ("Shakespeare's Hair: Staging the Object of Material Culture," *Shakespeare Quarterly* 52, no. 4 [Winter 2001]: 479-91, 480).

from one location to another, we can develop a description of its shifting value that helps to account for the complex interplay between sites such as the church and the marketplace, or the marketplace and the theater. In what follows I provide a few examples of what it might mean for a stage property to pass through multiple moments of commodification and singularization. These transformations speak to the ways in which individuals connect themselves to the transcendent figures of Shakespearean theater—the famous actors as well as the elusive author himself— while simultaneously reproducing the cultural values that effect that transcendence. If a close study of stage properties helps us understand the fluctuating status of objects in early modern London, an examination of stage relics shows us how the theatrical enterprise itself became an institution capable of endowing mere things with an almost religious sacrality.

Tinsel and Trumpery

One of the more enjoyable jobs I held during graduate school was at the Annenberg Rare Book and Manuscript Library at the University of Pennsylvania. There I was given the opportunity to help catalogue and re-house an eclectic group of theatrical relics belonging to Horace Howard Furness, the editor of the Variorum Shakespeare. Although his objects sometimes lack a detailed or distinguished provenance, in many cases Furness attempted to authenticate them—marking them as remembrances of specific actors and performances—and in this sense, his properties, like all relics, represent an effort to preserve the dead among the living. The exhibition card attached to a human skull in his collection is particularly revealing in this respect; it begins with the famous lines about Yorick and goes on to assert that this particular object once belonged to a licensed pharmacist named Mr. Carpenter, "who had loaned it to many actors playing at the Walnut Street Theatre." By way of proof, the signatures of some of these actors who used the skull as a property when playing the title role in *Hamlet* are still visible on the cranium. Furness's project, one that the gravedigger undertakes in a more ironic fashion when speaking about Yorick to Hamlet and Horatio, is to prove that the skull is not just any skull.[21] This property, now a relic with its own archivally-approved reliquary, provides a link between generations of actors while connecting modern readers and theatergoers to the lives of famous performers.

We can define stage relics, then, as a particular class of theatrical relics, objects that would not necessarily be of any value to players or playgoers during

---

[21]   Citing Joseph Roach, Carol Chillington Rutter calls this type of connection a "genealogy of performance" ("'Her first remembrance from the Moor': Actors and the Materials of Memory," in Peter Holland, ed., *Shakespeare, Memory, and Performance* [Cambridge: Cambridge University Press, 2006]: 168-206, 191). Rutter's astute meditation on stage relics overlaps in many ways with my own, but she focuses mainly on the way in which these objects function within the theatrical environment.

the moment of performance but accrue meaning, both affective and economic, as traces of that performance once it has ended. They accrue value because of rather than despite the ephemeral nature of dramatic performance, linking collectors to the fleeting moment of a particular production and allowing repeated access to the experience of being in the theater with Irving or Modjeska or Terry. In subsequent decades, of course, relics with a moderate degree of authenticity, or a compelling narrative of any kind, have become valuable as historically interesting curiosities, and have continued to resist desingularization. The Folger Shakespeare Library owns an especially well-documented set of stage properties and costumes. Among these objects is the prayer book property discussed in Chapter 4; other noteworthy items include a dagger that Henry Irving carried in *Hamlet*, a set of fake noses used to create his Shylock, and countless dresses, belts, hats, and swords worn by a range of modern performers.

Although I cannot explore the life histories of each of these objects in detail here, I want to sketch out the kinds of things we can learn by looking at the printed inventories and catalogues—most of which are from the nineteenth century—that document the value of stage relics. In contrast to early modern inventories of stage properties, all of which are tantalizingly incomplete, these texts give us vital information about both the singularization and the commodification of objects. Pasted into the middle of the Folger Library's copy of Henry Irving's estate sale catalogue, for instance, is a clipping which notes that among his personal effects, "[t]he relics of theatrical lineage naturally attracted much attention." The author of the newspaper article also comments that "[t]he stage relics associated with Irving himself were generally fought for with heartiness."[22] The enshrining of such "relics" in museums and private collections represents a reversal of the processes through which religious objects were brought onto the early modern stage, while continuing to demonstrate the difficulty of assigning a stable value—either economic or religious—to objects that are in constant circulation.

Originally, of course, the properties gathered by Furness, Folger, and other collectors of Shakespeareana were part of the profit-making venture that originated in the professional theaters of early modern London, but these collectors' efforts also assume a type of value that collides with the realities of theatrical production. On the stage, any attempt to attach a coherent meaning to the handkerchief in *Othello* is further complicated by the fact that the actual handkerchief is itself a mere commodity. The napkin deployed in a production of *The Spanish Tragedy* could easily reappear in a subsequent production of *Othello*, and therefore the meaning of the property is necessarily determined by the dramatic contexts in which it is placed. Similarly, Catholic relics only took on value once they were placed within a particular geographic setting, such as a chapel or cathedral. "Relics,"

22 On the back a later collector has noted in blue crayon that the header was "Sale of Irving Relics / Over 2,500 Pounds Realised," and that the date was Tuesday, December 15, 1905. Henry Irving, *Catalogues of theatrical collections sold by Christie* (London: Manson and Woods, 1905).

as Patrick Geary writes, "are most peculiar sorts of symbolic objects—symbols without intrinsic significance."[23] The relic only becomes sacred once it has been authenticated and enshrined within a community, but relics can also circulate as commodities, objects with economic rather than religious value. Geary admits elsewhere that "[a]ny consideration of sacred relics as commodities in the Middle Ages may seem to be pushing to the extreme the definition of commodities as 'goods destined for circulation and exchange,'" but it is also true that commodification is not a one-way street—on the contrary, the commodity can only be labeled as such at the precise moment of exchange.[24] Thus, both Catholic relics and theatrical relics reinforce Igor Kopytoff's revised definition of the commodity as an object's life phase rather than its predestined identity.

Though many Catholic relics are venerated as actual body parts, other articles, labeled relics of touch or *brandea*, "acquired miraculous powers through contact with the holy remains." Mary's tunic, for instance, was deemed valuable because of its proximity to the body of the Virgin; along with a substance said to be her milk, it became the main attraction at Chartres. In Hans Belting's formulation, "[t]he relic as *pars pro toto* was the body of a saint, who remained present even in death and gave proof of his or her life by miracles."[25] Thus the finger of Saint Theresa connects worshipers to the mysterious power of the historical personage, allowing them to contact her directly to ask for her help. Similarly, theatrical relics were described in terms of their closeness to the original actor or moment of performance. It is no accident, therefore, that many of the theatrical relics now housed in literary archives are clothes and pieces of clothing. Furness's library, for example, contains several pairs of gloves supposedly worn by Henry Irving in *Much Ado About Nothing* and one pair that enthusiasts have traced back to the bard himself.

The challenge for the collector, of course, lies in the difficulty of tracing the relic to the absent body—especially Shakespeare's. In reference to Catholic ornaments, William Pietz notes that, "anyone can manufacture an object intended for worship, but only the priestly lineage or the church can empower them for the community of the faithful."[26] In the case of theatrical properties, there is no officiating priest, but the power of stage relics does rely upon a community of believers, namely avid playgoers and collectors, and great weight is placed on authenticating evidence. In the Folger collection, for instance, the object identified as Irving's dagger is accompanied by a letter that reads: "Dear Mr. Brooks, This is the dagger used by the late Sir H Irving in Hamlet, see Picture. Yours truly, J. Bald [?] 20 years in his

---

[23]   *Furta Sacra: Thefts of Relics in the Central Middle Ages* (Princeton: Princeton University Press, 1978), 152.

[24]   *Living with the Dead in the Middle Ages* (Ithaca: Cornell University Press, 1994), 194.

[25]   *Likeness and Presence: a history of the image before the era of art* (Chicago: University of Chicago Press, 1994), 59, 299.

[26]   "The problem of the fetish, II," 30.

employ as stage hand." Two engravings of Henry Irving in the role of Hamlet, both showing his dagger, are included with the object, testifying to its lineage.

Irving was among the most popular figures of the nineteenth-century stage, and in 1938 the London Museum displayed a range of his theatrical memorabilia, including a feather he plucked from Ellen Terry's fan during a production of *Hamlet* in 1877. The feather, which was subsequently pasted to a photograph of Terry taken by Edward Bell, is a particularly vivid example of the desire to preserve some material trace of a theatrical performance. The photograph authenticates the feather as belonging to Ellen Terry, while the feather itself is the physical remainder of an actual event. The same London Museum exhibition also displayed a handkerchief "spotted with strawberries" from Irving's production of *Othello*.[27] This object is not an artifact of a particular production, nor is it associated with any individual actor. The catalogue entry simply identifies the item using the language of the play itself, which is understandable, given that the handkerchief passes from character to character rather than being tied to any particular individual. In one sense the property is Desdemona's, but it is also a token used to fabricate her guilt. In another sense it is Othello's, but he never appears on stage with it, except when it is in Cassio's hands. Cassio adopts it, but only to order a copy of the workmanship. The anonymity of this stage object is ironically confirmed by the description of a "strawberry handkerchief" in the Folger collection that was used by "various actors."[28] The handkerchief associated with the Irving production is unique in that it commemorates a specific director, while at the same time its relatively anonymous afterlife seems to have been predetermined by its fluctuating status in the play.

Even in the medieval period, however, the process of designating sacred objects as genuine relics was fraught with difficulty. As Jonathan Sumption points out, "the trade in relics reached epidemic proportions after the sack of Constantinople in 1204, when the market was inundated with objects whose authenticity it was impossible to prove."[29] Ironically, the proliferation of relics in the marketplace caused many competing monasteries to steal each other's relics so as to preserve them from the threat of commodification and duplication. By removing them from the marketplace altogether, relic thieves temporarily masked the embarrassing overlap between an object's sacrality and its economic value. The dual processes

---

[27] Irving, 23, 28.

[28] The object, which is described only on a card in the "Costume Collection" drawer in the special collections alcove, is number 11-1-51-1.

[29] *Pilgrimage: an image of mediaeval religion* (London: Faber & Faber, 1975), 31. "From the merchants' point of view," Patrick Geary argues, "relics were excellent articles of trade. They were small and easily transported . . . . As highly desirable luxury items, they brought excellent prices in return for little capital investment." "The best aspect of all," he goes on to say, "owing to the difficulties of communication between communities involved, was that the body of a popular saint already sold might be sold again to another customer" (*Furta Sacra*, 63).

of theft and reconsecration provided a viable solution to the excesses of the relic trade, but from a Protestant point of view, relics continued to present a broad spectrum of ethical and theological problems. The reformers were concerned about the alarming way in which relics tended to multiply, but they also worried about the fact that their authenticity could only be determined by church authorities, who often had an interest in the profits made by selling or displaying relics to pilgrims. It was a commonplace of Reformation-era satire that all the pieces of the true cross, if gathered together, would easily sink the best English ship—the implication being that there are too many relics for them all to be authentic, but also that relics are bad for the nation as a whole. In many ways, however, the Protestant use of the term "relic" actually collapsed the distinction between the problem of worshiping false relics and the problem of worshiping objects that should never have been designated as holy in the first place. Nineteenth-century hoarders of stage relics, like Furness, seem to have inherited some of this embarrassment about the potential for worshiping the object (the stage property) rather than the divinity (the genius expressed in the plays), and consequently their use of the language of relics to describe their endeavors is remarkably multivalent.

One of the better documented nineteenth-century stage relics is a Maltese cross "enamelled and set with pastes" that John Philip Kemble used in his production of *Hamlet*. This item passed first to Mrs. Kean, who wore it as Queen Katherine, and then to her husband, and it was eventually sold in a 1904 event at Christie's for forty-four guineas. Yet a newspaper reviewer, pointing out the object's lack of commercial value, labeled it a "piece of tinsel."[30] Tinsel, like pasteboard, is a prop-making technology that dates back to the guild-sponsored drama. The term, which originated around the year 1500, eventually came to be "applied to a cheap imitation [of gold or silver] in which copper thread was used to obtain the sparkling effect" (*OED* "tinsel," 2). Writing nearly four hundred years later, the London reporter was still picking up on the antitheatrical resonances of the word "tinsel." The pervasive attitudes that continue to associate stage properties with mere ornamentation were thus in direct competition with the theatrical subculture associated with the growth of the Shakespeare industry, which sought to enshrine them as relics.[31] Even within the community of the faithful, however, documents such as the sale catalogues for the estate of American drama critic William Winter are quite explicit about the relative value of individual items. One object is categorized somewhat dismissively as "nice personal relic" while another, a girdle worn by Helena Modjeska in the role of Cleopatra, is "a most interesting and desirable relic of the great actress," and yet another is labeled a "treasured relic." Still other items, such Ada Rehan's paperweight, are classed as "association

---

[30]   Irving, 8, 18.

[31]   For more on the Shakespeare industry and some of the other relics associated with it, see Barbara Hodgdon, *The Shakespeare trade: performances and appropriations* (Philadelphia: University of Pennsylvania Press, 1998), and Graham Holderness, ed., *The Shakespeare Myth* (Manchester and New York: Manchester University Press, 1988).

relics" because they link the owner to the actor but are not necessarily connected to the theater itself.[32]

Although not all the properties described in sale catalogues relate thematically to the question of a stage property's status as a relic, a number of other entries shed light on the issues outlined elsewhere in the book, especially in Chapter 3, because they describe the diachronic trajectories of individual items. Although stage relics might pass directly from actors to their family members, or to collectors, they took on even greater weight if they could be said to have first passed from one performer to another: such objects possessed a double resonance and could be linked to an even older theatrical past. Thus a sword described in one of the Folger catalogues is recorded as having passed from Kean, who stabbed Caesar with it, to Irving, who did the same. Another sword, used by Kean as Richard III, was given to Irving when he took over the role. One circassian dagger apparently had a lengthier journey, passing—so the catalogue claims—from Byron to Charles Kean, and thence to Ellen Tree, who gave it to Mrs. Kean. For her part, Mrs. Kean gifted it to her niece Patti Chapman, who gave it to Irving. The piece sold for thirteen guineas at the 1904 sale, significantly less than the "tinsel" cross that had been traced back to Kemble, perhaps because it was less of an antique.[33] On the other hand, the Charles Kean sale catalogue indicates that swords which could be identified with a particular historical moment or play were significantly more expensive than swords that were generically described as "Kean's." The 1898 sale is particularly useful for thinking about the diachronic lives of stage relics, for many of the items in it originally were listed in the catalogue describing his father's possessions. When Edmund Kean died penniless in 1833 many of his effects were sold off at a public auction, but at the sale his son Charles was encouraged to buy back some of his father's property, including a sword presented to the senior Kean in 1819 by a group of admirers from Edinburgh who approved of his *Macbeth*; this same property was resold upon Charles's own death in 1898 for almost five times the original sum.[34]

If any of these relics were to appear without its museum label in a London pawnshop, it would be worth no more nor less than any other similar commodity. It would be disingenuous, however, to say that there is no institutional authority behind the value of such theatrical objects. Although performances themselves are ephemeral, the theater as it emerged in Shakespeare's England was a capitalist enterprise driven by the prestige of companies, actors, and theater managers, and the Shakespeare industry, as it arose in the eighteenth and nineteenth centuries, is anchored in the cultural capital associated with his name. Objects such as Booth's sword, Irving's beard, and Modjeska's satin dress were elevated to the status of

---

[32] Anderson Galleries, Inc., *The Library of the Late William Winter Sold by Order of His Son Mr. Jefferson Winter. Books, Letters, Manuscripts and Dramatic Memorabilia* (New York: Anderson Galleries, 1921), 2b, 258, 220, 77, 2e, 198.

[33] Irving, 26-7.

[34] Munby, 377, 422

relics by those who collected them because they had once been associated with the living stage, which was itself a commercial medium as well as an artistic one. In other words, theatrical properties provide perhaps the clearest example of the claim that objects can be commodified in one phase of their social lives and sanctified in another. The documentary history of the stage relics available to collectors in the nineteenth century demonstrates the complex ways in which emotional and monetary value corroborate one another, both within the theater and outside it. These objects indicate the fervor with which theatergoers sought to connect themselves to Shakespeare, but they also suggest the ways in which that worshipful attitude was often tinged—as in the case of Catholic relics—with consumerism.

Remainders

Dora and Nora Chance, the protagonists in Angela Carter's fifteenth novel, *Wise Children*, spend much of their lives studiously avoiding their connections to the Shakespeare industry. Rejected by their father, a famous Shakespearean actor, they have chosen to pursue happier and more remunerative careers in the music hall. The novel opens with the two sisters growing old together and telling stories about their girlhood, stories that inevitably involve their progenitor, Sir Melchior Hazard. To say that this book is a re-writing of *King Lear* is to belittle its inventiveness, but *Wise Children* does circle around Shakespeare's play, revealing the centrality of stage properties both inside and outside the dramatic fiction. I end with Carter, therefore, as a tribute to the imaginative power of the theatrical relic. I have been arguing that the playing companies of Shakespeare's day were unusually invested in the shifting status of religious objects, and in the processes of valuation and devaluation that made them available to theater practitioners. But *Wise Children*, which both mocks and eulogizes the materialistic pomp of nineteenth-century Shakespearean productions, demonstrates that stage objects can also take on compelling roles in modern fictions, especially when we consider their entire life histories.

In many ways, Carter's novel is about heirlooms, for Melchior has inherited his profession from his father Ranulph while leaving his own illegitimate daughters nothing. More importantly, the girls' grandfather left his son a stage property crafted by Melchior's mother during a particularly disastrous repertory tour:

> Props and costumes were lost or stolen or fell to pieces and then were begged or
> improvised or patched and darned. Ranulph drank and gambled and declaimed;
> he was going to pieces, too. He shouted at America but it would no longer listen
> to him. One night, at a bar at Tucson, Arizona, he gambled away his crown from

Lear and Estella put together a new one for him out of a bit of cardboard. She dabbed on some gold paint. 'Here you are.'[35]

This short piece of narration cannily reflects what scholars have recently learned about the early modern repertory companies. The properties used by Ranulph and his colleagues were immanently replaceable, and although they might be repeatedly restored, they could just as easily be discarded when they were no longer worth the expense of patching. Moreover, like the early modern costumes described by Ann Rosalind Jones and Peter Stallybrass, they could move in and out of the pawnshop when the actors needed ready cash.[36] What is most interesting about this fictional anecdote, however, is that the metal crown—which presumably had a monetary value attached to it—was replaced by one made of cardboard. It is this crown, the supposedly worthless one, which continues to circulate from generation to generation and throughout the novel. For, as the sisters report, Melchior "took away from the grand catastrophe of his parents' lives only one little souvenir—the pasteboard crown that Ranulph wore for *Lear*, the one Estella made" (22). The other aspect of this novel that echoes recent discoveries in early modern scholarship is that it reveals the role of women in the production and maintenance of costumes, sets, and properties. Although Estella was not a professional member of the acting troupe, it is tempting to read her contribution in light of Natasha Korda's work on women's involvement in the public theater of Shakespeare's day.[37]

Despite the feminist aspects of the novel, however, the crown seems to symbolize a patriarchal inheritance system from which the sisters, born out of wedlock, are systematically excluded. They glimpse the crown only fleetingly, for it is ensconced in "a glass case on the mantelpiece" in the manorial home to which they are seldom admitted (99). Melchior's jealous hold over the object is shaken, however, by a fire that consumes the entire estate. In a climatic exchange, he bewails his loss to Dora, who simultaneously bewails her own:

> 'You've lost your eyebrows,' he remarked.
> 'Worse than that,' I said, and sobbed. 'I've lost my sister.' 'I've lost,' he said, 'my crown.'
> From the way he said it I knew the loss of a natural daughter weighed less heavy on his heart than the loss of the old Hazard heirloom I'd just seen in his bedroom. For a weak moment, there, my unreconstructed daughter's heart wished I could have saved it for him. … 'My crown, my foolish crown, my paper crown of a king of shreds and patches,' he lamented. 'The crown my father wore as Lear—to have survived so many deaths, so much heartbreak, so many travels … and now, gone up in smoke! Oh, my dear girl, we mummers are such simple folk … superstitious as

---

[35] *Wise Children*, 1st ed. (New York: Farrar, Straus & Giroux, 1992), 20.

[36] *Renaissance Clothing and the Materials of Memory* (Cambridge: Cambridge University Press, 2000), 26-32.

[37] "Household Property/Stage Property: Henslowe as Pawnbroker," *Theatre Journal* 48, no. 2 (May 1996): 185-95.

little children. The fire was welcome to take everything, the frills and furbelows, the toys and gewgaws, the oil paintings, the cloisonné, the Elizabethan oak … but, oh, my crown! That cardboard crown, with the gold paint peeling off.' … I was amazed to see him so much moved, and on account of what? A flimsy bit of make-believe. A nothing. (104-5)

Dora, for all her perceptiveness, misses the point in labeling the crown a "nothing." For Melchior it is an object with immense personal and professional significance: it is simultaneously Lear's, his father's, and his mother's, and it links him to all three of them as well as to his self-identity as a famous actor. For Melchior, the crown is worth more than "oil paintings" and "cloisonné," luxury items he ironically labels "gewgaws," a word that along with "toy" was later linked to the discourses of the trifle and the trinket discussed above. The novel thus manages to reference a particular moment in time when the entire theatrical apparatus was considered idolatrous, while simultaneously layering this historical reality on top of the personal story of Melchior's inheritance from his father, a narrative that works against these long-standing stereotypes. The fact that the paint on the crown was peeling was a sign of its significance, not its worthlessness, and for all his pomposity, Melchior is quite serious about the loss of an object with such a history behind it.[38]

As it happens, however, the crown is not lost, for Melchior's volatile younger brother, Peregrine, has rescued both it and Nora from the flames. Dora relates this happy ending with a mixture of disbelief and excitement: "for one dreadful minute, I thought that he was dead and it was his haloed ghost approaching, but as he left the fire behind him, I saw what it was he'd got on his head. In his arms a girl" (105-6). This revelatory scene in turn sets the reader up for the final meeting between the four characters: Melchior, his bastard daughters, and his bastard younger brother. Near the end of his life, Melchior gathers his family around him for one final dramatic appearance at his one-hundredth birthday. He has dressed up like his father Ranulph for the occasion, but, as the sisters observe, in his dotage he has forgotten the crown which once meant so much to him. Like the old man himself, it has fallen into some neglect, but Peregrine manages to spruce up the "battered and tattered" crown, and Dora presents it to her father on a cushion: "I stood up

---

[38] This novel also includes a significant nod to bardolatry *per se*, as the twins are entrusted with a piece of Stratford soil to take to America: "See that thing in Nora's arms, that looks like a decapitated doll? You'll never believe it. It was a pot, a sort of jar, about the size of ones they use for ashes in the crematoria, and it was hollow inside and in the shape of a bust of, that's right, William Shakespeare; our father had had it specially made, in Stoke-on-Trent, and the bald patch lifted off, that was the lid. And what did this bizarre vessel contain? Earth. We travelled with a box of earth, like Dracula, and never let it out of our sight. Earth from Stratford-upon-Avon, dug out of the grounds of that big theatre by some reverential sidekick and then entrusted to Nora and myself, a sacred mission, to bear the precious dust to the New World" (112-13).

on tiptoe. I placed the crown on his long, grey hair. Sometimes you know it's sentimental and sometimes you just don't care. I was a touch long in the tooth for Cordelia but there you are" (225-6). It is tempting to read this scene—in which the virtuous daughter, formerly exiled from the house, re-crowns her aging father—as an indication that the property serves as a bond between the generations. Carter makes it clear, however, that Melchior has forgotten all about the object; only his daughters, formerly so skeptical about his attachment to his own theatrical image, are able to give his crown back to him, endowing it with a new set of meanings in the process. The reunion scene is pointedly not one in which the daughters and their father are able to affirm that they see the meaning of the crown, and therefore their relationship, in the same way. Rather, this strange inheritance registers the degree to which relics survive as a result of change, both their own transformations and the shifts in attitudes toward them.

Nowhere is John Sommerville's account of secularization as the segmentation of religious experience more powerfully manifested than in the subcultures that have sprung up in both Great Britain and America, as well as in countless post-colonial sites, around the veneration of Shakespeare.[39] To compare theatrical relics such as cardboard crowns and handkerchiefs to Catholic ones such as bones and locks of hair is not to belittle either faith system, but I can think of no better explanation for the profusion of Shakespeareana than Sommerville's notion that religion has become "a thing to think about rather than a way of thinking."[40] Ultimately, I suspect that the analogy between theatrical objects and religious ones works only because of the distance between them. Antiquarians such as Furness were no more convinced that their relics constituted a link to the "real" body of Shakespeare than playgoers in early modern England were convinced that the religious objects they saw on stage were identical to the ones they had grown up with. The pleasure of the relic comes from the speculation about its origin, and the pleasure of the theater's appropriation of religious objects, I would argue, arose from the obvious difference between the stage property and the thing it was designed to represent. Like all relics, stage properties were valued because of the stories people told about them, and in the case of the early modern theater, those stories included both the theatrical fictions and the complex range of experiences each playgoer brought with her to the theater. These meanings were not naively consolidated in the act of performance, but were rather aggregated upon one another as the object circulated throughout the company's repertory and within individual plays. Sixteenth- and seventeenth-century reformers frequently contrasted the static icon with the godly

---

[39]   In addition to the nineteenth-century examples cited above, there are several noteworthy relics associated with the lions of the twentieth-century stage. In the Sotheby's catalogue of Ralph Richardson's personal effects, for instance, collectors were offered the chance to buy the gloves worn by Henry Irving when he played Cardinal Wolsey in 1892. The asking price was 500-700 pounds. *The Ralph Richardson Collection* (London: Sotheby's, 2001), 86.

[40]   Sommerville, 70, 11.

narrative, preferring depictions of Christ's interactions with the disciples to the potentially idolatrous spectacle of the crucifixion. The relic, however, is both image and story, and thus provides an apt metaphor for the incredible variety of meanings religious objects took on as they moved from one sphere of exchange, one community of faith, to another.

Select Bibliography

Primary Sources

Anderson Galleries, Inc. *The Library of the Late William Winter Sold by Order of His Son Mr. Jefferson Winter. Books, Letters, Manuscripts and Dramatic Memorabilia.* New York: Anderson Galleries, 1921.

Anderson, J. J., ed. *Newcastle Upon Tyne*. Records of early English drama. Toronto: University of Toronto Press, 1982.

Anon. *The passage of our most drad Soveraigne Lady Quene Elyzabeth through the citie of London to westminster the daye before her coronacion Anno 1558.* London: Tottill, 1558.

——. *The Tragedy of Master Arden of Faversham*. Edited by Martin L. Wine. London: Methuen [Distributed in the U.S.A. by Harper & Row Publishers, 1973].

——. *The true chronicle historie of the whole life and death of Thomas Lord Cromwell*. London: [Read], 1602.

——. *The Two Noble Ladies*. Edited by Rebecca Garrett Rhoads. London: Printed for the Malone Society by J. Johnson at the Oxford University Press, 1930.

——. *Vox borealis, or the northern discoverie: by way of dialogue between Jamie and Willie*. [London or Edinburgh]: Margery Mar-Prelat, 1641.

——. *A Warning for Fair Women. A Critical Edition*. The Hague: Mouton, 1975.

Barbour, Philip L., ed. *The Jamestown Voyages Under the First Charter, 1606-1609, Documents Relating to the Foundation of Jamestown and the History of the Jamestown Colony up to the Departure of Captain John Smith, Last President of the Council in Virginia Under the First Charter, Early in October 1609*. London: published for the Hakluyt Society [by] Cambridge University Press, 1969.

Barlow, William. *The summe and substance of the conference ... at Hampton Court. January 14. 1603*. London: John Windet [and T. Creede], 1604.

Beaumont, Francis, and John Fletcher. *The Dramatic Works in the Beaumont and Fletcher Canon*. Edited by Fredson Bowers. 10 vols. Cambridge: Cambridge University Press, 1966.

——. *The Knight of Malta*. Edited by Marianne Brock. Bryn Mawr, 1944.

Becon, Thomas. *The Catechism of Thomas Becon. With Other Pieces Written by Him in the Reign of King Edward the Sixth*. Cambridge: Printed at the University Press, 1844.

Berkeley, William. *The lost lady a tragy comedy*. London: Jo. Okes, 1638.

Brewer, Anthony. *The love-sick king, an English tragical history with the life and death of Cartesmunda, the fair nun of Winchester*. London: n.p., 1655.

Brome, Richard. *The Antipodes*. Edited by Ann Haaker. Lincoln: University of Nebraska Press, 1966.

Buckeridge, George. *A sermon preached before His Maiestie at Whitehall, March 22. 1617. being Passion-Sunday, touching prostration, and kneeling in the worship of God*. London: Bill, 1618.

Carter, Angela. *Wise Children*. 1st ed. New York: Farrar, Straus & Giroux, 1992.

Charke, William. *An answere to a seditious pamphlet lately cast abroade by a Iesuite with a discoverie of that blasphemous sect*. London: Barker, 1580.

Chettle, Henry, and Anthony Munday. *The death of Robert, Earle of Huntington Otherwise called Robin Hood of merrie Sherwodde*. London: [Bradock], 1601.

Church of England. *Articles to be enquired of, within the province of Canterburie*. London: [H. Denham], 1576.

——. *The Booke of common praier*. London: Jugge and Cawode, 1559.

——. *Certain sermons or homilies appointed to be read in churches in the time of Queen Elizabeth of famous memory and now reprinted for the use of private families, in two parts*. London: n.p., 1687.

——. *Documentary Annals of the Reformed Church of England, Being a Collection of Injunctions, Declarations, Orders, Articles of Inquiry, &c. from the Year 1546 to the Year 1716, with Notes Historical and Explanatory*. Edited by Edward Cardwell. 2 vols. Oxford: University Press, 1839.

——. *Formularies of Faith, Put Forth by Authority During the Reign of Henry VIII*. Edited by Charles Lloyd. Oxford: At the Clarendon Press, 1825.

——. *Visitation Articles and Injunctions of the Early Stuart Church*. Edited by Kenneth Fincham. Vol. 2. Woodbridge, Suffolk [England]: Boydell Press, 1994.

——. *Visitation Articles and Injunctions of the Period of the Reformation*. Edited by Walter Howard Frere. 3 vols. Alcuin Club Collections. London, New York: Longmans, Green & Co, 1910.

Clopper, Lawrence, ed. *Chester*. Records of early English drama. Toronto: University of Toronto Press, 1979.

Cranmer, Thomas. *The Works of Thomas Cranmer*. Edited by John Edmund Cox. Cambridge: Printed at the University Press, 1844.

Crashaw, Richard. *Steps to the temple sacred poems, with other delights of the muses*. London: T. W., 1646.

Crashaw, William. *A Sermon Preached in London before the right honorable the Lord Lawarre ... Feb 21, 1609*. London: Lownes, 1609.

D'Avenant, William. *The cruell brother A tragedy*. London: M[athewes], 1630.

Daborne, Robert, and Philip Massinger. *Three Turk Plays from Early Modern England: Selimus, A Christian Turned Turk, and The Renegado*. Edited by Daniel J. Vitkus. New York: Columbia University Press, 2000.

Dekker, Thomas. *The Dramatic Works of Thomas Dekker*. Edited by Fredson Bowers. 4 vols. Cambridge: University Press, 1953.

————. *The Spanish Gipsy by Thomas Middleton and William Rowley: A critical edition.* Edited by Kate Parker Smith. Northwestern University Dissertation, 1944.

Donne, John. *The Divine Poems.* Edited by Helen Louise Gardner. Oxford: Clarendon Press, 1959.

Durand, Guillaume. *The Symbolism of Churches and Church Ornaments, a Translation of the First Book of the Rationale Divinorum Officiorum.* Leeds: T. W. Green, 1843.

Elizabeth I. *Elizabeth I: Collected Works.* Edited by Janel M. Mueller, Leah S. Marcus, and Mary Beth Rose. Chicago: University of Chicago Press, 2000.

Erasmus, Desiderius. *A dialoge or communication of two persons . . . intituled [the] pylgremage of pure devotyon. Newly tra[n]slatyd into English.*

Fletcher, Giles. *The policy of the Turkish empire. The first booke.* London: Windet, 1597.

Fludd, Robert. *Utriusque Cosmi Majoris Scilicet Et Minoris Metaphysica, Physica Atque Technica Historia: In Duo Volumnina Secundum Cosmi Differentiam Diuisa.* Oppenhemii: Acre Johan-Theodori de Bry, 1617.

Ford, John. *The Broken Heart.* Edited by Donald K. Anderson. Lincoln: University of Nebraska Press, 1968.

Foxe, John. *Actes and Monuments of These Latter and Perillous Dayes.* Imprinted at London: By John Day, dwellyng over Aldersgate. Cum privilegio Regi[a]e Maiestatis, 1563.

————. *The First[-Second] Volume of the Ecclesiasticall History.* London: Printed by John Daye, 1570.

Galloway, David, ed. *Norwich, 1540-1642.* Records of early English drama. Toronto: University of Toronto Press, 1984.

Garter, Bernard. *A new yeares gifte, dedicated to the Popes Holinesse.* London: Bynneman, 1579.

Gee, John. *New Shreds of the Old Snare Containing the Apparitions of Two New Female Ghosts.* London: Printed [by J. Dawson] for Robert Mylbourne, 1624.

Gibson, James M, ed. *Kent: Diocese of Canterbury.* Records of early English drama. Toronto: The British Library and University of Toronto Press, 2002.

Goad, Thomas. *The friers chronicle: or, The true legend of priests and monkes liues.* London: for Robert Mylbourne, 1623.

Gosson, Stephen. *Playes confuted in five actions.* London: n.p., 1582.

Great Britain. *Documents Relating to the Office of the Revels in the Time of Queen Elizabeth.* Edited by Alfred Feuillerat. Vaduz: Kraus Reprint, 1963.

————. *Documents Relating to the Revels at Court in the Time of King Edward VI and Queen Mary.* Edited by Alfred Feuillerat. Louvain: A. Uystpruyst, 1914.

Green, Mary Anne Everett, ed. *Calendar of State Papers, Domestic Series, of the reigns of Edward VI, Mary, Elizabeth and James I.* 12 vols. London: Longman, Brown, Green, Longmans & Roberts, 1856.

Harington, John. *Epigrams both pleasant and serious, written by that all-worthy knight, Sir John Harrington: and never before printed.* London: [Purslowe], 1618.

Harsnet, Samuel. *A Declaration of Egregious Popish Impostures.* London: Roberts, 1603.

Heywood, Thomas. *An apology for actors.* London: Okes, 1612.

——. *The first and second partes of King Edward the Fourth Containing his mery pastime with the tanner of Tamworth, as also his love to faire Mistrisse Shoare.* London: K[ingston], 1600.

——. *The foure prentises of London with the conquest of Jerusalem.* London: Okes, 1632.

——. *If you know not me, you know no bodie: or, The troubles of Queene Elizabeth.* London: Purfoot, 1605.

Ingram, R. W., ed. *Coventry.* Records of early English drama. Toronto: University of Toronto Press, 1981.

Irving, Henry. *Catalogues of Theatrical Collections Sold by Christie.* London: Manson & Woods, 1905.

Jonson, Ben. *Ben Jonson.* Edited by C. H. Herford and Percy Simpson. 11 vols. Oxford: Clarendon Press, 1925.

——. *Sejanus His Fall.* Edited by Philip J. Ayres. Manchester: Manchester University Press, 1999.

Kyd, Thomas. *The Spanish Tragedy.* Edited by David M. Bevington. Manchester: Manchester University Press, 1996.

Lambarde, William. *Dictionarium Angliae Topographicum et Historicum: An Alphabetical Description of the Chief Places in England and Wales.* London, 1730.

Lithgow, William. *A most delectable, and true discourse, of an admired and painefull peregrination from Scotland, to the most famous kingdomes in Europe, Asia and Affricke.* London: Okes, 1614.

Loarte, Gaspar. *Instructions and advertisements, how to meditate the misteries of the rosarie of the most holy Virgin Mary.* London: Carter, 1597.

Lumiansky, R. M., and David Mills, eds. *The Chester Mystery Cycle.* London: published for the Early English Text Society by Oxford University Press, 1974.

——. *The Chester Mystery Cycle: Essays and Documents.* Chapel Hill: University of North Carolina Press, 1983.

Malcolm, James Peller. *Londinium Redivivum, or, An Antient History and Modern Description of London.* 4 vols. London: Printed by J. Nichols, 1802.

Marlowe, Christopher. *Christopher Marlowe's Doctor Faustus 1604-version.* Edited by Michael Keefer. Peterborough, Ont: Broadview Press, 1991.

——. *Dido Queen of Carthage and The Massacre at Paris.* Edited by H. J. Oliver. London: Methuen, 1968.

——. *Tamburlaine: Parts One and Two.* Edited by Anthony B. Dawson. 2nd ed. London: A. C. Black, 1997.

Massinger, Philip. *The maid of honour*. London: I. B., 1632.

——. *A new way to pay old debts*. London: E[lizabeth] P[urslowe], 1633.

Mayer, John. *A patterne for women: setting forth the most Christian life, & most comfortable death of Mrs. Lucy late wife to the worshipfull Roger Thornton.* London: Griffin, 1619.

Middleton, Thomas. *A Game at Chess*. Edited by T. H. Howard-Hill. Manchester: Manchester University Press, 1993.

——. *The Second Maiden's Tragedy*. Edited by Anne Begor Lancashire. Manchester: Manchester University Press, 1978.

Morris, John. *The Troubles of Our Catholic Forefathers Related by Themselves. First [-Third] Series*. Vol. 3. London: Burns and Oates, 1872.

Munby, A. N. L., ed. *Sale Catalogues of Libraries of Eminent Persons*. London: Mansell with Sotheby Parke-Bernet Publications, 1971.

Munday, Anthony. *A Critical Edition of Anthony Munday's Fedele and Fortunio*. Edited by Richard Hosley. New York: Garland Pub., 1981.

Nichols, John Gough. *Narrative of the Days of the Reformation: Chiefly from the Manuscripts of John Foxe the Martyrologist; with Two Contemporary Biographies of Archbishop Cranmer*. Westminster: Printed for the Camden Society, 1859.

Perkins, William. *A warning against the idolatrie of the last times And an instruction touching religious, or divine worship*. [Cambridge]: Legat, 1601.

Prothero, G. W., ed. *Select Statutes and Other Constitutional Documents Illustrative of the Reigns of Elizabeth and James I*. 4th ed. Oxford: Clarendon Press, 1913.

Prynne, William. *Histrio-Mastix: The Players Scourge, or, Actors Tragdie, Divided into Two Parts*. London: Printed by E[dward] A[llde, Augustine Mathewes, Thomas Cotes] and W[illiam] I[ones], 1633.

Rainolds, William. *Th'overthrow of Stage-playes*. London: Schilders, 1599.

Randolph, Thomas. *The muses looking-glasse*. London: n.p., 1643.

Rowley, William. *A Shoemaker, a Gentleman*. Edited by Trudi Laura Darby. New York: Routledge, 2003.

Rymer, Thomas. "A Short View of Tragedy." In *Shakespeare the Critical Heritage*. Edited by Brian Vickers. London and Boston: Routledge and Kegan Paul, 1974. 1: 51-4.

Sandys, George. *A relation of a iourney begun an: Dom: 1610 Foure bookes. Containing a description of the Turkish Empire, of AEgypt, of the Holy Land, of the remote parts of Italy, and ilands adjoyning*. London: [Field], 1615.

Scot, Thomas. *The Workes of the Most Famous and Reverend Divine Mr. Tomas Scot. Bachelor in Divinitie: Sometimes Preacher in Norwich*. Holland: n.p., 1624.

Shakespeare, William. *The Riverside Shakespeare*. Edited by G. Blakemore Evans and J. J. M. Tobin. 2nd ed. Boston: Houghton Mifflin, 1997.

——. *The Tragedy of King Richard III*. Edited by John Jowett. Oxford [England]: Oxford University Press, 2000.

Simpson, W. Sparrow. "Churchwardens Accounts for the parish of St. Matthew, Friday Street, in the City of London, from 1547-1603." *Journal of the British Archaeological Association* 25 (1869): 356-81.

Smart, Peter. *The Vanitie & Downe-Fall of Superstitious Popish Ceremonies*. London: Heyres of Robert Charteris, 1628.

Sotheby's (Firm). *The Ralph Richardson Collection: Sold by Orders of the Trustees of the Ralph and Meriel Richardson Foundation*. London: Sotheby's, 2001.

Sparke, Michael. *The crums of comfort with godly prayers. Corrected and amended*. London: n.p., 1628.

Taylor, Thomas. *The Pilgrims profession, or a sermon preached at the funeral of Mrs Mary Gunter by Mr Thomas Taylor*. London: Dawson, 1622.

Tourneur, Cyril. *The Revenger's Tragedy*. Edited by Lawrence J. Ross. Lincoln: University of Nebraska Press, 1966.

Tyndale, William. *Expositions and Notes on Sundry Portions of the Holy Scriptures, Together with The Practice of Prelates*. Edited by Henry Walter. Cambridge [Eng.]. Printed at the University Press, 1849: Johnson Reprint Corp, 1968.

Webster, John. *The Duchess of Malfi*. Edited by John Russell Brown. Manchester: Manchester University Press, 1997.

——. *The Duchess of Malfi*. Edited by Brian Gibbons. 4th ed. London: A. & C. Black, 2001.

——. *The White Devil*. Edited by John Russell Brown. Manchester: Manchester University Press, 1996.

Wilkins, David. *Concilia Magnae Britanniae Et Hiberniae, a Synodo Verolamiensi A.D. CCCCXLVI. Ad Londinensem A.D. [MDCCXVII] Accedunt Constitutiones Et Alia Ad Historiam Ecclesiae Anglicanae Spectantia*. 4 vols. Bruxelles: Culture et Civilisation, 1964.

Wright, Thomas, ed. *Churchwardens' Accounts of the Town of Ludlow, in Shropshire, from 1540 to the End of the Reign of Queen Elizabeth*. New York: AMS Press, 1968.

Wriothesley, Charles. *A Chronicle of England During the Reigns of the Tudors, from A.D. 1485 to 1559*. Westminster: Printed for the Camden Society, 1875.

Secondary Sources

Ackroyd, Peter R., Christopher Francis Evans, G. W. H. Lampe, and S. L. Greenslade, eds. *The Cambridge History of the Bible*. 3 vols. Cambridge: University Press, 1963.

Anstruther, Godfrey. *Vaux of Harrowden: A Recusant Family*. Newport: R. H. Johns, 1953.

Aston, Margaret. *England's Iconoclasts*. Oxford: Clarendon Press, 1988.

Bakhtin, M. M. [Mikhail Mikhailovich]. *The Dialogic Imagination: Four Essays.* Austin: University of Texas Press, 1981.

Barish, Jonas A. *The Antitheatrical Prejudice.* Berkeley: University of California Press, 1981.

Barton, Anne. "Perils of Historicism—Learning to Curse: Essays in Early Modern Culture by Stephen J. Greenblatt." *The New York Review of Books* 38, no. 6 (March 28, 1991): 53.

Bawcutt, N. W. *The Control and Censorship of Caroline Drama: The Records of Sir Henry Herbert, Master of the Revels 1623-73.* Oxford: Clarendon Press, 1996.

Beckwith, Sarah. *Signifying God: Social Relation and Symbolic Act in the York Corpus Christi Plays.* Chicago: University of Chicago Press, 2001.

Belting, Hans. *Likeness and Presence: A History of the Image Before the Era of Art.* Chicago: University of Chicago Press, 1994.

Devington, David, ed. *Medieval Drama.* Boston: Houghton Mifflin, 1975.

Boulter, Charles Bevois. *History of St. Andrew Undershaft, St. Mary Axe, in the City of London, with Description of the Monuments and the Coloured Glass Therein.* [London, Privately printed], 1935.

Brigden, Susan. *London and the Reformation.* Oxford: Clarendon Press, 1991.

Burton, Jonathan. "Anglo-Ottoman Relations and the Image of the Turk in *Tamburlaine.*" *Journal of Medieval and Early Modern Studies* 30, no. 1 (Winter 2000): 125-56.

Butler, Martin. *Theatre and Crisis, 1632-1642.* Cambridge: Cambridge University Press, 1984.

Carlton, Charles. *Archbishop William Laud.* London: Routledge & Kegan Paul, 1987.

Cave, Richard Allen. *The White Devil and The Duchess of Malfi: Text and Performance.* Basingstoke, Hampshire: Macmillan Education, 1988.

Cavell, Stanley. *Disowning Knowledge: In Six Plays of Shakespeare.* Cambridge: Cambridge University Press, 1987.

Chakravorty, Swapan. *Society and Politics in the Plays of Thomas Middleton.* Oxford: Clarendon Press, 1996.

Chambers, E. K. *The Elizabethan Stage.* 4 vols. Oxford: The Clarendon Press, 1974.

Clopper, Lawrence M. *Drama, Play, and Game: English Festive Culture in the Medieval and Early Modern Period.* Chicago: University of Chicago Press, 2001.

Collinson, Patrick. *The Birthpangs of Protestant England: Religious and Cultural Change in the Sixteenth and Seventeenth Centuries: The Third Anstey Memorial Lectures in the University of Kent at Canterbury, 12-15 May 1986.* New York: St. Martin's Press, 1988.

Comensoli, Viviana. *'Household Business': Domestic Plays of Early Modern England.* Toronto: University of Toronto Press, 1996.

Crawford, Patricia. *Women and Religion in England, 1500-1720.* London: Routledge, 1993.

Cressy, David, and Lori Anne Ferrell, eds. *Religion & Society in Early Modern England: A Sourcebook.* 2nd ed. New York: Routledge, 2005.

Croft, Pauline. "The Religion of Robert Cecil." *The Historical Journal* 34, no. 4 (December 1991): 773-96.

Dailey, Alice. "Easter Scenes from an Unholy Tomb: Christian Parody in *The Widow's Tears.*" In *Marian Moments in Early Modern British Drama*, 27-139. Aldershot, England: Ashgate, 2007.

Davidson, Clifford. "'The Devil's Guts': Allegations of Superstition and Fraud in Religious Drama and Art during the Reformation." In *Iconoclasm vs. Art and Drama*, edited by Clifford Davidson and Ann Eljenholm Nichols, 92-144. Kalamazoo, Mich.: Medieval Institute, 1989.

Dawson, Anthony B. "The Secular Theatre." In *Shakespeare and the Cultures of Performance.* Edited by Paul Yachnin and Patricia Badir. Aldershot, England; Burlington, VT: Ashgate, 2008. 83-100.

——, and Paul Edward Yachnin. *The Culture of Playgoing in Shakespeare's England: A Collaborative Debate.* Cambridge: Cambridge University Press, 2001.

Dendy, D. R. *The Use of Lights in Christian Worship.* London: S.P.C.K, 1959.

Dessen, Alan C., and Leslie Thomson, eds. *A Dictionary of Stage Directions in English Drama, 1580-1642.* Cambridge: Cambridge University Press, 1999.

Diehl, Huston. "'Strike All That Look upon with Marvel': Theatrical and Theological Wonder in *The Winter's Tale.*" In *Rematerializing Shakespeare: Authority and Representation on the Early Modern English Stage.* Edited by Bryan Reynolds and William N. West. New York: Palgrave Macmillan, 2005. 19-34.

——. "Observing the Lord's Supper and the Lord Chamberlain's Men: The Visual Rhetoric of Ritual and Play in Early Modern England." *Renaissance Drama* 22 (1991): 147-74.

——. *Staging Reform, Reforming the Stage: Protestantism and Popular Theater in Early Modern England.* Ithaca: Cornell University Press, 1997.

Duffy, Eamon. *The Stripping of the Altars: Traditional Religion in England, c.1400-c.1580.* New Haven: Yale University Press, 1992.

Egan, Robert. *Drama Within Drama: Shakespeare's Sense of His Art in King Lear, The Winter's Tale, and The Tempest.* New York: Columbia University Press, 1975.

Emmison, F. G. *Elizabethan Life: Morals & the Church Courts.* Chelmsford: Essex County Council, 1973.

Ferrell, Lori Anne. *Government by Polemic: James I, the King's Preachers, and the Rhetorics of Conformity, 1603-1625.* Stanford: Stanford University Press, 1998.

Foister, Susan. "Paintings and other works of art in sixteenth-century English inventories." *Burlington Magazine* CXXIII (May 1981): 273-82.

Forker, Charles R. *Skull Beneath the Skin: The Achievement of John Webster.* Carbondale: Southern Illinois University Press, 1986.

Gaskell, Ian. "*2 Tamburlaine*: Marlowe's War against the Gods." *English Studies in Canada* 11, no. 2 (June 1985): 178-92.

Geary, Patrick J. *Furta Sacra: Thefts of Relics in the Central Middle Ages.* Princeton: Princeton University Press, 1978.

———. *Living with the Dead in the Middle Ages.* Ithaca: Cornell University Press, 1994.

Gibson, Gail McMurray. *The Theater of Devotion: East Anglian Drama and Society in the Late Middle Ages.* Chicago: University of Chicago Press, 1989.

Grantley, Darryll. "*The Winter's Tale* and Early Religious Drama." *Comparative Drama* 20, no. 1 (Spring 1986): 17-37.

Graves, R. B. *Lighting the Shakespearean Stage, 1567-1642.* Carbondale: Southern Illinois University Press, 1999.

Greenblatt, Stephen. *Learning to Curse: Essays in Early Modern Culture.* New York: Routledge, 1990.

———. *Renaissance Self-Fashioning: From More to Shakespeare.* Chicago: University of Chicago Press, 1980.

———. *Shakespearean Negotiations: The Circulation of Social Energy in Renaissance England.* Berkeley: University of California Press, 1988.

Groves, Beatrice. *Texts and Traditions: Religion in Shakespeare, 1592-1604.* Oxford: Clarendon Press, 2007.

Gurr, Andrew. *Playgoing in Shakespeare's London.* 2nd ed. Cambridge: Cambridge University Press, 1996.

———. *The Shakespearean Stage, 1574-1642.* Cambridge: University Press, 1970.

Haigh, Christopher. *English Reformations: Religion, Politics, and Society Under the Tudors.* Oxford: Clarendon Press, 1993.

———. *The English Reformation Revised.* Cambridge: Cambridge University Press, 1987.

Hall, Peter. *Peter Hall's Diaries: The Story of a Dramatic Battle.* Edited by John Goodwin. 1st ed. New York: Limelight Editions, 1985.

Hardison, O. B. *Christian Rite and Christian Drama in the Middle Ages; Essays in the Origin and Early History of Modern Drama.* Baltimore: Johns Hopkins Press, 1965.

Harris, Jonathan Gil. "Shakespeare's Hair: Staging the Object of Material Culture." *Shakespeare Quarterly* 52, no. 4 (Winter 2001): 479-91.

———, and Natasha Korda, eds. *Staged Properties in Early Modern English Drama.* Cambridge: Cambridge University Press, 2002.

Hodgdon, Barbara. *The Shakespeare trade: performances and appropriations.* Philadelphia: University of Pennsylvania Press, 1998.

Holderness, Graham, ed. *The Shakespeare Myth.* Manchester and New York: Manchester University Press, 1988.

Hopkins, Lisa. *John Ford's Political Theatre.* Manchester: Manchester University Press, 1994.

Howard, Jean E. "Other Englands: The View from the Non-Shakespearean History Play." In *Other Voices, Other Views: Expanding the Canon in English Renaissance Studies.* Edited by Helen Ostovich, Mary V. Silcox, and Graham Roebuck. Newark; London: University of Delaware Press; Associated University Press, 1999. 135-53.

——. *The Stage and Social Struggle in Early Modern England.* London: Routledge, 1994.

——, and Phyllis Rackin. *Engendering a Nation: A Feminist Account of Shakespeare's English Histories.* New York: Routledge, 1997.

Jackson, Ken, and Arthur F. Marotti. "The Turn to Religion in Early Modern English Studies." *Criticism: A Quarterly for Literature and the Arts* 46, no. 1 (Winter 2004): 167-90.

Johnston, Alexandra F. "Cycle Drama in the Sixteenth Century: Texts and Contexts." In *Early Drama to 1600*, edited by Albert H. Tricomi, 1-15. Acta (Acta): 13. Binghamton: Center for Medieval and Early Renaissance Studies, State University of New York, 1987.

Jones, Ann Rosalind, and Peter Stallybrass. *Renaissance Clothing and the Materials of Memory.* Cambridge: Cambridge University Press, 2000.

Kearney, James. *Matters of the Book: The Incarnate Text in Renaissance England.* University of Pennsylvania Dissertation, 2001.

——. "Trinket, Idol, Fetish: Some Notes on Iconoclasm and the Language of Materiality in Reformation England." *Shakespeare Studies* 28 (2000): 257-61.

King, John N. "The Godly Woman in Elizabethan Iconography." *Renaissance Quarterly* 38, no. 1 (Spring 1985): 41-84.

——. *Tudor Royal Iconography: Literature and Art in an Age of Religious Crisis.* Princeton: Princeton University Press, 1989.

Koerner, Joseph Leo. *The Reformation of the Image.* London: Reaktion, 2004.

Kopytoff, Igor. "The cultural biography of things: commoditization as process." In *The social life of things: commodities in cultural perspective.* Edited by Arjun Appadurai. Cambridge, New York: Cambridge University Press, 1986. 64-91.

Korda, Natasha. "Household Property/Stage Property: Henslowe as Pawnbroker." *Theatre Journal* 48, no. 2 (May 1996): 185-95.

Lake, Peter, and Michael C. Questier. *The Anti-Christ's Lewd Hat: Protestants, Papists and Players in Post-Reformation England.* New Haven: Yale University Press, 2002.

Lee, John. "The Man Who Mistook His Hat: Stephen Greenblatt and the Anecdote." *Essays in Criticism: A Quarterly Journal of Literary Criticism* 45, no. 4 (October 1995): 285-300.

Leggatt, Alexander. *Jacobean Public Theatre.* London: Routledge, 1992.

Maltby, Judith D. *Prayer Book and People in Elizabethan and Early Stuart England.* Cambridge: Cambridge University Press, 1998.

Matar, N. I. *Islam in Britain, 1558-1685.* Cambridge: Cambridge University Press, 1998.

McClain, Lisa. *Lest We Be Damned: Practical Innovation and Lived Experience Among Catholics in Protestant England, 1559-1642.* New York: Routledge, 2004.

McCullough, Peter E. "Out of Egypt: Richard Fletcher's Sermon before Elizabeth I after the Execution of Mary Queen of Scots." In *Dissing Elizabeth: Negative Representations of Gloriana.* Edited by Julia M. Walker. Durham: Duke University Press, 1998. 118-49.

Meredith, Peter, and John E. Tailby. *The Staging of Religious Drama in Europe in the Later Middle Ages: Texts and Documents in English Translation.* Kalamazoo, Mich: Medieval Institute Publications, Western Michigan University, 1983.

Moore, Roger E. "The Spirit and the Letter: Marlowe's *Tamburlaine* and Elizabethan Religious Radicalism." *Studies in Philology* 99, no. 2 (Spring 2002): 123-51.

Mullaney, Steven. *The Place of the Stage: License, Play, and Power in Renaissance England.* Chicago: University of Chicago Press, 1988.

Mullany, Peter F. "The Knights of Malta in Renaissance Drama." *Neuphilologische Mitteilungen. Bulletin de la Societe Neophilologique/Bulletin of the Modern Language Society* 74 (1973): 297-310.

——. *Religion and the Artifice of Jacobean and Caroline Drama.* Salzburg: Institut fur Englische Sprache und Literatur, Universitat Salzburg, 1977.

Neill, Michael. "'Feasts put down funerals': Death and Ritual in Renaissance Comedy." In *True Rites and Maimed Rites: Ritual and Anti-Ritual in Shakespeare and His Age.* Edited by Linda Woodbridge and Edward Berry. Urbana: University of Illinois Press, 1992. 47-74.

——. *Issues of Death: Mortality and Identity in English Renaissance Tragedy.* Oxford: Clarendon Press, 1997.

O'Connell, Michael. *The Idolatrous Eye: Iconoclasm and Theater in Early-Modern England.* New York: Oxford University Press, 2000.

——. "Vital Cultural Practices: Shakespeare and the Mysteries." *Journal of Medieval and Early Modern Studies* 29, no. 1 (Winter 1999): 149-68.

Orlin, Lena Cowen. *Private Matters and Public Culture in Post-Reformation England.* Ithaca: Cornell University Press, 1994.

Phillips, John. *The Reformation of Images: Destruction of Art in England, 1535-1660.* Berkeley: University of California Press, 1973.

Pietz, William. "The problem of the fetish, I." *Res* 9 (1985): 5-17.

——. "The problem of the fetish, II: The origin of the fetish." *Res* 13 (1987): 23-45.

Pollock, Linda A. *With Faith and Physic: The Life of a Tudor Gentlewoman, Lady Grace Mildmay, 1552-1620.* London: Collins & Brown, 1993.

Roach, Joseph R. *Cities of the Dead: Circum-Atlantic Performance.* New York: Columbia University Press, 1996.

Rowlands, Marie B. *English Catholics of Parish and Town, 1558-1778: A Joint Research Project of the Catholic Record Society and Wolverhampton University.* London: Catholic Record Society, 1999.

Rutter, Carol Chillington. "'Her First Remembrance from the Moor': Actors and the Materials of Memory." In *Shakespeare, Memory and Performance*, edited by Peter Holland, 168-206. Cambridge: Cambridge University Press, 2006.

Scarisbrick, Diana. *Jewellery in Britain 1066-1837: A Documentary, Social, Literary and Artistic Survey*. Wilby: Michael Russell, 1994.

Scarisbrick, J. J. *The Reformation and the English People*. Oxford: Blackwell, 1984.

Sheingorn, Pamela. *The Easter Sepulchre in England*. Kalamazoo, Mich.: Medieval Institute Publications, Western Michigan University, 1987.

Simpson, W. Sparrow. "Churchwardens Accounts for the parish of St. Matthew, Friday Street, in the City of London, from 1547-1603." *Journal of the British Archaeological Association* 25 (1869): 356-81.

Smith, Bruce R. "Sermons in Stones: Shakespeare and Renaissance Sculpture." *Shakespeare Studies* 17 (1985): 1-23.

Sofer, Andrew. *The Stage Life of Props*. Ann Arbor: University of Michigan Press, 2003.

Sommerville, C. John. *The Secularization of Early Modern England: From Religious Culture to Religious Faith*. New York: Oxford University Press, 1992.

Southern, A. C. *Elizabethan Recusant Prose, 1559-1582. A Historical and Critical Account of the Books of the Catholic Refugees Printed and Published Abroad and at Secret Presses in England Together with an Annotated Bibliography of the Same. With a Foreword by H. O. Evennett*. London: Sands, 1950.

Sumption, Jonathan. *Pilgrimage: an image of mediaeval religion*. London: Faber & Faber, 1975.

Targoff, Ramie. *Common Prayer: The Language of Public Devotion in Early Modern England*. Chicago: University of Chicago Press, 2001.

Taylor, Gary. "Divine [ ]sences." *Shakespeare Survey: An Annual Survey of Shakespeare Studies and Production* 54 (2001): 13-30.

Teague, Frances N. *Shakespeare's Speaking Properties*. Lewisburg: Bucknell University Press, 1991.

Twycross, Meg. "Playing The Resurrection." In *Medieval Studies for J. A. W. Bennett, Aetatis Suae LXX*. Edited by P. L. Heyworth. Oxford: Oxford University Press, 1981. 273-96.

Tyacke, Nicholas. "Archbishop Laud." In *The Early Stuart Church, 1603-1642*. Edited by Kenneth Fincham. Stanford: Stanford University Press, 1992. 51-70.

Wabuda, Susan. "The woman with the rock: the controversy on women and Bible reading." In *Belief and practice in Reformation England: a tribute to Patrick Collinson from his students*. Edited by Caroline Litzenberger and Susan Wabuda. Aldershot and Brookfield, VT: Ashgate, 1998. 40-59.

Walsham, Alexandra. "Jewels for Gentlewomen: Religious Books as Artefacts in Late Medieval and Early Modern England." In *The Church and the Book*. Edited by R. N. Swanson. Woodbridge: Boydell and Brewer, 2004. 123-42.

——. "The parochial roots of Laudianism revisited: Catholics, anti-Calvinists and 'parish Anglicans' in early Stuart England." *Journal of Ecclesiastical History* 49, no. 4 (1998): 620-51.

——. "Unclasping the book? Post-reformation English Catholicism and the vernacular Bible." *Journal of British Studies* 42, no. 2 (April 2003): 141-66.

——. "'Yielding to the Extremity of Time': Conformity, Orthodoxy, and the Post-Reformation Catholic Community." In *Conformity and Orthodoxy in the English Church, c. 1560-1660*. Edited by Peter Lake and Michael C. Questier. Woodbridge, Suffolk: Boydell Press, 2000. 211-36.

Watt, Tessa. *Cheap Print and Popular Piety, 1550-1640*. Cambridge: Cambridge University Press, 1991.

White, Paul Whitfield. *Theatre and Reformation: Protestantism, Patronage, and Playing in Tudor England*. Cambridge : Cambridge University Press, 1993.

White, Peter. "The via media in the early Stuart Church." In *The Early Stuart Church, 1603-1642*. Edited by Kenneth Fincham. Stanford: Stanford University Press, 1993. 211-30.

Whiting, Robert. *The Blind Devotion of the People: Popular Religion and the English Reformation*. Cambridge: Cambridge University Press, 1989

Wickham, Glynne William Gladstone. *Early English Stages, 1300 to 1660*. London: Routledge and Paul, 1959.

Williams, Raymond. *Marxism and Literature*. Oxford: Oxford University Press, 1977.

Yule, George. "James VI and I: furnishing the churches in his two kingdoms." In *Religion, culture, and society in early modern Britain: essays in honour of Patrick Collinson*. Edited by Anthony Fletcher and Peter Roberts. New York: Cambridge University Press, 1994. 182-208.

Index